"Margaret has written the first book not simply about money and the Enneagram, but about money as an expression of consciousness. This is a powerful topic, deserving of wide attention and further development."
– Don Richard Riso

MONEY:

FROM FEAR TO LOVE

USING THE ENNEAGRAM TO CREATE
WEALTH, PROSPERITY, AND LOVE

Margaret H. Smith, PhD, CFP™

To my teacher, Russ Hudson,
for transmitting the heart
and wisdom of the Enneagram.

To my eldest son, Chaska, 12,
who is young enough to be
curious about money and love,
but old enough to be doubtful
about things he cannot see, hear, and touch.

To my husband, Gary,
who has always helped me
follow my dreams and shine.

The quotations in this book are real, but the names of those quoted have been removed to protect their privacy.

CONTENT

ACKNOWLEDGEMENTS

I am grateful to so many people for supporting me. It takes a village to raise a child, and it takes a village to write a book. First, I thank the hundreds of individuals who participated in the interviews. I would like to name each of you individually, but don't want to compromise your privacy. I want each of you to know that your participation mattered and you made a real difference. You taught me to trust the power of a sincere request, and you taught me that I am supported. I wanted to do something that seemed impossible at first. But step by step, with your blessed participation, everything came together. Please know you are in my heart. You made this book possible and your spirit lives in these pages. I also thank Donna Fowler. When I first started thinking about this book, all I had was the kernel of an idea. I didn't know where to start, who to interview, or what to do. Donna assured me that it was an important topic and gave me the initial encouragement to write this book.

I thank my financial planning clients through the years who taught me about how money moves through our lives and gave me the curiosity to figure out how our personalities affect our financial behavior. Thank you Gayle Scott for the support you have given me through the years, and your insistence on incorporating the instincts into this work on money. And I thank my friends who gave me extra encouragement and moral support. Your enduring interest gave me the drive to stay focused. Thank you Brian, Catherine, Cece, Christine, Cindy, CJ, Connie, David, Debbie, Don, Heather, Maria, Mario, Mark, Mary, Moreah, Karin, Kathryn, Katy, Kevin, Laura, Lee, Peleg, Robin, Scott, Sondra, Zitta. Thank you Christine and David for brainstorming the title of the book with me. Thank you to my friends who journeyed with me in Egypt back to a time where Spirit moved civilizations. Thank you Peleg for your enthusiasm about the book, designing the cover, helping me with the subtitle, sketching out some of the illustrations, and keeping me on my toes and fresh through the final stretch of writing. I thank my parents, Lucy and Wei, and brother, John, for always supporting me. An extra thank you to my mom for watching baby Claire so I could think and write.

We each stand on the shoulder of giants. I am grateful to Don Riso for the pioneering work he has done on the Enneagram. He clarified the nine personality types, the kernel of which was first suggested by Oscar Ichazo, discovered the Levels of Development, and worked out the specifics of the Nine Domains and their relationship to the personality types. Don is one of the most creative thinkers in the Enneagram field, and I am grateful to have him as my teacher and friend. I am also grateful to Don for creating a thriving Enneagram community at the Barn and for supporting a joyous atmosphere of creativity and discovery.

This book would not be complete without my deep acknowledgement to my teacher Russ Hudson. I have been transformed by my time with him. Not only has Russ so effectively transmitted the heart and wisdom of the Enneagram to me, but he has also modeled compassion, dignity, and integrity. He is an unbelievable force in this world and the positive impact he has had on thousands of lives is staggering. He continues to forge his legacy to this world with his stunningly clear teaching and thoughtful leadership. It was when I was meditating deep inside the Great Pyramid (on a trip to Egypt led by Russ and John Anthony West) that I got the flash of inspiration that became the core idea of this book. We cannot be present and thrive when we are worried about survival. The idea is so crystal clear, yet our perception of this fact is clouded by our very survival strategies.

Lastly, I thank my husband, Gary Smith, not only for his tireless and patient editing, but also for his love and continual support. He's given me the time, resources, and space to research, learn, think, write, day after day, year after year. He's always believed in me, supported my growth, and walked alongside me as I took my own journey home.

Margaret H. Smith
Claremont, January 2011

PREFACE

A few hours ago, I saw *Inside Job*, a movie about the players from Wall Street, government, and academia who contributed to the devastating global financial crisis of 2008. Right now, we're living the consequences of that financial meltdown. It's a terrific movie that illustrates how our human greed and potential for wretched excess can build, but also unravel, economies. It illustrates vividly how connected we are, and how markets in the U.S. can impact markets in Iceland, Singapore, and China. It shows us how a system that has unbelievable potential for good as a lubricant of economic growth can so easily be corrupted to serve the selfish interests of a few powerful players, and how the government and the rest of us could stand by and let it happen.

The movie shows us a striking example of the difference between wealth and abundance. The guys on Wall Street making millions of dollars in bonuses and salaries had no sense of abundance or real prosperity. They had what I call "fake prosperity" – money without love. They were driven by their basest instincts. Their selfish Self-Preservation instinct led them to forget about the larger society around them. Their competitive Sexual instinct drove them to take insane risks with other people's money. These guys wanted to dominate and didn't care that they were taking bigger and bigger risks because they were playing with house money and rewarded for the risks they took. They wanted more jets, more houses, more women. They didn't stop to think about how their actions would impact the lives of billions.

Who was culpable? I want to say the greedy Wall Street executives, hedge fund traders, and derivatives engineers. I want to say Presidents Obama, Bush, and Clinton, who each brought in conflicted Wall Street executives to serve in the nation's most important financial and economic posts. The movie makes their culpability clear. The movie also rightly points the finger at economists from the nation's most elite academic institutions who were once my peers and teachers. These academic economists were "experts" who were supposed to know how markets work best. They themselves had no real understanding of how our selfish instincts could implode deregulated markets. They were just as co-opted as the rating agencies that were supposed to tell the public what was safe to invest in. Like doctors who don't disclose their conflict of interest when they recommend drugs made by the pharmaceutical companies that pay them, economists and academic consultants were paid huge sums of money to tell one side of the story. And they let their ideology about free markets and their hubris shape pronouncements.

What about the rest of us? Are we just victims? If we think that we have nothing to do with the economic collapse of 2008, we are deluded too. Perpetrators and victims alike played a role. Some whistle blowers and insiders saw the corruption and knew things had gone awry. But no one could stop the train. We partook of the easy money and allowed our herd mentality to get the best of us. We need to admit that we all have the capacity for greed, excess, herd behavior, and corruption.

I am part of what happened just as much as the Wall Street execs who used fake invoices to pay for high-end prostitutes and cocaine. As a Harvard graduate student, I bought into the culture of economists who knew everything, were all head and no heart, and not only never questioned the excesses of Wall Street, but benefited from it in various ways. I never questioned the responsibility of economists in government, nor did I use my good mind and training to look more deeply. I let my improving financial situation in the 2000s lull me into a false sense that everything was fine. I was co-opted.

Why did this happen? When we live in a system marked by this much fear, greed, and lack of love, we are all affected and all brought down by it. When we let our society be corrupted by a culture of excess, we are all culpable. Our relationship to money individually and collectively makes a bigger difference than we could ever imagine. We are both part of the problem and part of the solution. We need to wake up to our own accountability. If we continue to think that we are the victims rather than the perpetrators, nothing will ever change.

This book emerged from my journey to understand our relationship to money and how we can grow. Recognizing our underlying fear, the direction of my work has become clearer and clearer. How can I participate in the shift of our collective consciousness from one based on Fear to one based on Love? What tools do we need to see and understand ourselves, and then heal and grow? I believe that this work can help heal the world, for when one person wakes up, we all wake up.

I am the product of a middle-class immigrant Chinese-American family in which sacrifice, thriftiness, and hard work were valued. My dad was always working. My mom had her day job and made sure everything else was taken care of. My job was to be a good daughter, be responsible, get good grades, and go to a prestigious university that would earn the family status and honor. Our religion was upward mobility. Leaving their respective families behind, speaking almost no English, with less than a hundred dollars in their pockets, my parents came here to live the American dream. They believed they could have a higher standard of living, more stability, and better educational opportunities for themselves and their children. A better life in terms of material well-being was the compelling goal. My family's immigrant story echoes the story of millions of other immigrants over many generations from all over the world who came to America in search of a better life. The importance of a higher standard of living and better opportunities for material well-being cannot be denied.

If a better standard of living could make my parents move to the frozen tundra of Winnipeg, where they knew no one, with nothing but hope for a better life, then money must be a powerful thing indeed! My parents didn't understand much about this new culture, but they did know to pay the bills and (mostly) balance their checkbook. As a child of immigrants, I was determined to master American culture. America seemed to be a place where commerce ruled, so I figured that I would better navigate life if I learned about money. I majored in Economics at Yale as an undergraduate, and then went on to get a PhD in Business Economics at Harvard. I was taught about financial markets, international trade, labor economics. I was taught that humans are basically rational, though sometimes make errors that can impact markets in unpredictable ways. After graduating, I taught finance and economics for a decade as an economics professor. Then, because I had always been interested in upward mobility, I became a fee-only Certified Financial Planner™, helping people save and plan more effectively for college and retirement. I was a good student of economics and financial planning. Not only did I learn the rules, I believed in them.

As I began my own family, I also dreamt the American Dream. By my late twenties, I was married, a homeowner, with a good job and a kid. By my late thirties, I had re-married, had three more kids, and now owned two homes. I believed in meritocracy, democracy, and the market system. My kids would have the luxuries I didn't have growing up. We moved several times, each time for a bigger, better house. We saved for education, saved for retirement, monitored our net worth, made profitable investments. Everything conspired to make me feel smug – I understood this market system, I knew how to play the game. I could even help others navigate the system.

I felt confident in my knowledge, my abilities, my wisdom. It was simply a matter of applying basic economic and planning concepts. Understand your budget. Don't live beyond your means. Save 10% (or maybe 25%) of your income. Think about the future. Set goals and work diligently towards them. Make good investment decisions. Apply common sense, persistence, will power, and you'll be on your way. The recipe had worked for me, so it seemed appropriate for others. I believed in the value of understanding money, tax laws, retirement options, mortgage rates. I believed in long-term planning and saving. I believed in moving in a logical, linear fashion towards goals. I got a great deal of satisfaction giving people the confidence to make their material lives work for them. This worked until it stopped working. Then I couldn't do it anymore. I had to regroup and figure things out.

In retrospect, I think what I was really after was some understanding of how this mythic market system could motivate people to make big sacrifices and do difficult things for the sake of money. None of what I learned in college or graduate school really shed much light on this question. What I have come to realize is that we interact with this mythic market system in a way that makes sense for our instincts and personalities but not our rational minds. We mostly operate from fear. Through my real life engagement with people and their money, I discovered just how non-rational we all are when it comes to money. And it turns out, most of the fundamental assumptions of economics and financial planning don't necessarily serve us well either. These discoveries have transformed my own life and have been the impetus for my writing a book about money.

Little did I know that my journey would lead me to question the very foundations of economics and financial planning including the assumptions of planning, trade-offs, and scarcity that had been bread and butter for years. Everything I had preached seemed misguided. After twenty years breathing these fundamental assumptions, I began to realize that perhaps I had completely missed some deeper truths and that these assumptions were at the root of my yearnings and discontent. I came to recognize that economics and planning are based on an egoic perspective of the material world based on fear, and that this is the fundamental reason we have a difficult time with money.

As I began to explore my own relationship to money and ask how I might work with others in a more meaningful way, I also began to explore the Enneagram. The Enneagram is a symbol embedded with ancient wisdom about the laws of the universe that, in the last forty years, has been applied to understanding human personality. More powerful than the Myers-Briggs personality system, because it describes deeper structural motivations, the Enneagram can be used to reveal potential directions for growth and transformation. It describes our strengths, weaknesses, and helps instill in its students compassion and respect for all human beings. It became increasingly apparent to me that the Enneagram had a lot to say about people's relationships to money. The Enneagram shows us how we fall asleep and also shows us how to wake up. As I used the Enneagram in my financial coaching, I was increasingly stunned by its power.

Starting from an entirely different vantage point than economists, the Enneagram explains how our unconscious beliefs, fears, and instincts cause us to relate to money in distinct and patterned ways. The Enneagram has not yet been systematically applied to money and financial matters, but it can and should be. It can help us understand how we get into trouble with money, and also show us how to move towards greater balance and well-being. I believe that this book is the first attempt to do so, and I've spent the last three years interviewing, documenting, and analyzing the various Enneagram personality types and how they relate to money in unique ways.

We can transform our mindsets to work for and not against us by becoming more aware of the unconscious beliefs that keep us from living our best lives. If we collectively work on healing and transforming our relationship to money, our world will surely be a better place. I believe this topic is of utmost importance because so much of the strife in our world is caused by our greedy struggle for resources, and this acquisitive behavior is ravaging our planet. The less people feel fearful, needy, and hungry, the less people will feel compelled to eat up the planet. If we do not awaken to how our impulses are driving our economic motives and actions, then we are doomed to live out the consequences of our own greed. We need to examine our individual relationships to money and consider how we might move from fear and scarcity thinking to love and abundance. Then we might be able to act collectively from a more conscious, connected and holistic place to steward our planet into the next centuries, if not for our planet's sake, then for our children's and children's children's sake.

INTRODUCTION

Money is a powerful mirror of who we are and where we are on our personal journeys. In this book, I will show you how to take a personal approach to understanding and improving your relationship to money. You will learn why you don't do what's best for you and get a better understanding of the challenges that hold you back from living your best life.

In **Part I** on the Nine Domains of Money, we will talk about the nine-stage process that you must master in order to have a healthy relationship to money. Each of us tends to focus on a few areas but neglect others, creating imbalance and frustration, and blocking us from wealth, prosperity, and love. In **Part II** on Our Relationship to Money, we will talk about our human instincts and personality types and how they impact our relationship to money. We will explore how three basic instincts operate in us unconsciously. We will also explore the ramifications of having a dominant instinct and an instinct that gets ignored. Lastly, we will discuss the nine distinct personality strategies around money, based on the Enneagram system.

The Enneagram system posits that there are nine archetypal energies that not only explain universal laws, but personality differences as well. Our personality types are a launching pad from which to understand ourselves more deeply. As we become more conscious of who we really are, we can begin to move towards abundance and love, and away from scarcity and fear. We can become more confident of our value and less afraid of our own power. We can find our way back home to a place where there is no fear.

There has been a long religious tradition warning of the allure of money. Jesus said on the Sermon on the Mount:

Lay not up for yourselves treasures upon earth, where moth and rust doth corrupt, and where thieves break through and steal. But lay up for yourselves treasures in heaven, where neither moth nor rust doth corrupt, and where thieves do not break through nor steal. For where your treasure is, there will your heart be also... No one can serve two masters, for either he will hate the one and love the other; or else he will be devoted to one and despise the other. You can not serve both God and Mammon. — Matthew 6:19-21,24.

For at least two thousand years, there has been a strain in Western culture that has been deeply suspicious of wealth. Those who worship mammon are greedy, selfish people who worship a false god. The Bible says that "It's easier for a camel to go through the eye of a needle than the rich man to enter heaven." It is saying that if we make money our God, then we will never look for the real heaven. Thomas Aquinas describes the sin of Avarice as "Mammon being carried up from Hell by a wolf, coming to inflame the human heart with Greed." Dante describes the Greek God Plutus as a wolf-like demon of wealth. Milton describes a fallen angel who values earthly treasures above all else.

But mammon has not been summarily dismissed by all churches. An alternative gospel known as the "prosperity gospel" proselytizes the belief that "God wants His children to enjoy health, happiness, and wealth now and not as an eternal reward in Heaven." Televangelical churches encourage people to believe that the more they give, the more they will receive, promising that "giving would release angels into their lives and help make them prosperous." Their assertion that the things people possess is a measure of their godliness sets believers up for disappointment. Some churches explicitly link donations to forgiveness, saying things like, "As soon as a coin in the coffer rings, a soul from purgatory springs."

In our fear, we cleave meaning to money that money intrinsically does not have. Money becomes a symbol of good and evil, worth, security, love, freedom, power, comfort. Even though money is neutral, we are not neutral about money because we are not neutral about ourselves. We project our fears, anxieties, shame, guilt, and hopes onto money. We think that we can be "measured" by how much money we have. We project our insecurity onto the economic system and believe that our security can be ensured by saving and investing. We project our fears and sense of scarcity by believing that we live in a zero-sum world. If you have more, then I have less, so we must fight for resources.

Because we are not neutral about money, money pushes us off center. When we lose our ability to hold the truth of scarcity together with the truth of abundance, we allow money to become our master. We cede power to an inanimate object that only has the power with which we infuse it. We set up a divide between ourselves and our true nature. Money reflects back to us what we hold ourselves to be.

The market system can be very confusing. Supposedly, higher prices reflect scarcity while lower prices reflect abundance, thereby helping us efficiently allocate resources. But something that has a high price is not intrinsically more valuable or meaningful to us than something with a low price. Many of the best things in life are free. We can't put a price on the love we feel for a child, or the feeling we get when we see the clouds pierced with a ray of sunlight. Even though prices signal value in the market system, they do not measure value in our human system.

Traditional economic models are based on scarcity; indeed, economics is often defined as decision making in a world of limited resources and unlimited desires. In such a world, we have a fixed amount of time and money. We are constrained by scarcity and frustrated by tradeoffs. If I buy this, I won't be able to buy that. If I work today, I won't be able to play today. In a world of scarcity and unavoidable tradeoffs, we are anxious about decisions and fearful of the consequences. Paradoxically, many people feel that they have to work hard so that they can take vacations and retire. But then vacations are a nuisance because they take us away from our work, and retirement is death because we don't know what to do with ourselves when we aren't working. The whole system doesn't square with our humanity. This traditional epistemology no longer serves us.

The rational market system was created by an egoic mind that objectifies human lives and natural resources. To the ego, everything, including our parents and our children, are objects that exist to serve the ego. To the egoic mind, any and all sacred things are objects that can be priced and traded. Once an economic system conceptualizes all things as objects, it becomes a moral order based on the ego's moral order: a price can be put on everything, including a human life, a human organ, a lake, fresh air. All resources can be efficiently allocated by prices and we should not disrupt this moral order.

Naturally, the egoic mind would desire that its creation operates in unfettered fashion, thus promulgating the very values that the ego understands – scarcity, fear, competition, efficiency, productivity, hoarding. In contrast, fairness, compassion, and equality threaten this egoic moral order. The ego cannot let go of its belief in scarcity. It understands an impersonal market system that creates winners and losers. The ego understands the ruthless logic of markets. The ego understands that more is better, that comfort and conveniences equal happiness. The ego understands a system that feeds the body but does not feed the soul.

Economists are not sure what to think about our selfish instinct. The selfish instinct seems to be an important part of what makes the free market system work efficiently. In the rational market system, we pay market prices, buy what advertisers push, believe we need what others have, and never feel satisfied. We are bribed into accepting the market system because we get shiny cars and plasma TVs. We don't question why the things we care most about are neglected. What the ego does not perceive is that this impersonal market system can cause us to lose our basic humanity. It cannot perceive that the market system charms and allures us with bright and shiny things, but does not feed our souls. We underestimate the ruthless logic of markets and forget that nature and human life have a sacred dimension, an intrinsic value that doesn't have a price. The market system can operate like a black hole in the way it can suck us into doing work we hate so that we can buy things we don't need. We forget our connection to other people and become selfish, indifferent, numb. A system that can do this to us is not okay. Can our egos see this?

A different kind of relationship to money and to life is possible. The material world does not have to be an end in itself. If we could transform our fear-based relationships to money to love-based relationships, we could become the forces that heals the world's sicknesses. We could do so by participating consciously in a market system that is, in truth, neutral, based on money that is neutral but can be manipulated out of fear or love, depending on how we choose to interact with it. If we hold money lightly, then money can regain its proper place as a valued companion on our journey here. But when we are in ego, we are bound to experience fear and scarcity. Only when we move to a place beyond ego can we experience Love and abundance. When we are awake, we can be with the contradictions between scarcity and abundance, and hold both the no and yes simultaneously. In this place, we would not feel compulsion to over consume. We would not feel compulsion to hoard and not share. We would save naturally for rainy days. We would take resources as we need them, at a pace that the world can sustainably support. We would know that we can create more resources tomorrow out of our continuously creative impulses.

The problem is that we are each asleep to our relationship to money in some way. Waking up requires intervention. We need a map of the ways in which we are asleep. This is the fundamental beginning point for improving our relationship to money. How can a person who is asleep diagnose the ways in which he is asleep? He cannot. Asking people to explore their family history with money, their childhood money messages, and their money values will bring them some distance, but not all the way. Eventually, we will hit a wall. Without a map, we cannot see ourselves more clearly. This is precisely why a system that can help people find themselves is so useful.

We don't know why or how we got so confused, fearful, and ambivalent about money. We may try to create a story, but the truth is probably much more complex and nuanced than we can realize on our own. This book can help us see our own unique patterns from a higher vantage point. It gives us a map to penetrate the depths of our money psyches in a way we could not do on our own, using the framework of the Enneagram.

The Enneagram system pioneered by Oscar Ichazo in the 1960s was a psychospiritual personality system. He was the first to assign the nine passions and ego fixations to the Enneagram symbol. He was inspired by three influences: a Neo-Platonist work of the second century called *The Enneads and The Nine Mystical States*, the Kabbala's tree of life as a map of divine and human consciousness, and Pythagoras' writings. Oscar Ichazo and George Gurdjieff both placed the Enneagram system within the context of personal and spiritual development. Claudio Naranjo expanded the descriptions of the nine types and correlated them to known psychiatric categories (the unhealthiest aspects of each type) using panels of exemplars. Don Riso pioneered the vertical dimension of the Enneagram, deepening our understanding of the average and healthy traits of each type. Don Riso and Russ Hudson together have further developed our understanding of how the Enneagram can be brought into clearer coherence with modern psychology.

"I am personally convinced that the future of the Enneagram lies primarily in the quality of its teachers and in their ability to be present; further, the future of the Enneagram also lies in the quality, range, and applicability of material derived from the system." – Don Richard Riso, 2010.

I believe the Enneagram system is the best explanatory framework for understanding our money and economic decisions. It is both general and specific. It has an internal coherence that is general enough to be pertinent to all people while specific enough to be relevant to individuals. It is able to explain both why we don't do what we know we should do and how we differ in our relationships to money. It is holistic in that it is not just based on our cognitive head center, but integrates our emotions, our hearts, and our bodily instincts. It is from here that modern psychology and economics can begin to understand the black box of human decision making. We do not need shorthand heuristic psychological models. The Enneagram model clearly outlines a basis for decision making and behavior. What might seem irrational from the outside does not seem irrational from the inside.

As we make this exploration of different money styles, not only will we come to see ourselves more clearly, but we will also develop greater compassion for, and understanding of, our fellow humans. We will discover why money is so difficult for all of us in different ways. We will explore why some feel so strongly that they need money while others believe money is evil, some feel money is boring while others feel money is fascinating, some feel money is a burden while others feel money is to be enjoyed. We will explore why some people save easily while others don't. We will explore why some of us stay in cycles of debt and poverty, and others live hand to mouth without relief. Money is a charged topic for so many of us because it reflects our internal struggles on the grand stage of life. This book is unique in using the Enneagram symbol as a framework for understanding money. This framework helps illuminate the nature of wealth creation and prosperity, as well as the connection between money, fear, and love. I hope to inspire you to understand that your work with money is really work on yourself, and that the two paths are intertwined.

May you move past
false beliefs and unhelpful patterns
towards freedom and spaciousness
on your journey home to
wealth, prosperity, and love.

PART I:

NINE DOMAINS OF MONEY

CHAPTER 1

MONEY AS A JOURNEY

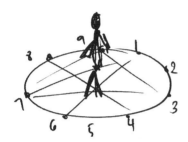

Where are you in your journey with money? We all begin from a place of scarcity, lack, and fear. And we all have the potential to journey to a place of wealth, prosperity, and love. How far we go depends on how much we allow money to teach us. Money is a medium for each of us to learn about ourselves and touch real truths about what is possible for our lives. It forces us to address questions about what we are doing with our lives, what our purpose is, and whether we are living fully, with vigor and joy. If we do not take the time, effort, and care to learn what money has to teach us, we will not travel far in our journeys with money. If, on the other hand, we allow money to be our teacher, we will eventually recognize that we directly impact our own wealth and prosperity by how open we are to the truth of love and abundance. So, a large part of each of our journeys with money is to discover the myriad ways we have blocked the truth of Love.

LIFE AND DEATH

When we were born, we were given life, but we were also threatened with the prospect of death. We had to develop faculties that would enable us to cope with this duality. In addition to our human instincts that enable us to survive and reproduce, we developed clever psychological structures to help us adapt and survive. As soon as we became capable of feeling hunger and desire, we could also feel dissatisfaction, frustration, sorrow and fear. With our animal instincts and human consciousness came our ability to experience pleasure, but also pain and suffering. As humans with survival instincts and a consciousness of our separate identities, we could be deluded and make mistakes, but we could also be brave, control our animal nature, and awaken to a higher level of consciousness.

At birth, we could not distinguish between ourselves and others. But quickly, we recognized that I am me and you are you, and we have survival needs. This ability to perceive ourselves as separate grew out of our ego consciousness and helps us survive and function in this physical world. If I could not perceive myself as separate, I would find it puzzling that I need food to eat and clothes to keep warm because it would seem these things should be a part of me. Our egos motivate us to get our needs met. Our egos are therefore critical to our ability to operate effectively and intelligently in this physical world. But at the same time, our egos cause us to embrace our separation from others and our fear of dying, and not recognize our habits as habits.

Our personalities are manifestations of our ego consciousness. Some of us are particularly attached to our parents. Some of us feel rejected by one or both of our parents. Some of us are frustrated by one or both of our parents. When we separate and individuate, we tend to do so in particular ways. This allows us to get our needs met, function in this physical world, and live our life. As such, there is nothing wrong with our egoic minds or our personalities.

THE EGO FEARS

Our egos and instincts are both actively engaged to avoid death. Fear, at its core, is an avoidance of death. However, if I am actively avoiding death, then I cannot be wholly alive. I cannot be in the flow, I cannot let go, surrender, trust. When I am in a state of fearfulness, I cannot appreciate, relax, and enjoy because fear keeps my thoughts, feelings, and body rigid. Fear keeps me in a fixated state, compelling me to act in my own self-interest. The ego is afraid of physical death and its own obsolescence. Our ego has every incentive to keep us scared, and on a straight and narrow personality path, so that it never loses its job. It doesn't want us to try anything new, or ask questions of ourselves.

Our egos also cause us to think dualistically. The ego thinks in terms of I am me, you are you. By extension, it also thinks: this is black and that is white, this is good and that is bad, this is yes and that is no. You are either with me or against me. The ego has its own powerful zero-sum logic. It's either mine or it's yours. If you have something, then I can't have it. If I have something, then you can't have it. If I don't take it, you will get it. I must take care of number one first. I come first, my family comes second because they help me, and everyone else comes a distant third. When I am coming from this egoic consciousness, I can't help but be selfish.

When our egos take our survival instincts and wield them to their own agenda, we feel like we need more money than we really do. Our egos have insatiable appetites. We are compelled to work more than we must and consume more than we need. But the more we indulge this thinking, the worse the situation becomes. We can never work enough or consume enough to satisfy our ego and fill our emptiness. The problem of scarcity is a problem of the egoic perspective. If all we can perceive is the physical reality that our five senses recognize, scarcity will indeed be the ultimate truth, because there is only so much oil in the ground, so many diamonds in the earth, and so much gold to be mined. To the extent that I steadfastly deny the existence of anything beyond the realm of the five senses, scarcity will always be reality.

When we are not awake, we use and relate to money in ways that only perpetuate the hunger in our soul. Rather than help us live better lives, the ego distorts and warps our behavior. Our egos prevent us from seeing that we live not only in the material world where there is scarcity, but also in a world where there is abundance and love. Why are we given survival mechanisms that induce such suffering?

OUR EVOLUTIONARY JOURNEY

We were given survival tools that induce suffering so that we will not settle for simply surviving. We were meant to ask what our lives are supposed to be about. Am I just this separate being that eats, sleeps, and survives? Or am I meant to experience something more in my conscious life? We are meant to recognize that the beliefs and assumptions of our egoic minds that protect us also hinder our living fully. We are meant to question the protective armor of our personalities and egos, and we are meant to shed this protective armor as we mature. This transformational process is not fun or easy, but it is necessary for our growth and development. We are each meant to suffer so that we will discover the source of our suffering.

We are all initially blocked by our egos to the truth of abundance and love, and it is up to us to wrest control back from our egos. By looking closely at our relationship to money, we can see the strategies we use to get what we want. By starting with the most superficial facts about our financial lives, we can begin to uncover our unconscious instincts and beliefs about ourselves and the world, what we believe we can and can't have. We all tend to have unconscious beliefs about money that keep us tethered to scarcity. By seeing how we are blocked from abundance and love, we begin to have choices. Seeing ourselves accurately and honestly gives us the freedom to break out of vicious cycles based on fear and resistance. As you read the book, ask yourself how you are blocked from wealth and love.

Our egos resist change. Love and abundance threaten the ego. To complete our journeys, we must overcome the strong pull of our egos. When we work with the Nine Domains of Money as a transformational process, we participate in an unfolding journey back to our true selves. This journey will lead us to discover our hearts, our capacities, and who we are meant to be. This process will help put us back in harmony with the flow of Being and ultimately enable us to feel, perceive, and experience Love.

MONEY AS OUTER WORK

The work on the Nine Domains of Money is part of our Outer Work. Outer Work is the work we do on our material lives to have well-being in realms such as health, relationships, and money. It is the work we do on our external selves to move past habitual, unhealthy patterns to live more balanced lives and realize our fullest potential. Inner Work, in contrast, is the work we do inside to take stock of ourselves, release fixations, move past limiting beliefs, wake up, and connect to our true selves behind our masks. While the practices of Inner Work help us experience the various aspects of Essence or Being, the practices of Outer Work help us experience the various aspects of abundance. Both Inner Work and Outer Work help us become more aware of how we have been asleep and how to wake up to our true potential. It is impossible to release our inner distortions without addressing our actual behaviors. As we become more successful in living our lives, we become more confident and less reliant on our ego programming. Inner Work and Outer Work, done together, support the emergence of our true capacities, and help us really show up and participate in our lives. From this perspective, doing the Outer Work of cultivating a healthier relationship to money supports our journeys back to ourselves.

MONEY AS A SYSTEM

Money. What is it? Is it a dollar bill? Is it a *thing*? Money is a medium of exchange that allows us to transact more easily. With it, we don't have to barter and store goods that may be bulky and difficult to transport. We can simply exchange bills and coins to get what we want. If I am a pumpkin grower, I don't have to haul around my pumpkins in a big wheelbarrow to trade for the things I need. Instead, I can sell my pumpkins for this thing called money, and then walk around with bills and coins in my pocket to buy what I need. Money is also a store of value that enables me to obtain valuable goods and services now or later. If I put a wad of bills under my mattress, I can take them out ten years later and still buy things with these bills. Money is a thing that makes our lives easier and more convenient, both as a medium of exchange and as a store of value.

But money is more than a *thing* – more than just paper or metal. Money supports our economy, the sea we swim in. It is part of the very fabric of our lives, underpinning our assumptions, motivations, and behaviors. Although money starts off as a *thing*, it quickly morphs into something much more complex and dynamic. Why? Because our interactions with this thing collectively change the thing itself. What we value, and how we spend, save, and invest all affect the value money has. If, collectively, we desire more gold, we will push the price of gold up. If we spend our dollars more quickly, we will push the overall prices up. If we work more productively, we will dampen the overall rise in prices. Money mirrors our communal values. What we believe in, pay attention to, have preferences for, spend on, invest in – these things materialize and grow. What we neglect will wither and fail to grow.

If we are collectively motivated by fear and scarcity, our system of exchange will mirror this belief. The discipline of economics began with Adam Smith who observed that people are selfish and greedy. He surprisingly concluded that if everyone acted in their own self-interest, the laissez-faire outcome would be optimal. Fear, greed, selfishness, and scarcity were taken as a starting point for individual behavior in explaining how the trading of scarce resources could result in optimal collective outcomes. However, just because economists assume humans are selfish doesn't necessarily make it so. If we each had a healthier, more enlightened relationship to money, then the entire discipline of economics would have to be reconstrued. The only reason that economists can legitimately assume fear, selfishness, and scarcity as underpinnings of the market system is because we allow these things to be true. We have not done the hard work to make them *not* true.

THE ELEMENTS OF MONEY

To have a precise and complete way to talk about our relationship to money, we must identify the essential aspects of this relationship. As a symbol of universal laws describing archetypal patterns, the Enneagram offers a powerful framework for helping us think about these essential elements. With the Nine Domains of Money[1] framework, we are able to talk about the nature of money as a system, and understand the concept of wealth and prosperity in a holistic way.

We have a relationship to each of the Nine Domains of Money, whether we are aware of it or not. If our relationship to each of these Nine Domains is healthy, then we will experience a sense of abundance and prosperity, whether we are "wealthy" by conventional standards or not. However, if we pay attention to certain Domains while ignoring other Domains, then our relationship to money will almost surely suffer.

From this model of money, we will see that wealth and prosperity are really about a state of being, and not just about money in the bank. The Nine Domains of Money help us see where we are in our journey with money,

---

[1] This concept of the Nine Domains of Money applies the Nine Domains of the Enneagram to the topic of money. It is based on the Nine Domains idea that was first publicly described by Don Riso at the 2010 International Enneagram Association (IEA) conference. The application, naming, and interpretation of each of the Nine Domains of Money is entirely my own.

and provide us with a guidepost to what is possible.   True wealth and prosperity is about being aligned in our three centers – having a clean heart, a clear mind, and a centered state of being. In the heart center, it is about being nurtured, of value, and connected to meaning. In the head center, it is about clarity, faith, and mindfulness. In the belly center, it is about vitality, wholeness, and balance. When we do not have these qualities, we will inevitably experience fear and scarcity, and no amount of money will enable us to feel wealthy and prosperous.

WHAT'S YOUR REACTION?

As you review the diagram of the Nine Domains of Money below, beginning at Domain 1 and moving clockwise around the circle, track your reactions. Are certain Domains especially interesting or intriguing? Are other Domains boring or unsettling? This is very useful information because each Domain is crucial to having a healthy relationship to money. What makes it difficult to sustain interest in a particular Domain? Why do you lose focus and turn your attention elsewhere?

It is natural and normal that we will not relate uniformly well to each of the Nine Domains of Money. When we operate from ego, we operate from fear, and our fears distort our beliefs, attention, and behavior. We will understandably enjoy and be more competent at certain Money Domains while having aversions and weaknesses in other Money Domains. Some of us love budgeting while others disdain it. Some of us focus on earning and wealth building, while others focus on meaning and understanding. These Nine Domains of Money help us to see more clearly areas that we are strong at, proud of, and possibly a bit fixated on. They also help us identify areas we resist, neglect, or downright resent. Can we simply farm out some Domains to others to manage on our behalf? Not really! Each of these Domains connects to our own growth process. If we fail to have a substantive connection to each Domain, we will not be able to progress around the circle. Domain 5 specifically follows Domain 4 which specifically follows Domain 3, and so on.

BALANCE
Domain 9

WEALTH BUILDING
Domain 8

BUDGETING
Domain 1

PLANNING
Domain 7

SPENDING
Domain 2

RISK MANAGEMENT
Domain 6

EARNING
Domain 3

KNOWLEDGE
Domain 5

BELIEFS
Domain 4

A TRANSFORMATIONAL PROCESS

By consciously addressing each Money Domain, the process of working through the Nine Money Domains becomes a transformational process. We begin to recognize that there are specific ways in which we are blocked from wealth and prosperity. Once we identify these blockages, we begin to see how to free ourselves so that we can move from surviving to thriving. In this transformational process, we will be forced to question our habits and ask whether they are truly serving us. We begin to see, perhaps for the first time, that we have choices. There isn't just one way to do budgeting, or one way to do planning. In each Domain, we will begin to make distinctions between ways that feel constricted and ways that feel spacious and full of possibilities. No matter where we have been or where we are in our relationship to money, it is always possible, in this moment, to choose something new, and to heal and grow.

We always have a choice – we can choose to engage life in a jaded way or in an enthusiastic way. The same is true of money. "Alright, I'll pay the bills, keep track of papers, check the bank balances. But, gosh, I really hate doing these things. There are so many more interesting things to do right now." If we take on a task in a perfunctory manner, just doing what we have to do, we will continue to come from a place of fear and scarcity and feel constricted. But if we take on each of the Nine Money Domains as a spiritual practice, we will be challenged to change our perspective. This is a powerful shift, not just for our relationship to money, but to life in general! We are accepting the possibility that everything might have something to offer us. If we do this, money becomes a vehicle for personal growth and transformation that shows us the possibility of a world of abundance and love as opposed to scarcity and fear.

THE INITIAL SHOCK

George Gurdjieff talked about the Enneagram as a process and how the process always began with an initial shock. An initial shock is required to begin examining your relationship to money. It is what brought you here to read this book and begin looking at your relationship to money. Be grateful for what brought you here.

DOMAINS 1, 2, 3 – SURVIVING

Domains 1, 2, and 3 are about the basics of survival. When we only pay attention to these first three Money Domains, we are living hand to mouth, making money, spending money, and approximately making ends meet. We are not ascribing much meaning to money or to our existence. Nor are we curious or knowledgeable about how the larger system works. We are not planning ahead or aware of our role in the bigger picture. We are merely surviving. *Stop and inquire:* Have I only been aspiring to survive? If so, what more is possible for my life? How can I move from surviving to thriving?

A second shock is required to move us out of survival mode. Perhaps a mid-life crisis makes things seem meaningless and inconsequential. Perhaps an existential shock makes us realize that we have no real direction in our lives. Whatever form this second shock takes, we can be grateful to it as well for egging us along on our journey back to ourselves and our true nature.

DOMAINS 4, 5, 6 – PURPOSING

Domains 4, 5, and 6 are about connecting to our purpose. This intermediate stage is critical for bridging from survival mode to thriving mode. Without a clear definition of our purpose and mission in life, it is impossible to thrive. Thriving means living every day believing that our life matters, that what we do and how we do it matters, and knowing that we are utterly supported in our journeys. *Stop and inquire:* How clear and connected am I to my purpose and mission? Does a lack of clarity and commitment affect my ability to create wealth and experience abundance and prosperity?

A third shock is required to move us from purpose to action. Without this third shock, we can get stuck at the gate, all dressed up but not going anywhere. This third shock is the stimulation we need to make good on our full potential. It's about acting, not just dreaming, being bold and fully alive.

DOMAINS 7, 8, 9 – THRIVING

Domains 7, 8, and 9 are about thriving. These Domains are about taking our survival skills and life's purpose and bringing our mission to fruition. This requires joyful participation, active engagement, and harmonious balance. When this part is missing, our dreams and plans cannot be fulfilled. *Stop and inquire:* How effectively am I manifesting my life's purpose with solid planning, engagement, and balance? How does lack of planning and follow through affect my ability to create wealth and experience abundance and prosperity?

This process does not end when we have gone through the Nine Domains once. In fact, the process is so continual that it is difficult to say that there is an exact beginning point at all. It is helpful to understand that there is a sequence from surviving to thriving. But there is no starting point or finish line. It is an ever deepening process. In order to do the work of budgeting in Domain 1, for example, we need to be clear about the meaning of money in our lives, which is the work of Domain 4. If we glide though life with superficially-held beliefs about money, it is difficult to envision greater possibilities for our lives, which is the work of Domain 7. Similarly, in order to do the work of Domain 2 and spend in a way that is nurturing, we need to understand how money works in our lives, which is the work of Domain 5. If we glide through life ignorant, without confidence about money, it is difficult to create wealth and manifest our plans, which is the work of Domain 8. And in order to do the work of Domain 3 and earn in a way that reflects our full potential, we must be able to make commitments, which is the work of Domain 6. And we can only keep our commitments and do our best work when we can maintain stability and balance in the midst of all kinds of change, which is the work of Domain 9. Therefore, to do the work of Domains 1, 2, 3, and begin the transformative process, we must actually call upon the other six Domains. The process is continual and iterative. In taking the wisdom of the Enneagram, and applying it to our relationships to money, we can move from surviving to thriving, from Fear to Love, and begin to create new wealth and prosperity in our lives.

"We think there are different categories of life, such as money, health, relationships, and then for some of us, another category called 'spiritual life.' But only the ego categorizes. There is only one drama going on in life: our walk away from God, and our walk back. Money is an area where we need, individually and collectively, a radical healing of our mental habits."
– Marianne Williamson, *A Return to Love.*

The Nine Money Domains and the Transformational Process

CHAPTER 2

SURVIVING:

DOMAINS 1, 2, 3

We can choose whether to relate to Domains 1, 2, 3 at the level of surviving or as part of a larger process of thriving. It is up to us to step into a more connected and purposeful life.

DOMAIN 1: BUDGETING

We have an intrinsic need to be able to account for our resources, and make sure that we have enough coming in to support the expenditures going out. Domain 1 is ostensibly about budgeting and making ends meet. But it is really about paying attention, about bringing awareness to our financial situation – how we manage money and how we stay within financial boundaries. There are three essential parts to this Domain:

1. **Data and Monitoring:** In order to know our financial situation, we need bank statements, credit card statements, pay stubs, receipts. We need to keep records, organize our papers, know where things can be found. We have to track this data over a full year at least because some expenses (like insurance or property taxes) are lumpy. The most important question is whether our income covers our expenses – literally whether we can afford our lifestyle.

2. **Prioritizing:** This is about interpreting the data and making choices. Which expenses are absolutely necessary? Which are we willing to forego? If spending exceeds income and we are living on credit card debt, how do we get out of this expensive sinkhole? If income exceeds spending, how do we invest our savings? What criteria will we use to make difficult calls about spending priorities?

3. **Staying within limits:** This is about making choices and adjusting our behavior so that we can stay within budget. What factors get in the way when it comes to staying within limits? What attitudes and behavioral patterns do I see in myself vis a vis this Domain? What kind of resistance do I have to staying within limits. How does this play out in my life and around money?

While Domain 1 is relatively straightforward, many of us are resistant to this Domain. When you read about these aspects of budgeting, did you experience some negativity? If so, can you stay with your feelings for five minutes without reacting? What do you learn about yourself when you stay with your feelings? We can have pretty strong reactions to budgeting. We rationalize that it is confining, tedious, boring, even unnecessary. We rationalize that we can budget intuitively without having to look at actual numbers. At the same time, we have a small niggling sense that our resistance to this Domain causes us pain. When we resist Domain 1, we tend to feel scattered, out of control, held back, guilty and ashamed.

A budget on paper feels confining. I won't keep to it.

I don't budget and am bad about tracking spending. I don't check on it and never did the checkbook balancing thing. I worry about over spending. But I mostly figure things will average out. My system is fuzzy, not clear. I operate on my intuition. I have an intuition about my spending over a month period. If I had more disposable income, I would be willing to take more risk.

I have a general idea and I do stuff online, but I hate accounting and find it boring and it is one of the biggest breakdowns in my life. I had six months of filing and bills. What was the charge? I wasn't paying attention to the details. I needed someone else to pay attention to it. It is the bigger things that I care about. Little problems are not interesting.

We help each other cheat. When we are so disciplined in our diet, then we feel like we deserve a cocktail. There never is not a great reason to go to a restaurant. There's a giddiness to it, but has the consequence of guilt and shame. I deal with it by forgetting about it completely. I have no budget, no commitment to a bigger thing. But I feel I need that. It's a foreign vocabulary for us.

I don't like details. I don't budget. Just hearing about it makes me cringe. I detest it. I don't see the point. I have no idea how much money we save or spend per month.

I have a certain arrogant attitude – I can make the money, so don't make me manage it too! I don't keep records. I'm too busy. I don't pay any attention to tracking things. A budget review confirmed my gut instinct that we needed to slow down.

Do any of these comments sound familiar? I invite you to relax your beliefs about Domain 1 for a moment and consider what Domain 1 might offer you. Domain 1 is about our need for order, accuracy, and self-regulation, all of which enable our financial lives to be self-sustaining. It provides us with the means to keep things in balance so that there is neither too much nor too little spending. Too much spending means that we are spending by borrowing money that must eventually be repaid. Too little spending means that our income has not been fully earmarked for priorities, which include consumption, but also investments for the future. It might seem strange that spending too little could be as bad as spending too much, but spending too little means that you are underinvesting in areas that could benefit from greater investment. Either you are not enjoying the benefits of your resources today or you are not investing for the future. When we live in imbalance, we are not living to our fullest potential.

Without Domain 1 being operational, the system cannot be healthy because there won't be a strong mechanism in place to ensure that the system stays in balance and is self-sustaining. Domain 1 is like having an organized desk that clears our mind and allows us to start fresh. Who isn't cheered by a clean, organized desk where they can find what they are looking for? It gives us the strong, organized foundation to do our work. Knowing and understanding your income and spending and making conscious choices about your spending and earning priorities has that same power to free you. You can earmark certain expenditures without feeling it is wrong. And you no longer have to operate in a fog of uncertainty about whether you are doing something that threatens your financial health. By budgeting, you actually put yourself in a position to get what you want from life. It relieves you of worry, stress, and fear, and allows you to feel more clear and spacious.

Doing the work of Domain 1 requires a shift in energy. For some of us, it will require a downshift; others, it will require an upshift. What it will require in all of us is an ability to sit still, focus, and pay attention. It is very much like meditating. In fact, I offer Domain 1 as a modern day meditation practice that has the power to calm our nerves, center us, and cultivate our inner observer. As you begin to engage Domain 1 as a modern day meditation practice, I offer these questions to guide you.

1. How do I pay attention?

How do I pay attention to my money? How do I know what I know about how much comes in and goes out? Do I just check what is left over each month? Do I obsess about the checking account balance daily or try to input everything into a software program daily? How can I be informed and stay in balance, but not be anxious or obsessed?

2. What beliefs do I have about Budgeting?

1. What do I believe about record keeping and staying organized?
   a.   They are unnecessary burdens.
   b.   They are necessary evils.
   c.   They are a lot of fun to do.
   d.   None of the above. I believe _____

2. What do I believe about creating a budget with spending priorities?
   a.   I don't want to plan ahead because I want to be spontaneous.
   b.   My spouse will not cooperate with me.
   c.   It will be an opportunity to have more freedom, less fear and guilt.
   d.   None of the above. I believe _____

3. What do I believe about my current financial situation?
   a.   I don't want to know because I might have to change my lifestyle.
   b.   I know we spend too much and need to cut back.
   c.   I have a general idea and everything will work out fine.
   d.   None of the above. I believe _____

4. What do I believe about staying within a budget?
   a.   It will cramp my style and force me to deny myself things I want.
   b.   Budget? What's a budget?!!
   c.   I just won't be able to do it.
   d.   None of the above. I believe _____

3. How do I actually behave around Budgeting?

Do my beliefs about budgeting cause me to avoid it altogether? Do I procrastinate? Do I do it sporadically but without enthusiasm? Do I do it regularly but resentfully? Do I do it anxiously and obsessively? What assumptions create resistance in me? Do I have some story about being too busy: "There's not enough time in the day to do what I need to do, let alone waste my time doing budgeting." Do I have some story about there not being enough charge: "Budgeting is so tedious and boring." Do I have some story about there not being enough understanding: "The budget is so complicated that I'll never be able to sort it out." Or do I have some story about there not being enough support: "My wife will never cooperate with me on this exercise. She just spends what she wants to." These are just a few examples of the possible stories that keep us tied to scarcity.

4. What could shift if I relaxed some of my old beliefs about Budgeting?

If I could relax some of my beliefs about budgeting, what might shift in my life? How might paying attention help to release anxiety, guilt and shame? How might it enable me to have healthier conversations with my spouse about money? How might it enable me to be more confident and hopeful about my financial future? How might it enable me to have a relationship to money that is more relaxed and engaged? Domain 1 creates the bedrock foundation from which we can experience prosperity in our life. Avoidance and fear make the unknown scarier than it really is.

5. Budgeting as a Spiritual Practice

I call the spiritual practice for this Domain "in breath out breath, inflow outflow." It is about paying attention to the money that comes into and goes out of your life. This spiritual practice is akin to the meditation practice of paying attention to your breath. We breathe in and out over six million times a year. It's repetitive, continual, perhaps boring. But it keeps us alive! Rather than being resentful or bored, we should be grateful for every in breath and out breath we take. In the same way, money comes in and goes out of our life continuously. It is a bit tedious to track. Possibly boring. But at the same time, it signifies that we are alive. We are using resources and generating new resources. There is nothing to resent and everything to be grateful for. Whenever you hear the word boring, think "ego!" It's your ego making up stories to keep you focused on what it wants you to focus on. Your ego believes that your survival depends on not paying attention to the "boring" stuff. But what's boring? In truth, nothing is boring. Life is alive, wondrous, real. If you really pay attention, it's all interesting. The entire world is fascinating, down to your in breath and out breath. What happens when you pay attention to your breath? It's not easy to do at first. But when you do, you calm down. Your nervous system relaxes. Your mind clears. You stop holding on to things mentally and emotionally. You are here, present, peaceful. The same thing happens when you begin to relate to Domain 1 like this. When you pay attention to the inflow and outflow of your money like you pay attention to your in breath and out breath, without judgment, you will feel clear headed, clean hearted and present. You will begin to notice things about your life and your choices, without fear or shame. Cultivating a practice of "in breath out breath, inflow outflow" will enable you to pay relaxed attention to money and is the foundational piece for creating wealth and experiencing prosperity.

DOMAIN 2: SPENDING

We have an intrinsic need to feed, clothes, and shelter ourselves. We must obtain what we need to care for ourselves and others. Domain 2 is ostensibly about spending, but it is really about nurturing. Once we have established an ability to pay attention to the inflow and outflow of money, we can turn our attention to how we spend money to nurture ourselves. Domain 2 is about nourishing our bodies and souls so that we can be healthy and well. In order to have a healthy relationship to this Domain, we must bring awareness to our spending behavior and motivations. There are three parts of this Domain to consider:

1. **The Nature of Expenses:** Do I track spending? Can I track spending by category, by recipient, by type of expense, by form of payment? All are interesting in their own ways. By category, do I know how much goes to food, clothing, shelter, health, transportation, travel, gifts, and various other areas? By recipient, do I know how much goes for my spending versus others' spending? By type of expense,

do I know how much is spent on absolutely necessary, medium necessary, unnecessary things? By form of payment, do I know how much is spent with various credit cards, versus checks or cash?

2. **Spending Motivations:** What drives my spending? Am I driven by a need for security, social connection, social status, or stimulation? Am I driven by my ideas about what is correct, meaningful, or smart? Am I driven to be frugal or to keep up with the Jones?   Is my spending driven by fear – fear of not having enough or not being good enough? How do I discern what is appropriate to spend on and what is not?

3. **Spending patterns:** What patterns and spending cycles do I observe in myself? Is my spending consistent or volatile? Am I planful or spontaneous, even reckless? Do I mostly buy things with my credit card or with cash? How does this impact my spending behavior? What is my attitude towards those I buy from? Am I grateful for their goods and services? Do I use money to be self-sufficient, or possibly to separate myself from others?

Domain 2 tends to be an area we like to talk about. It makes us happy to think about the things we buy. But a deeper inquiry into this Domain can trigger some strong reactions. How we spend our money can be a charged and sensitive topic touching something deep inside us, because the spending choices we make reflect our sense of identity and core values. Have I ever tried to buy happiness, love, friendship?

I have a dysfunctional relationship with money. Either I spend and then feel guilty, or don't do it and then feel deprived and angry.

I'm really in debt. I'm fixing it and working on it, and have had tough conversations with creditors. How did I get into debt so bad? I'm still amazed and don't understand how this happened. I got myself completely out of debt, and then within a year, I was back in the hole – what happened?

My spending depends on my mood. I love creating a celebration wherever I go. Let's enjoy this moment and live and fully indulge and share the moment and the joy of it and forget the scarcity. When I go out to shop, I can get a real high and buzz from it.

I am back and forth with spending. I will spend the money – even if it is unnecessary, but it is comforting to do. I go from frugal to carefree. I feel like, no, we don't have enough, to blowing it. I want to be carefree. But then I am racked with guilt about spending money that could have gone to paying off the debt. I do a lot of second guessing.

There has always been adequate money for me to do stuff. But when I go shopping and buy too much, I always feel guilty. My story was – it was his money and I didn't earn it, so I really shouldn't be spending it.

When we avoid taking a deeper look at spending, it is often because we are overwhelmed with self-judgments about what is appropriate. It is easier to continue doing what we have been doing than to examine the implications of our choices. But our resistance to this Domain causes us pain because we feel unnourished without understanding why.

The idea that we are *supposed* to be nourished by our spending can be at once comforting and startling. It is comforting because we yearn to be nourished, but it can be startling because we so often feel unnourished. The challenge of Domain 2 is to learn to come to a place of groundedness where we can admit not only our longing for nourishment, but also how we have denied ourselves that nourishment.

Our consumption patterns, collectively, have powerful ripple effects that drive the way farmers farm, the way animals are raised, and impacts international shipping routes, migration patterns, waste disposal, wars, global warming, and so on and so on. When we do not spend in a way that nourishes ourselves, it is a tragic waste of the labor, resources, and energy that went into delivering those goods or services to us, for our benefit. The world nurtures us, but it is our obligation to think seriously about how we are nurtured by our spending. When we don't spend in a way that nourishes our body and souls, we compromise ourselves and our ability to experience the love and abundance that truly exists around us, while at the same time wasting valuable resources. Changing our spending orientation from acting out impulses and habits to nurturing ourselves requires a shift in our energy. For some of us, it will require greater self-care, while for others, it will require pruning. What it requires is an ability to listen to our bodies and our inner voice so that we can tune in to what is really needed. Consider these five questions.

1. How do I pay attention?

How do I pay attention to my spending? Do I know what categories I spend on? Do I have a sense of my spending patterns and how they fit together with my income patterns? Am I conscious about where my money goes? Do I feel grateful and nourished by what I buy? Or do I feel anxious and guilty about my spending?

2. What beliefs do I have about Spending?

1. What do I believe about spending money?
   a.   Money is to be spent and shared, not hoarded.
   b.   It is best to be frugal (and save for a rainy day).
   c.   Nothing is going to stop me from living well.
   d.   None of the above. I believe _____

2. What do I believe is the right approach to spending?
   a.   I ought to be disciplined about spending.
   b.   I want to be spontaneous and respond to what comes up.
   c.   I ought to spend only when I deserve it.
   d.   None of the above. I believe _____

3. What do I believe about my spending needs?
   a.   My spending needs are very limited. I just need food and shelter.
   b.   My spending needs are very high and difficult to constrain.
   c.   My spending needs are indistinguishable from my wants and therefore unlimited.
   d.   None of the above. I believe _____

3. How do I actually behave around Spending?

Looking truthfully at our actual behavior is a powerful act that alone can often change our behavior. Is my spending consistent from month to month? Do I bring discipline and forethought to my spending? Or am I a spontaneous spender? Do I spend even when I don't have the money? Do I spend more when I feel giddy? Do I spend more when I want to make myself feel better? Do I get a rush from buying things on sale? Do I give myself permission to spend only when I am "deserving"? Do I spend more when I am with friends and cannot say no? Do I love to treat everyone to a good time or am I incredibly tight? Do I use spending to make myself better than others? Do I use spending to connect to others? When we spend out of a sense that we are missing something or need to block something out, we presume scarcity – scarcity of joy, satisfaction, worth, acceptance, respect. These are just a few of the ways that spending can keep us tethered to an experience of scarcity.

4. What could shift if I only spent money on things that nourish me?

If we don't feed and nurture ourselves, we have to turn to others to get our needs met and be takers rather than givers. If we cannot be honest about our own needs and address them directly and honestly, then we will stay hungry, frustrated, resentful, hurt and ashamed. When we deny our need for nourishment, we become broken-hearted and it is impossible to experience what is real and available to us.

So we must take the time to figure out what really nurtures us. This is not to be confused with self-indulgence. What do you really need to be fed, body and soul? What power would you gain by being really clear about what you need? How would this enable you to live in balance, having security, connection, and stimulation? When we listen to ourselves, and give ourselves what we really hunger for, whether that be a vacation, a hot cup of coffee, or time to listen to a beautiful piece of music, we feel cared for and loved.

5. Spending as a Mundane vs Spiritual Practice

A helpful spiritual practice for Domain 2 is "deep listening." Rather than spending reflexively, we can choose to spend consciously from a place of deep listening to our bodies and inner voices. Listening deeply takes practice. Messages come in at us from all directions. It requires attention to tune in. What do I really want and need in this moment? When we allow ourselves to listen deeply to our needs and the world's needs, we will be fed, supported, loved, and touched by how connected we really are. Cultivating a practice of deep listening will enable you to connect to what truly nurtures you, which is the second step on your way to creating wealth and experiencing prosperity.

DOMAIN 3: EARNING

We have an intrinsic need to bring resources into our lives and feel that we are of value. Domain 3 is ostensibly about how we make money. But it is really about how we work to our full potential. When I am nurtured and nourished, I am ready to take my place in the world. I can be of service and value to others. Domain 3 is about how we earn a living by offering our gifts. In order to have a healthy relationship to this Domain, we must recognize that we have something to offer that is valued by others. There are three parts of this Domain to consider:

1. **Making money:** How do I make a living? What motivates me to make money? How did I choose this work?

2. **Skills assessment:** What are my strengths? What are my gifts? What type of work ethic do I have? Am I a good team player? How well do I learn and adapt?

3. **Full potential:** How can I earn a living in a way that feeds my soul and enables me to work to my fullest potential? Am I doing what I am meant to be doing? Am I able to shine every day?

Domain 3 can be an area where we feel resigned and even trapped. How we make a living can be a difficult topic because it can reflect the limits we feel we are up against, our survival fears, and how we are valued. It forces us to confront the question of whether we are living to our fullest potential.

> When I was younger, I was a single mom working to make ends meet. Now I want to find work that fits me. But I am scared about marketing myself and getting people to pay me for my services.
>
> I can't figure out what I want to do and I keep changing jobs. I want to keep my options open and some options are bound to be good options.
>
> I've lived many years as a poor starving artist. I didn't want to have an ordinary job with regular hours. For many years, I was practically giving away my services for free. But lately, I have been raising my prices and standing up for my value. I am doing this for a lot of reasons. Mainly I want to grow up.
>
> I took a job that was expedient, but not my passion. I just wanted to make a decent living so I could have a good life, never considering for a second the cost of doing a job that was not my passion.
>
> I don't know how to offer my gift to the world and make money. I just don't believe it could work out, and I'm scared of trying. My dreams feel out of my reach.

We may avoid doing what we love because we feel we have no choice. Maybe we believe that changing careers would be like changing tires on a moving bus. Or that we are too old to learn new tricks. Or that we just need to put in a few more years till we can retire. We are tempted to continue doing what we know without really asking whether this is the most we have got in us. Our inertia in this Domain causes us pain because we continue to live a life that not as fulfilling as it might be.

The idea that we are *supposed* to live and work to our fullest potential may be obvious to some and yet completely foreign to others. Some perhaps know this to be true but feel they cannot afford to entertain the possibility. The challenge of Domain 3 is to ask ourselves if we are really doing what we are meant to be doing with the full set of skills and interests that define who we are.

When we aren't doing work that we love, we prevent ourselves from leaving fear behind and moving towards what is possible. We compromise our ability to experience the abundance that truly exists around us. Changing our orientation from default to intention requires our willingness to examine what we would like to offer of ourselves, and how that matches up with what is valued by the world.[2] What personal training or education do I need? What contacts will I have to make? What compromises will be needed in the short term? For some of us, a course change will require more confidence and engagement, while for others it will require a willingness to go slower and more humbly towards a new but more intriguing arena. As you begin to explore the possibility of stepping into your fullest potential, consider these five questions.

1. How do I pay attention?

How have I paid attention to making money? What is it that I have typically tracked? Am I tracking my pay? Am I tracking whether it is lighting me on fire? Am I tracking my reputation and status? Am I building my resume? Building my network? What's got my attention? Am I even thinking about reaching my fullest potential?

2. What beliefs do I have about making money?

1. What do I believe about making money?
    a. Money doesn't grow on trees. I'm grateful for the job I have.
    b. Being creative and making money don't go together.
    c. Making money is easy. There are a lot of ways to make money if you're willing to do it.
    d. None of the above. I believe _____

---

[2] This chapter applies to those who take care of others without pay, such as a stay-at-home mother or father, or those who choose to work in volunteer positions, to the extent that they have a means of viable financial support and they deem it to be the best use of their talents.

2. What is my attitude about work?
   a.   Just a few more years, then I can retire.
   b.   I work to put food on the table. That's all it's about.
   c.   I love what I do.
   d.   None of the above. My attitude is_____

3. What do I believe is the right approach to making money?
   a.   The best way to make money is to earn a stable salary.
   b.   The best way to make money is to work for yourself.
   c.   The best way to make money is to have a form of passive income
        that grows over time.
   d.   None of the above. I believe _____

3. How do I actually behave around Making Money?

Does my work stimulate me to be my best, intellectually, socially, energetically? Do I put in my best effort everyday? Do I have a sense that my best work will be rewarded, both now and in the future? Do I continue to hone my skills and talents? Do I secretly dream of doing something else? What stories do I tell myself about why I continue doing what I am doing? Am I secretly or not so secretly counting the days until retirement? Do I undervalue myself? Do I find myself doing what I love but not making enough money to make ends meet? Or do I continue to do work that I don't love because I don't know what else to do? These are just a few of the ways that we behave around the earning Domain that keep us tethered to an experience of scarcity.

4. What could shift if I made money in a way that fed and energized me?

What would be different if I made money in a way that really fed me and energized me? I would be excited every morning about getting up to do my work. I would be motivated to take care of my body and take care of myself so that I can continue to do my best work. I would not need to look outside of myself for validation, because I would know that I was doing good work. Because my work would be intrinsically satisfying, I would not be so focused on how much money I am paid. At the same time, though, I would not accept others undervaluing my services or disrespecting my work. When I hit a roadblock, I would persevere, believing that if I truly shine, there is no way others can resist what I offer to the world. If I made money in a way that really fed me and energized me, I would be confident in the two-way relationship between providing service and earning money. And because I value my energy and effort, I would not squander the money I make. I would not feel inclined to spend money thoughtlessly or foolishly. Instead, I would eat well and exercise and keep my energy up so that I could put in another great day of work. When we deny our ability to work to our fullest potential, it hurts our heart and we feel deprived. This forces us to find outlets for self-soothing. So we must take the time to figure out how to work in a way that we can truly shine. This is not to be confused with bragging and false glory. It is about finding a way to work and live to your fullest capacities so that you are inspired to be your best self and live in balance – grounded, secure, connected, and passionate. When we allow ourselves to work to our fullest capacities, we are doing what we are meant to do.

5. Earning a living as a Mundane vs Spiritual Practice

The spiritual practice for Domain 3 is "humble self-regard." Humble self-regard is about having an appropriate level of self-regard. Humility is required to never put ourselves above others. But we should never underestimate ourselves either. Humble self-regard is about perceiving our whole existence as a confirmation of the truth that our life is a gift and that we are meant to make good on this gift by becoming what we are meant to be. Cultivating self-regard is the opposite of selfish. By holding yourself back, you hold the whole universe back. The universe wants each of us to shine and make good on our promise. So it is our obligation to assess our gifts and honor these gifts by bringing them forth in our life and in our work. It is about having the confidence to know that the world awaits your arising. By cultivating a practice of "humble self-regard" we choose to earn a living in a way that not only allows us to shine but also serves others, and we begin to see that how we generate income must be integrally linked to who we can be.

CHAPTER 3

PURPOSING:
DOMAINS 4, 5, 6

Domains 4, 5, 6 enable us to articulate what matters to us and what our commitments are so that we can move from surviving to thriving. If, however, we do not connect meaning, understanding, and commitment of Domains 4, 5, 6 to planning, action, and balance of Domains 7, 8, 9, we will not be able to benefit fully from our purposing.

DOMAIN 4: BELIEFS

We have an intrinsic need to make sense of our lives, and making sense of money is part of this impulse. Domain 4 is ostensibly about our money beliefs, but it is really about moving from superficially-held beliefs to personal meaning. Domain 4 specifically follows Domain 3 about earning and being of value. Domain 4 is about connecting external value to what is of personal value to us. Making meaning and determining what is of personal value is a personal process. Meaning to you may be about developing yourself and your talents, doing something unique or creative, understanding things, doing what's right, being responsible, being free, enjoying pleasure, exercising your power, being comfortable, having integrity, maturing and growing. It may be about security and well-being. It may be about connecting with others, fighting for justice, making a contribution, living in harmony with nature. It may be about connecting with spirit, being inspired and awed. It is about distilling your beliefs down to ideas that resonate for you and inspire you. It is about creating a life that is worth living. In order to have a healthy relationship to this Domain, we must become aware of our inner selves. There are three parts to consider:

1. **Money Beliefs:** What do I believe to be true about money? Where do my beliefs come from? How did my family background and cultural context influence my money beliefs? What childhood messages did I receive about money? Do I believe that money is evil, a tool of the unjust, or that it disconnects me from others? Are my beliefs true to me or do they come from outside me?

2. **Making Meaning:** How do I get in touch with what is meaningful to me? How do I ascribe meaning to my experiences? Do things happen to me by chance? What is behind my success or failure? What possibilities are available to me? How do I know what is authentic and true? How do I listen to my inner voice?

3. **Meaning of Money:** What does money enable me to do and be? Why is money meaningful to me? What is the relationship between my beliefs about money, how I create meaning around money, and how I relate to money?

Domain 4 is about moving past superficial, inherited beliefs to something deeper and much more personal. Superficial beliefs persuade us to hold ourselves apart and judge things (including money) and people from afar. In contrast, making meaning forces us to participate and take responsibility.

> Money is a marker of how you are doing relative to others.
>
> Money doesn't grow on trees.
>
> Having more than you need feels vaguely sinful. Having too much brings out greed in people. Money can have a corrupting influence.
>
> There is a sense of vulgarity about money. I've avoided looking at the world through a money lens. Money is a hot issue for me and is about power and adulthood.

When we are young, we are flooded with messages about money that we take at face value. We inherit beliefs from our parents, our culture, and the outside world. But in the process of growing up, we begin to filter these messages through the lens of our own personal experience. Oh, yes, dad was right, "money doesn't grow on trees!" Or, "Money is not the tool of the corrupt." We reject some messages and old beliefs, while modifying others, and incorporating yet others. We begin to make meaning of the world that we live in. During the process of growing up and maturing, we begin to make personal sense of our lives, and we begin to craft a personal story about the significance, importance, and value of things. From a loosely detailed canvas, a rich and complex mosaic is created.

In the same way, with our money journeys, we must traverse a road from superficial, unexamined beliefs to personal meaning. If we do not take this journey, our relationship to money will forever be stuck in a childlike phase. When we take on the work of defining for ourselves the personal meaning money has, this will propel us forward to meaningful action. Buddha said "You must decide for yourself what you want to believe and where you want to invest meaning, and then you must commit to what you have chosen."

The idea that we are *supposed* to make meaning of our lives and make meaning of money in our lives may come easily to some, but be quite foreign to others. The challenge of Domain 4 is to ask ourselves whether our beliefs about money are superficial or authentic. When we don't take the time to create meaning, we end up mimicking the inherited beliefs of our parents and culture and making self-defeating choices out of guilt and misplaced loyalty to family stories and dramas. If we don't engage in this maturing process, we compromise our ability to experience the abundance that truly exists around us.

But changing our orientation from beliefs to meaning requires a willingness to question the status quo and our own beliefs. This process of making meaning and living authentically is a lifelong process. As the world around us changes, so too does our relationship to the world and to money. As you begin to explore your beliefs about money and how you might create meaning from these beliefs, consider these questions.

1. What beliefs do I have about money?

1. What do I believe about money?
   a. Money is boring and mundane.
   b. Money is embarrassing.
   c. Money is vulgar.
   d. Money is great.
   e. None of the above. I believe _____

2. What do I believe money can buy?
   a. Money gives you comfort, stability, security.
   b. Money gives you self-worth.
   c. Money gives you status and power.
   d. Money gives you freedom and independence.
   e. None of the above. I believe _____

3. What do I believe about the importance of money?
   a. Money is a means to an end.
   b. Money is a way to avoid problems and not worry.
   c. Everything I want and need requires money.
   d. Without money, I will starve.
   e. None of the above. I believe _____

4. What do I believe about deserving money?
   a. Having money would make me selfish.
   b. A certain amount of money is okay, but too much is greedy.
   c. I am entitled to the money I earn.
   d. I am entitled to money in general.
   e. None of the above. I believe _____

5. What do I believe about what money does to people?
   a. Money takes people away from experiencing life.
   b. Money creates divides between people.
   c. Money makes people greedy and powerful.
   d. Money makes people wise.
   e. None of the above. I believe _____

6. What do I believe is the correct way to relate to money?
   a. It's not right to have, want, or be driven by money.
   b. Saving money would require me to put my life on hold.
   c. Money will take care of itself.
   d. I must work hard and save money.
   e. None of the above. I believe _____

2. Do these beliefs serve me?

Do my beliefs serve me or do they block me? What do I gain from holding these beliefs? And what do I lose? How do my beliefs block me from living to my fullest potential? How am I blocked from bringing money into my life? How am I blocked from being the greatest service to the world? Are my beliefs about money supporting me?

3. How can I create meaning around money that serves me?

What would be different if instead of holding superficial and unexamined beliefs, I worked to create meaning around money that really served me? What difference might it make in my life? How could I begin to do this? The first thing I would explore is where my beliefs came from and how valid my beliefs are. The second thing I would do is examine how my beliefs serve me and don't serve me. The third thing I would do is explore what is meaningful to me and how money is connected to what is meaningful to me. When we deny the value of money, we cut off vital energy, and we feel deprived. This forces us to justify why we are so blocked, frustrated, and envious. Creating meaning around money does not mean putting money on a pedestal. It means finding a way to connect what is personally meaningful about money as an energy to what you wish to bring forth in your life. When we have meaning, we want to be here, participating and responsible for our lives.

4. Living authentically as a Spiritual Practice

The spiritual practice for Domain 4 is to live authentically by maintaining contact with our inner source – the place that gives us renewed inspiration, creativity, freshness and meaning. This spiritual practice means connecting to things fundamental and universal. When we live authentically, we can no longer stand apart and shrug our shoulders. When we live authentically, we actively participate in the unfolding of the universe. We become personally invested in the process of defining what is meaningful and we can no longer act as if we were free from responsibility. Once we have taken the adult journey to defining what is meaningful to us, we can no longer pretend to be victims or powerless bystanders. By living authentically, we choose to live in a way that makes life worth living.

Domain 4

Let me give an example of how this process might work. Carol came into my office, ostensibly to get help with her budgeting process. But as we began to look at her budget, it became apparent how charged money was for her. As we spoke about her charitable contributions, she began to sob. She felt that she could not give properly to the charities of her choice. She felt disempowered to make decisions herself. She felt that her relationship to her husband was deeply unequal and unfair, and she felt "victimized" by the fact that she had compromised her career to be the mother to their three children. She was very down on herself about the fact that she had "underperformed in the money arena," because she was not career-oriented, did not make as much money as he did, and was not as worthy as he was. Her relationship to money led to resentment and an unsatisfactory marriage.

Carol had inherited her beliefs about money and power from her parents. "It is deeply ingrained in me that it is his money and I need to petition for it." She felt that she did not have access to the household funds and felt diminished by this belief about her relationship to money, power and authority. She believed that who has money has power. She also believed that people who work for money are selling out. She believed that a lot of money equals bad and that if she had money, she would be a part of the bad people. She also believed that money is not righteous and it should go to charity. Carol had a lot of beliefs about money that she inherited from her childhood. But she had not had the opportunity to really mature her beliefs into something personally meaningful for her. Her beliefs kept her a victim, and held her away from personal responsibility.

When we went through a Domain 4 process of examining the meaning of money and what was deeply meaningful for her, she realized that what she cared about was being able to contribute and serve her community. We looked at how her beliefs about money prevented her from connecting money to what was meaningful to her, and she recognized that the lack of money served her because it allowed her to feel righteous and resentful and stay in the victim role. But she also recognized how holding on to her negative beliefs about money blocked her from an ability to contribute, feel of value, and be empowered. She recognized that by questioning the validity of her beliefs, she was also able to see a different perspective about her relationship to her husband's income. She realized that he was not the one with a separate checking account, she was! Then we discussed how she might create a meaning of money that resonated positively and powerfully for her. When we did this, Carol realized that money was a neutral thing, and that she could welcome it into her life as a way to empower her to make contributions that she valued and that make a positive difference in other people's lives. This freed her from the negative beliefs about money that kept her stuck, and allowed her to reach for her full potential as a physical therapist, serving others, while making a good income, developing a freer and healthier relationship to money.

DOMAIN 5: KNOWLEDGE

We have an intrinsic need to understand the world around us and how things work. Domain 5 is ostensibly about our knowledge of money. But it is really about moving from superficial knowledge to a deeper understanding of how money works in our lives and how to make good decisions about money. It is also about our integrity, self-confidence and deeper wisdom. The work of Domain 5 should be done after the work of Domain 4 because meaning precedes understanding. We are only motivated to understand that which is meaningful to us. Our hearts lead our good minds. If money is meaningful, and we have done the work of Domain 4, then we will be motivated to understand how money works. There are three parts to consider:

1. **Knowledge about Money:** What do I know about money and how money works? Do I understand how money grows? Do I understand the relationship between budgeting and savings? Do I understand my investment options? Do I understand the tradeoffs between risk and return? Do I understand the consequences of saving and not saving money for my future lifestyle?

2. **Learning about Money:** Where have I gotten my knowledge about money? Who do I trust to teach me? Do I have the confidence that I can learn what I need to learn? Do I learn by doing? Do I learn from books? Have I had opportunities in my life to learn about money? What have I done with these opportunities?

3. **Money Wisdom:** What does it mean to cultivate wisdom about money? What's the difference between knowledge and wisdom? How do I make sense of different things? How do different parts of my life fit together? How do I integrate what I know into my lived life?

Domain 5 can be an area we feel resigned about. We may believe that we are ignorant because the topic is too big, complex, and overwhelming. We may believe that we must stay ignorant so that we can stay focused on what matters and not get derailed into a pit of worries around money. We may believe that we are not capable or powerful enough to do anything, or that money is bad so there is no point in learning how money works. Whatever blocks us from understanding money also blocks us from a clarity about how to achieve what is meaningful to us. Knowledge is a gateway to fruition. Without knowledge, we deprive ourselves of the tools we need to turn what is meaningful to us into reality. Knowledge truly is power.

> I feel resistance to knowing about money. I fear finding out that my tastes are too expensive for what I can afford. I fear that I will not be able to continue my standard of living. I fear that if I learn, then things will necessarily have to change for the worse.

> At tax time, I find it quite stressful and I have a hopeless feeling that I can't do it on my own and I don't understand and it is scary. I feel quite ashamed that I have to ask for help around this area.

> I have a low understanding about money and lack interest in it. I trust others to manage my money because I don't want to take the time researching investment options, which would be too boring for me.

> The topic of money causes me to feel helpless and defiant at the same time. I don't trust myself, but I don't trust others either. I don't want to worry and micromanage money.

> I don't have a good head about money matters. I don't take it seriously, and have no experience, training, background in it, and it feels foreign to me. It hasn't been a priority.

To understand money is to have more than just information. To understand money is to have confidence that we can make something meaningful happen. When we understand how the larger forces around us work, we are less apt to feel swept to and fro, victimized by random events. We realize that things are not always personally directed towards us. Having knowledge and understanding enables us to navigate life more effectively. We are meant to understand the nature of things. This understanding adds to the richness of our lives and is part of what makes living worthwhile. Ignorance about money compromises our ability to experience the abundance that truly exists around us.

Having an orientation and desire to understand money requires a willingness to be curious. You must first care to know, recognizing the gift that exists in the knowing. Then, as you begin to take on the process of learning, you can integrate your understanding of money into your lived life, connecting it to what is meaningful for you. As you begin to explore the possibility of understanding money, consider these questions:

1. How do I work to understand money?

Do I want to understand money and how it works? Do I put any effort into understanding how money works in my life and in the larger economy? What blocks me from learning more?   Lack of interest, lack of confidence, lack of time? What are the consequences of my lack of understanding? Do I rely on others to manage things for me? Do I feel hindered in being able to make my life really work the way I want to because I fail to understand how money works or the support money can bring?

2. What could shift if I understood money better?

Ignorance about money induces feelings of shame and fear. We are ashamed that we are unable to control something that is important to us, and we are afraid that our ignorance will prevent us from reaching our true potential. When we understand, we feel less victimized and more in control of our own destinies. Understanding compels me to participate in life, in the world, in the economy. Once I perceive that money is a stimulant and a lubricant, I cannot deny how compelling it is. Not only does money stimulate people to try new things, think up new ideas, products, and services, and engage in innovative activity, it also is a lubricant of human relations that enables human society to function more smoothly so that we can take care of ourselves and our families and communities. Money is truly a gift, and when we can understand it as such, we want to honor it, respect it, and help it move powerfully through our own lives.

3. Understanding Money as a mundane vs spiritual practice

Understanding money can simply be about understanding the nuts and bolts of money and economics. For example, it can be about understanding supply and demand, the time value of money, unemployment, GDP, exchange rates, inflation, etc. All these aspects of knowledge about money help us to make more informed decisions. But understanding money can be about more than this. Understanding money can be a spiritual practice. When we cultivate understanding money as a spiritual practice, we cultivate our curiosity about money. When we are curious, we want to learn, and we are pleased and fulfilled by our understanding of things. Curiosity is critical to cultivating wisdom. Curiosity stimulates us to grapple with complexity and to try to unravel truth. As we penetrate into the deeper nature of things and how things work, we recognize that in the end, things are mysterious. The frontiers of our understanding about the economy are always evolving. Wisdom, as distinct from understanding, rests not on knowledge that could change, but on an abiding sense of what is fundamentally true. Money wisdom is the ability to discern what is true about the nature of money and have an abiding wonder about the ways in which money can manifest and work its magic in the world.

DOMAIN 6: RISK MANAGEMENT

We have an intrinsic need to orient ourselves in some direction and commit ourselves to something. Domain 6 is ostensibly about risk management, but it is more fundamentally about how we uphold the structures that support us and maintain our commitments to what really matters for us. It is rooted in a determination to not let life get the best of us. Domain 6 is about meeting life head on. It is about considering what could go wrong and managing risk in order to stay on course. The work of Domain 6 should occur after the work of Domain 5 because understanding precedes commitment. We can only commit ourselves to that which we understand and hold to be meaningful. Purpose is the sum total of meaning, understanding, and commitment. Without commitment, there is no fidelity to the intention. There are three parts to consider.

1. **Commitment:** Commitment requires a willingness to put ourselves into our work, to understand what it is we are dealing with, and risk whatever comes up in that process. This is about having a sense of purpose and mission that I commit myself to, take seriously, and invest myself in.

2. **Derailers:** These are the things that can throw us off our path: sickness, injury, illness, accident, job loss, crime, poor economic conditions, natural disaster, conflict.

3. **Managing Risk:** This is about cultivating various forms of support to help us weather the dangers and catastrophes that could derail us from our commitments. It is about being proactive about managing risks so that we can stay on our path.

Our commitment must start with ourselves. We must commit ourselves to the business of living our life fully, present, and awake. We must commit ourselves to caring deeply about that which is meaningful. If we cannot commit ourselves to living a serious life, we let ourselves down. Life will give us plenty of opportunities to fail. We are the only ones who can make a determination to stay the path despite difficulties, discouragement, and fear. It is only when we can make good on our commitment to ourself that we can extend our commitments outwards to those who depend on us. If we let ourselves down, there is no way we won't let others down as well.

Our lives our vulnerable. Danger lurks everywhere. But we wouldn't care to manage risks if it didn't matter to us which way our lives went. It is because we care about our lives that we cultivate financial, social, and energetic support. Insurance helps to guard against potential crises like major illness, accident, job loss, earthquake, and crime. But other dangers cannot be fully insured against. Even if we have life insurance, the death of a loved one will still be devastating. No amount of insurance will fully ease our suffering.

Domain 6 can be a difficult Domain for many of us. This Domain demands that we get serious about our lives. It demands fidelity to being awake, present, and courageous in the face of all the things that could go wrong. It demands that we try not to let ourselves down. Letting ourselves down can be seductive because it serves our ego purposes. If we let ourselves down, we can play the victim, we can deny accountability for our own lives, we can put it on others to make us okay. It can be a lot easier than taking on this responsibility for ourselves.

I would like to be able to save for emergencies, medical emergencies and big catastrophes, losing a job, earthquakes. But we are not as properly prepared for these contingencies as I would like us to be. What produces anxiety for me is not being able to control the stuff I want to control.

I don't want to depend on others for support. I want to be self-reliant. It's more of a vague and intangible sense, not a fear of a particular scenario. I want to hold the reigns myself.

I like to build a little security with others, so that if I am in trouble, they will support me. My security net is with all those people who I've done right by. I work really hard to receive support.

If something bad happened economically, what I care about is my body. I live in a state of semi-threat all the time because I don't know what will happen, but I don't worry about it so much.

> We try to build up emergency savings, but are not so strict about these goals – if other things come up, that's okay. It's not acceptable to be too pessimistic.
>
> There's a way in which I just can't get too activated or worried about money. I can have trouble making changes and anticipating problems.

There are so many ways that we can rationalize not engaging in the work of Domain 6 and risk management. We say that we cannot save, that risk management is not important, that security doesn't matter, that I am self-sufficient, that I refuse to think about bad things in advance. What we really mean when we say these things is that we don't want to take our lives seriously. On the other hand, if we pay too much attention to the potential risks we face, we can become paralyzed by fear. When we face our fears, take responsibility, and prepare ahead, we are expressing our commitment to do what it takes to see things through. Commitment and the willingness to stay the course require an ability to stand up to fear, uncertainty, and the unknown. Domain 6 is about finding the ground, in spite of our fears, that supports us so that we can honor our commitments. As you begin to explore how best to honor your commitments and manage the risks you face, consider these questions.

1. To what do I commit myself to?

Making and honoring commitments are distinct from having a plan of action for getting from A to B. Making a commitment is about setting my orientation to take seriously my good health, good energy, good relationships, and good economic foundation. To what have I committed myself? How have I prioritized my commitments? In what way is my relationship to money consistent with my commitments? And in what way does my relationship to money betray me? How has it prevented me from making good on my commitments?

2. What has prevented me from fully honoring my commitments?

Many things can stand in our way of honoring our commitments to ourselves and others. The first is internal sabotoge. It is all the ways that we undermine ourselves, by not honoring ourselves and our potential. The second is not taking seriously the potential derailers. The third is failing to cultivate support. Everyone needs support. We may think that it is best not to depend on anyone for anything. But we need the communities we are embedded in to care for us and help us make our way. How do I fail to rally support for myself and my commitments? How do I fail to acknowledge the importance of support?

3. What would shift if I honored my commitments?

When I fully honor my commitments, I honor myself and others. I commit to making my life and my relationships work, and I commit to fulfilling my promises to myself and others. I commit myself to staying through the difficulties because I believe in my purpose and mission. In this promise to honor my commitments to myself and others, I strengthen my integrity. I do not run away from difficulty. I stay with myself, present and awake. By cultivating the courage, fortitude, and ability to face whatever difficulties present themselves, I become an adult, ready to thrive. When I commit myself to my life, to others, to my relationships to money, I am signaling my readiness to be a real grown up. I commit to improving, enhancing, and deepening my relationships. I commit to living my life to the fullest.

4. Risk Management as a mundane vs spiritual practice

At the mundane level, risk management is about cultivating support to weather the storms of our lives and ensure ourselves against worst-case scenarios. It is about helping ourselves not be derailed. But at a deeper level, risk management can be cultivated as a spiritual practice of developing faith. Ultimately, there is nothing we can do to keep difficulties and hardships, even tragedies, from occurring. Cultivating faith is about recognizing that the best that we can do is to cultivate our inner sense of support. Faith gives us the solid sense that we are supported by the universe, no matter what happens to us. When we are thrown off track, derailed, lose our way, let ourselves and others down, it is faith that helps us come back home to ourselves. Without cultivating faith, we are always vulnerable to being shattered by a tragic or catastrophic event. Risk management at the mundane level will always leave us vulnerable. It is only by cultivating faith that we can know how utterly supported we are. It is what gives us our unshakeable sense that we are held, and allows us to stay true to ourselves and others.

Domains 4, 5, 6 taken together enable us to articulate our purpose. It is only when we know what matters to us, understand the nature of things, and cultivate support against the downturns of life, that we can know that we have a purpose. Having a purpose moves us from surviving to thriving.

When we take the effort to make meaning of money, understand money, and make a commitment to ourselves, we define the purpose of money in our lives. This makes our relationship to money more meaningful than mere survival. Our relationship to money now connects us to what we really care about and want to bring into fruition. We become ships with beacons to sail towards, and our lives are infused with meaning. If we stop here, though, nothing will be realized. We must continue to do the work of Domains 7, 8, and 9 if we hope to bring to fruition that which we care about. Domains 7, 8, 9 are about making our dreams, which are the universe's dreams, come true. It begins with visualizing what is possible, followed by implementation (using and building resources to make things happen), and balance. When we do the work of all Nine Domains, we create wealth and prosperity that aligns with our deep sense of purpose.

CHAPTER 4

THRIVING:
DOMAINS 7, 8, 9

Domains 7, 8, 9 are about the actions we must take to thrive. It is about stepping into our purpose and living life with meaning and vision. If we focus on Domains 7, 8, 9 alone, though, without connecting to the foundational work of surviving and purposing, we will not thrive. Action without meaning is wasted action. Thriving requires the integration of all Nine Money Domains.

DOMAIN 7: PLANNING

We have an intrinsic need to be happy and inspired. Domain 7 is ostensibly about financial planning, but it is more fundamentally about articulating a vision of what is possible. It is about seeing how our lives serve something more important than ourselves and can make the world a more joyful and satisfying place for everyone. The work of Domain 7 specifically occurs after the work of Domain 6 because commitment must precede planning. If we skip the work of Domains 1 through 6 and try to jump to planning, we will experience great difficulty. Planning requires knowing your purpose. If you don't know what you care about, what is meaningful to you, what you are committed to, it will be impossible to make plans that resonate for you and that you stick to. What is my heart's core, my heart's desire, what

I really care about? This is Domain 4 work. How do I understand the world? This is Domain 5 work. What do I commit myself to? This is Domain 6 work.

A third shock is required to move from the phase of purposing to the phase of thriving. Whereas Domains 4, 5, 6 are about waking up to the *personal* meaning of our existence, Domains 7, 8, 9 are about waking up to the *universal* meaning of our existence. It is about recognizing that our existence is meant to serve a bigger purpose and that the universe supports us. It is about harnessing our power to make things happen, knowing that we are cooperating with the universe's will and knowing that our power is derived from the universe's will. We thrive in this cooperation. There are three parts to this Domain:

1. **Visualizing possibilities:** This is about dreaming the undreamt. How might we live an unbelievably joyful, fulfilling and satisfying life? If we can't see it, we can't make it happen.

2. **Intention and goals:** This is about honing the vast possibilities down to something that becomes your intentions and goals. An intention is a direction of thought around something you want to have happen. A goal is more specific, attainable, and concrete.

3. **Strategic and Tactical Planning:** This is about translating goals into a plan of action. It is about determining what resources need to be corralled, what hurdles need to be cleared, what logistical arrangements need to be made.

Superficially, planning is about creating goals and establishing a plan for reaching those goals. Planning at this level involves both strategic and tactical thinking. Strategic thinking is seeing the big picture, having a vision of where we want to go, and then creating a roadmap. Tactical planning is about carrying out specific aspects of the strategic plan, and involves shorter-term goals such as scheduling and prioritizing. Strategic and tactical planning can be difficult because we have so many different rationalizations why we can't or don't want to plan ahead. We feel disconnected from the future, it seems too far away, it is unknowable, we're not worth it, it's too difficult. Being reactive is easier than planning.

I do not want to think too much into the future. It feels like too much of an encumbrance. I have never had a plan. I have always been very casual about and around money.

Retirement planning – I haven't thought about it – it seems so far away. What I think about is "Can I make it through this year?"

I have ideals, but not goals. Ideals don't really lend themselves to concrete goal setting. Being successful is ok, but it feels a bit dirty.

I am repelled by planning. It is so painful and overwhelming I can't stay with it, because I'd have to embrace the idea that I'm worth it.

Long-range planning is absurd because the future is unknowable and therefore unplannable.

Planning and savings seem difficult.   Things always come up. So many unexpected things. I know I should save more, but I never seem to make it a priority. Planning seems so futile. When there is so little money left over for savings, and there is only one pot for savings, if something comes up, then money has to be taken from that pot.

It's hard for me to think about financial goals. I have no intention around money. I haven't done a lot to provide for the future. I have trouble being 100% committed to anything. I have difficulty being focused on a future goal. I am not as connected to the future as I am to the now.

I am afraid of being stuck somehow when I do long-term planning. Long-term planning seems boring to me. The straight line projections for 5 or 10 years feels very limiting – I fear being limited to the same thing. I like it being blurry. It's exciting to not know what is going to happen – I like it that way. I like the future to be unpredictable. It's more exciting that way.

I don't go too far into the future because   I could get overwhelmed by it. Future holds all the worst-case scenarios. So I don't go too far. I am just concerned about setting things up so my near future bodes well. I don't know how things will go, so I only go so far as I have the skill for. I am not willing to venture further than this.

I have no long-range vision financially. I am very in the moment. I don't have a planned out plan or structure. I wish I was goal oriented, but I'm not. I am not so goal oriented as opportunity driven. I want to do a good job in an area that is meaningful to me. I take a more organic approach to life.

My planning is more like dreaming. There is a slight disconnect between my plans and dreams. I see the big picture on a lot of things. But I don't get actively involved in taking the steps with proactive energy. Even though I want it, it is difficult for me to make it happen.

I think one should save for oneself. But I am hindered in this process by my belief that there is plenty out there and that I can take advantage of things because I am gifted and have been given a lot of opportunities.

I tend to deal with things as I go. I am not really planful, but I do have an idea where I am trying to go. Once I hit that number, I slack off. When I have what I need for the short term, then I turn my attention to other things.

The horizon over which we plan can be the next minute or several decades ahead. When we plan, we anticipate what the future will be like and try to take actions that will be helpful. Planning stems from an impulse to optimize our life path. It requires an appetite for satisfaction and joy. It requires seeing what is possible, having a vision of success, and wanting to participate in the unfolding future. If we can't visualize the dream, the dream can't happen.

But our ability to visualize future possibilities and actions can be impeded. When we are too fearful, for example, we have a very difficult time letting our imaginations soar. And even if our imaginations soar, it may be difficult to have clarity about our purpose. Translating a goal into something more concrete requires focus, discipline and commitment. Many of us find it easier to simply react to things as they come up. What we forget is that we were given the capacity to plan so that we could make things turn out well for ourselves and others. Our capacity to plan gives us a mental tool for living a fulfilling life. But it requires that we be proactive. Domain 7 is about making our lives better, in spite of all the unknowables, so that we can live our lives to our fullest potential. As you begin to explore how best to honor your life's potential, consider these questions.

1. How do I plan?

What attention do I pay to planning? Do I think ahead? Am I motivated to think ahead in some areas but not in others? For example, do I plan in the social arena? Do I cultivate social connections? Do I try to avoid conflicts so as to not burn bridges? Do I plan ahead in the sexual arena? Do I plan ahead to be attractive to others? Do I plan ahead to cultivate intimate connection? Do I plan ahead to be comfortable, not hungry, have money in the bank for bills? Do I dream big and and set big goals without figuring out what my needs are? Do I try to move into action before I have clarified my vision? Do I like short-term tactical planning but resist strategic long-term planning? Do I think that plans are always derailed by unexpected events? Do I think that I should not plan because my life is in God's hands? Do I believe that because the future is unknowable, I cannot plan?

2. How and why do I resist planning?

What blocks me from setting goals? What blocks me from planning to achieve goals? Do I believe that a life of ease is impossible, and therefore planning is futile? Or do I believe that there is no need to plan because opportunities always exist? Is my resistance to planning due to a fear of failure? Do I worry that trying and failing is worse than not trying at all? Or do I harbor an unconscious fear that if I made my life easier, I would not know what to do with myself? Do I resist planning because I cannot afford to let myself think expansively and optimistically about what is possible? Am I afraid of wanting more than I can have? Do I believe that planning will reduce my spontaneity? Am I more comfortable in crisis mode and reactive mode than I am in thriving mode? Do I fear being at ease?

Think back to high school. As 15-year-old sophomores, most of us had absolutely no idea what college we wanted to go to, where we might get in, where we would be happiest, or what would happen once we got to college. We also had no way of knowing whether something completely unexpected might happen just before we went to college. But none of these reasons justified not trying our best. Would our parents have accepted our excuse that we didn't want to try because we were afraid of failing, or afraid of being successful? Would our parents have accepted our excuse that life would turn out terribly no matter what, or that life would be fine no matter what we did? Would our parents have accepted our excuse that we wanted to keep things fresh, so there was no point in following a plan? By thinking ahead, we gave ourselves options as seniors. What parent wouldn't want their child to plan ahead?

The same logic applies to us as adults, though it feels different when the tables are turned. We don't see how we give up on ourselves when we fail to plan. If our own teenagers didn't try to make the best of their imminent futures, it would be tragic and sad. Yet, when we act the same way, we have difficulty seeing it. For example, planning ahead for college and planning ahead for retirement both require tradeoffs. Saving a little each month is like studying a few hours more each week in school. It is a cost, but it's not a big cost, and the benefits down the road can be enormous. And like planning ahead for college, retirement is an unknowable – we don't know how we will feel, what we will want to do, where we will want to live, how long we will live, whether we will be healthy or not. But that is not a valid excuse for not trying to create options and opportunities. Just as it would be tragic if our

15-year-olds squandered their opportunities, it is tragic when we shut off our opportunities. When we turn away from planning, we turn away from giving ourselves the most opportunities to thrive.

3. What could shift if I embraced planning?

At the deepest level, planning requires a willingness to participate in life and care enough about how it unfolds. It is about having the hope and willingness to make life work out the best we can, even if we might be disappointed, even if it might not go our way. Planning is an expression of our innate sense that we can make a difference, and that how we participate in the unfolding makes a difference for the unfolding itself. It is an optimistic impulse. The real point of planing is that we care enough to try to make things better, and that we don't give up on ourselves. We are confused when we think it is the achievement of the goal that generates fulfillment and satisfaction. Fulfillment and satisfaction come from trying. If we plan, we embrace life's possibilities.

4. Planning as a mundane vs spiritual practice

At the mundane level, planning is about making plans to achieve goals. But at a deeper level, planning can be cultivated as a spiritual practice of visualizing and creating prosperity and heaven on earth. To our egoic minds, living fully today and planning ahead seem oppositional. We think that if we are living fully right now, planning ahead will take us out of the moment. But in truth, planning ahead and living fully are not only complementary, but actually one and the same. When we plan ahead from a mindful place, our planning ahead *is* about living fully in the moment. When we live fully in the moment, mindful of everything that we are experiencing, we recognize how we are meant to be savoring this moment *and* how we are meant to be a part of the glorious unfolding of each moment. In this recognition, we see that we can only be a part of this glorious unfolding if we participate in the process. Planning is about visualizing a better world, and if we do this, the world in fact becomes better. Grace comes to us when we break through our blockages to perceive that heaven on earth is possible and think about how to make this possibility reality. Planning is about adjusting course, not about getting somewhere fast. When we are living in the present and oriented to planning as part of the unfolding, what matters is the unfolding not the final outcome.

DOMAIN 8: WEALTH BUILDING

We have an intrinsic need to make a difference and have an impact on the world. Domain 8 is ostensibly about implementing our plans and building wealth. But it is more fundamentally about turning possibilities into reality. Our wealth is made up of all the tangible and intangible resources that support us and allow us to thrive. It includes money, but also our good health, our strong bodies, our good minds and hearts, our family and friends, the beauty that exists all around us, the love that holds us. Domain 8 specifically occurs after Domain 7 because vision and planning must precede creation and implementation. If we skip the work of Domain 7 and jump to action, we risk action without intentionality, wasting energy and resources. The wealth creation process must be connected to our purpose and vision of how wealth will enable us to thrive. Domain 8 is about making things happen in our lives, making a difference, and having an impact. It is about developing our capacity to engage with energy, discipline and focus to make our dreams come true. There are three parts to Domain 8.

1. **The nature of wealth:** It is important to acknowledge the broader concept of wealth. We are wealthy when we have strong relationships, healthy bodies, good minds, and loving hearts. The wealth we have in our lives encompasses both the tangible and intangible resources that we possess. It's not just about having money, houses, cars, shoes. It's about everything that allows us to thrive.

2. **Creating wealth:** Creating wealth is about implementing a plan and turning a concept into reality. As you turn a plan into reality, you create wealth, not only for yourself, but for others as well. Whether the plan is to buy a car, build a house, have a retirement nest egg, or travel around the world, the implementation of this plan generates wealth.

3. **Building wealth:** Building wealth is a process that follows the initial creation of wealth, and is about maintaining and enhancing your wealth through good stewardship. This phase is about maintaining and building wealth through wise investments, and involves trade-offs and risk-taking.

Superficially, wealth building is about creating more money. But, at its core, wealth building is about creating greater abundance in the world. You could say that we are wealthy when we have the power and capacity to turn plans into reality. When we lack vigor and maturity, we cannot translate our dreams into something real. We cannot create abundance. When we set goals, but can't quite get to them, we fail in Domain 8. When we want something for ourselves, but cannot bring it into our lives, we fail in Domain 8. Domain 8 is the moment of truth – it's where our character gets put to the test. Can we make it happen? Do we fail for lack of courage? Lack of energy? Lack of boldness? Lack of willpower? Lack of determination? Lack of passion? What holds us back from making good on our dreams?

> Savings has been difficult for me because I felt that money was bad and could cut me off from others. I felt that it was selfish to save, and that others might be disappointed in me for being too snobby. Better just to stay small. If I had a lot of savings, people might envy me or not like me. I felt it would be better just not to try to have savings.

> Before, I rejected money and wealth in my life. There was a self-sacrificing nobility about being poor. I felt I could do without. I believed my own story. Now, however, I see the virtues of having wealth.

> I have trouble taking care of myself first. I've been careless with money. I haven't been good at saving it – feeling that I don't deserve to have it. I've spent it, given it away.

> I never managed to accrue for myself. It usually goes to the business and others. It's been frustrating for me. It's scary. I don't have a backup. I am in my 50s. I have shame around this.

> It is difficult for me to save. I know savings sounds safe and secure, and I believe it. But if I can't see it and touch it, then it doesn't feel real. It is frustrating to know that it's there and not able to use it. Money burns a hole in my brain and my pocket. My parents gave me a lot of money at sixteen. I can't even tell you where it all went. Part of me wishes I could save it, but savings doesn't resonate with me.

> I feel badly about this area of our lives. I feel irresponsible. For me, it's a matter of focusing my energy better. I know what I am supposed to be doing, and I know what life wants from me. I have a general sense of optimism that "I'm going to be fine." and it's difficult for me to get worked up thinking about retirement that seems so far down the road.

> I can be fairly inertial about taking action to change investment positions, believing that buy and hold makes more sense. I'm willing to wait things out than get too panicky about things. I don't get too activated about making changes to the investment portfolio unless someone else prompts me to. I just couldn't be bothered. I am not so proactive about decisions with investments.

Wealth creation is the first part of Domain 8, and has to do with implementing a plan that contributes to our thriving. When we move towards a worthwhile goal, we begin to create something valuable. When I build a company, I create wealth by creating valuable goods and services that serve others, and by employing people and paying wages. When I build a house, I create wealth by creating something of greater value than the raw inputs I started with. When I build a retirement nest egg, I create wealth by investing my money in companies that are creating real products and services.   To the extent that I carry forth a plan that contributes to my thriving, I create wealth even if my bank account doesn't grow. As I travel around the world, for example, I participate in both the creation of intangible wealth in the form of my greater emotional well-being, and in the creation of tangible wealth by supporting the transportation and tourist industries.

In contrast to wealth creation, wealth building is about maintaining and building wealth so that it is not dissipated. Whereas wealth creation requires activation energy and courage, wealth building requires discipline, stewardship, and fortitude. We invest wealth to beget further wealth. It requires discipline to forego some spending today in order to invest in something that will have a future payoff. It requires stewardship to watch over the process of investing and growing wealth. It requires fortitude because investing is never risk-free. The simplest investment is a bank account that earns little by little. There is little risk but little return. Even though the interest may be guaranteed, there is no guarantee that inflation will not erode the value of our investment. And the more complex investments may yield higher returns, but are riskier.

Why should we care about wealth building? Isn't it enough to make ends meet? At the individual level, when we do not save and invest, we cannot make bigger things happen in our lives. We cannot afford to retire, go on vacation, pay for college, enjoy other big-ticket items. When we don't save and invest, we cannot bring to fruition larger goals that we have such as making a truly meaningful donation. In the aggregate, if no one saved money, there would be no public investment in roads, hospitals, and schools, and no private investment in homes and businesses. Even when you simply put money in your savings account, the bank lends the money out and fuels somebody's dream. The true engine of growth in our economy is savers channeling money to households (so that they can buy homes) and to entrepreneurs (so that they can start new enterprises or expand existing ones). An economy's vibrancy and dynamism depends on financial markets that mobilize saving, lending, and investing.

Wealth building, contrary to our popular beliefs, is an inherently generous impulse. When we only make ends meet, we only take care of ourselves, feeding our bodies to survive. When we engage in wealth building, not only are we making good on our own plans, we are also contributing to the larger society in which we live and making a difference. When our private wealth is saved and invested, it begets greater wealth, not only for ourselves but for the entire economy. It may be difficult to connect our individual lives to this big idea, but the truth is that when we create wealth, we are engaged in the building of schools and hospitals, businesses, banks, financial systems, and the infrastructure that sustains billions of lives. When we build wealth, we are helping to build families, communities, societies. We are turning plans into reality and making real things happen, not only for our generation, but for future generations. We are making a positive impact on the world around us.

When you really think about it, wealth building is a miraculous act that we engage in every day. It is almost impossible to fathom how miraculous this is. By applying our cleverness, creativity, and labor to raw natural resources, we beget wealth that begets more wealth and more wealth. What one generation invests, future generations reap. Our ability to create wealth almost at will is remarkable. Each individual on this planet embodies the power to manifest wealth simply by applying their skills, passion, knowledge, vision and creativity to generate something completely new and heretofore unimagined. When we create and build wealth, we should celebrate this miracle. When we deploy our wealth to create more wealth, we create abundance not merely for ourselves but for others today and tomorrow. As you begin to explore creating and building wealth in your life, consider these questions.

1. How do I create wealth and build wealth?

We create wealth by doing something productive that a company pays us for. We create wealth by providing a service that others value. We create wealth when we build a firm that produces goods or services that the market desires. In every case, we step forward and sell ourselves to potential employers, customers, or financiers. Creating wealth requires boldness and a blast of energy. It requires that we step into our power to make things happen. But it also requires harnessing our will power to engage with discipline, focus and persistence. It requires a strong desire to bring things to fruition and a strong confidence that we deserve the fruits of our labor. If you start, but cannot finish things, set goals but never reach them, you will have difficulty creating and building wealth. In order to stay on track, we need to maintain our boundaries and structures, personally and physically.

Wealth building is the accumulation phase of wealth creation, the phase where wealth is used to beget more wealth. To build wealth, I must invest some portion of the wealth that I have created to create more wealth. There are many ways that we can invest our wealth. We can put it in a savings account or a money market account. We can invest our wealth in higher risk, higher return financial assets such as bonds or stocks. Or we can invest our wealth in real estate, commodities, or business ventures. There are a myriad of ways that we can invest our wealth and harness the power of compounding. If our wealth never grows, then our standard of living will be forever tied to our income level alone, and we have less cushion against economic setbacks and fewer future options.

2. How am I resistant to creating wealth and/or building wealth?

What beliefs do I have about creating and building wealth that impede my progress in this Domain? Do I believe that wealth building is not important? Do I believe that I can't do it, that I can't discipline myself to save? Do I believe that I can't understand how to invest? Do I think that it is more fun, interesting and juicy to spend than to save money? How am I resistant to creating and building wealth? What things get in my way? Do I procrastinate? Do I get distracted? Do I indulge in a story of victimhood that stymies my self-reliance, self-confidence, and sense of agency? Do I quit when the going gets tough? Do I get lazy when things are too difficult or boring? If I cannot own my power to turn plans into reality, to achieve goals and make good on my dreams, then I cannot build wealth. Building wealth requires all the strength, confidence and boldness we can muster, and requires that we stare down our fears and resistances. Building wealth is grown-up work and it requires showing up with our grown-up game.

3. What could shift if I could create and build wealth?

If I could create and build wealth, I would be a grown-up. I would set boundaries and goals that would enable me to be effective and productive. I would show up even when things were difficult. I would not play the victim. I would do what needs to be done without making excuses or whining. I would be patient, resolved, and persevering. I would be organized, focused, and strong. I would be comfortable with the circulation of money in and out of my life. I would know that to make money, you need to use money, that wealth begets further wealth. I would invest in myself, my family, my community, my world. Being a grown up about money would shift not only my relationship to money, but to my friends, my family, and myself. I would be confident about my impact on the world, accept the consequences of my actions, and fight for what I believe in. I would not put up with crap, from myself or others. I would demand of myself good health, good support, and good relationships. I would take myself and my life seriously.

4. Wealth building as a mundane vs spiritual practice

At the mundane level, wealth building is about making money, creating resources, and making more money and resources. But at a deeper level, wealth building can be cultivated as a spiritual practice of doing God's work. To our egoic minds, making money and doing God's work seem completely oppositional. We believe that if we are in the business of making money, we could not possibly pay attention to our inner lives and must necessarily be worshipping a false god. But in truth, cultivating a healthy relationship to money is absolutely aligned with our Inner Work and journey back to ourselves. When we create wealth, we are manifesting plans into reality and creating abundance. We are creating the conditions that enable us to thrive. When we do our good work, taking ourselves seriously, making our lives work well, we are actually doing God's work. When we labor in devotion, we labor in love, we create in love, and we build in love. We let the work come through us, but we also let it go back into the world and light it up. We are merely instruments of God, doing God's work. The wealth and abundance that we manifest is to support the manifestation of not only ourselves but everyone else as well.

DOMAIN 9: BALANCE

We have an intrinsic need to have stability and balance in our lives so that we can function and keep our commitments. Domain 9 is ostensibly about maintaining our stability and balance in the midst of constant change. But it is really about being in the flow, functioning effortlessly, from a place of internal balance and connection to the universe. The work of Domain 9 specifically follows the work of Domain 8 because manifesting precedes integration, balance, and flow. Domain 9 is about being in the flow of life, being in the flow with what manifests, maintaining our composure and balance in the face of the inevitable ebb and flow of wealth and material resources. In order to have a healthy relationship to this Domain, we must be able to relax, be balanced, and be centered. There are three parts to consider:

1. **Relaxation:** This is about being and not doing. It is about appreciating our life, breathing, taking in the experience of being alive. It's about feeling that it is okay to let my guard down, breathe, trust, feel supported, relax.

2. **Balance:** This is about maintaining a sense of equilibrium, both emotionally and physically, amidst all of life's ups and downs. It is also about not being reactive to surprises and unexpected events, but absorbing the ups and downs with calmness and good cheer.

3. **Flow:** This is about being in the flow of life, functioning effortlessly, without being over-stressed or over-doing. It is about seeing all the endless possibilities and allowing life to take you where it will, recognizing that there are no sure losses or sure wins. It is about recognizing that you are at one with the universe, both its dynamism and its stability.

While Domain 9 sounds rather attractive and appealing, many of us resist this Domain. We rationalize that relaxation is for the weak and unambitious, that balance is impossible, and that being in the flow will not take us where we need to go. At the same time, we have a small niggling sense that our resistance to this Domain causes us pain. When we resist Domain 9, we tend to feel stressed, overworked, exhausted, and tense. When we resist Domain 9, we cannot be creative or replenished. Here are some quotations from people who do not experience the benefits of being relaxed, in balance, and inflow with money.

> I have always been aware of the finiteness of resources, that there is not a lot available, so my sense of scarcity is high. I am trying to discover the reality of abundance. I can allow myself to have certain comfort and nice time, but I don't feel my life is a life of endless possibilities.

> I am always oriented to what more I need to do. So it is difficult to be appreciative or grateful for what I do have. I can't relax, I have to keep striving forward, stay motivated and productive.

> In reality, I am abundant and grateful, but my perception of abundance is not there. I never feel content. I like to stay in the buzz and intensity. I am not comfortable with stability. With abundance, there would be no challenge, and I would lack direction and focus.

In contrast, here are some quotations from people who experience the benefits of being relaxed, in balance, and inflow with money.

> I am open to different outcomes unfolding. I basically allow myself to have what I want, within reason. I don't feel denied.

> I have no sense that I am struggling. I sense my life wouldn't change much even with more money. Maybe I would maybe travel more if I had more money.

> I feel abundant and know that I have a lot of blessings, with good family and good lifestyle, and I do not sit around thinking I should have more.

> I feel gratitude, trust and recognition of a stewardship of these resources I've been blessed with that aren't really mine – I take my responsibility seriously. I feel supported, directed, empowered, like there is a purpose to what I am doing.

> I do not equate abundance with money. I think about it in terms of friendships, groups and organizations, travel, food, beauty, nature, etc. I feel so lucky in my life. I feel I've had an abundant life and am very grateful.

> I come from a place of abundance and am happy to share with others. I can be resourceful, can make things from nothing. Some people are hungry. I am not.

> Money is not in abundance but there is enough money to pay bills. I do believe all my needs will be met if I do the right thing, and believe the universe will provide.

> Before, I felt a lot of jealousy and envy and feeling that I don't deserve things. Now I believe, if I want it, I will create it, and I believe all of us can be abundant and that we can stand up for our true value and let the money flow in.

I invite you to relax your beliefs about Domain 9 for a moment and consider what Domain 9 might offer you. Domain 9 is about living in the flow, and maintaining our sense of equilibrium. It provides us with the energy to persevere with a positive attitude despite setbacks and unexpected changes and disruptions. It is about having a sense of stability and balance, and a sense that everything is alright, which enables us to stay positively engaged in the face of good or bad, knowing that we are ultimately supported and loved. It is what gives us our sense of real prosperity and abundance, which is ultimately not tied to the amount of dollars in the bank or amount of material wealth in our life.

Without Domain 9 being operational, our relationship to money cannot be healthy because we cannot maintain our sense of stability and balance in the face of continual disruptions and change. We become over-stressed, reactive, and exhausted. Our nervous systems get fried. This Domain is about balance in the sense of having stability, harmony, and peace in our lives. This balance enables us to experience ourselves as part of it all, flowing with the experience of life, not having to push against things to get results. It is about balance in the way water flowing downstream finds balance. When something gets in the way of flowing water, water effortlessly moves around the obstacle and keeps going. There is a sense of patience, perseverance, and effortless flowing. There is a sense that, in the long run, I will get where I need to go. Being able to have a relationship like that to money enables us to stay on track, not be deterred, and persevere in the face of hardship, obstacles, difficulties. It allows us to maintain our equilibrium so that we can do the right thing and not be over-reactive in spending, investing, saving, learning, etc. By relaxing and maintaining our composure and balance, we put ourself in a position to get what we want from life. We feel more appreciative, relaxed, and at peace.

Doing the work of Domain 9 requires a shift in energy. For many of us, it requires a downshift; others, a change of focus. What it will require in all of us is an ability to be non-reactive, calm, and centered. It is about being at peace in our everyday life. As you begin to explore being in balance and flow in your life, consider these questions.

1. How do I orient energetically towards life?

What is my orientation to life? Do I effort? Is work stressful? Is my life frantic and overbooked? Do I get exhausted from pushing myself too hard? Do I believe that relaxation will make me lose my edge? Do I believe that relaxation is only for vacation time? Or do I believe that my whole life is relaxed? Is it difficult to get going? Do I lack activation energy?

2. How do I block relaxation, balance, and flow?

I block relaxation, balance and flow by keeping myself in a state of stress and reactivity, needing things to go a certain way, and being closed to different possibilities and options. I block relaxation, balance, and flow when I am anxious, doubting, cynical, and unable to let go. I block relaxation, balance, and flow when I cannot see the bigger picture behind the ups and downs, and let myself get continually tossed off center. I block relaxation, balance, and flow when I do not allow myself to have time-outs from work and the frantic motion of life.

3. What could shift if I could experience relaxation, balance, and flow?

If I could experience relaxation, balance, and flow, then I would experience abundance and prosperity, the sense that there is plenty for me now and always. I would recognize that scarcity exists, but abundance is true as well. I would be able to navigate the truth of scarcity and abundance simultaneously, and have a relationship to money that was relaxed, engaged, and optimistic. I would have a consciousness of the abundance and love that is always here. I would experience my wealth as sourced from an infinite fountain, a gift. I would feel appreciation and gratitude for the wealth that I have, humility to know that it is a gift, and trust that I am always supported. Because I experience abundance, I would not feel greed. Rather than hoarding my wealth and resources, I would want to make sure that it, like life blood, continues to circulate, supporting life everywhere. With a sense that there is plenty to go around, and plenty where this came from, I would not be afraid for my own survival. I would move with the cycles of the universe rather than resisting them. When there is a lot of wealth, I would feast and enjoy the plentitude. When there is little material wealth, I would enjoy the simplicity and express myself authentically without props and material things.

4. Prosperity as a mundane vs spiritual practice

Prosperity can be cultivated as a spiritual practice of active receptivity. When we cultivate active receptivity, we let go, surrender our will, and are actively receptive to grace. This spiritual practice of active receptivity enables us to receive love. To our egoic minds, prosperity is something we make happen, not something we receive. We believe that we are prosperous by our own efforts, and poor by our own failings. We do not consider the possibility that our prosperity is a grace that we receive when we work to our fullest potential, establish our commitments, do good work, and simply stay on track, like water flowing effortlessly downstream. When we are in the flow of our life, we are graced with an experience of prosperity. If we do not find our balance and our center, we might pretend that we are prosperous but our souls will feel the lie. When we cultivate active receptivity, we experience ourselves as part of the abundance.

The Nine Domains of Money arranged clockwise around the Enneagram symbol delineate a specific process for creating wealth and experiencing prosperity. When the Nine Domains of Money are taken on as a spiritual practice, money becomes a powerful vehicle for self-development and personal growth. From this perspective, we can see how our movement towards wealth creation and prosperity is a journey towards abundance and love, and away from scarcity and fear. The first Domain is about balancing inflow and outflow and developing a firm foundation for taking in nourishment. The second Domain is about nourishing ourselves so that we can work to our fullest potential. The third Domain is about discovering our outer value so that we will be stimulated to look for personal meaning. The fourth Domain is about discovering how money connects to what matters to us so that we will be motivated to understand money. The fifth Domain is about understanding money so that we can discern what we are committed to. The sixth Domain is about managing risk so that we can embrace larger possibilities. The seventh Domain is about envisioning possibilities that we manifest in reality. The eighth Domain is about manifesting our dreams so that we can experience abundance and prosperity. The ninth Domain connects our actions and wealth to our experience of balance, abundance, and prosperity.

Various books about money have treated subsets of these Nine Money Domains, but none have provided a treatment of this totality of Nine Domains. Financial planning books emphasize Domains 1, 5, 6, 7, 8, around budgeting, knowledge, risk management, planning, and wealth building, instructing us to be more organized, better budgeters, more knowledgeable, take account of contingencies, plan, and invest. Spiritual money books, in contrast, emphasize Domains 2, 3, 4, 9 encouraging us to be more charitable and service oriented, do what we love, be more aligned with what is meaningful to us, and think abundantly, but neglect to discuss the more "technical" Domains. The Enneagram symbol is the only system that provides us with the particular wisdom to understand wealth and abundance in this illuminating sequence and framework. It helps us to understand not only the nature of money, but also the nature of prosperity, and how to journey from scarcity and fear to abundance and love.

Nine Money Domains: Mundane vs Spiritual Practice

	Mundane Practice	Potential experience of scarcity due to:	What it is really about	Spiritual Practice
1	Budgeting	Limitations and constraints	Paying attention	In breath out breath, inflow outflow
2	Spending	Unlimited wants	Nourishing us	Listening deeply
3	Earning	Over striving	Working to full potential	Humble self-regard
4	Money Beliefs	Lack of accountability	Making meaning of money	Living authentically
5	Money Knowledge	Lack of curiosity and imagination	Understanding what money is, how it works	Cultivating curiosity
6	Risk Management	Inability to insure fully against danger	Supporting our commitments	Cultivating faith
7	Planning	Anticipation that grass is always greener on the other side	Visualizing what's possible	Participating in the unfolding
8	Wealth Building	Continual exerting	Creating and sustaining wealth	Doing god's work
9	Balance	Lack of engagement and vitality	Being relaxed and in the flow	Active receptivity

PART II:

OUR RELATIONSHIP TO MONEY

CHAPTER 5
INSTINCTS and MONEY

Our human consciousness makes us unique in the animal kingdom. Unlike other animals, human beings can have an awareness of their existence, and can reflect on their thoughts and feelings. At the same time, we share a lot in common with living organisms in our programming to stay alive, organize socially, and reproduce sexually. Our programming leads us to do certain behaviors automatically. Like birds that know how to build nests, ants that know how to self-organize to create a complex social organization, or drone bees that know to mate with a queen bee in the air, we have instincts to survive, socialize, and reproduce without thinking about it. Having evolved over millions of years, our preprogrammed instincts enable us to respond naturally to environmental stimuli as they arise, giving us a survival edge.

We can comprehend much of our human economic behavior and relationship to money in terms of our human instincts. There are a whole set of behaviors that we tend to do automatically at a level beyond our conscious thought even though in theory we could control them. For Maslow, an instinct is something that cannot be overridden, and therefore does not apply to human beings who can override the instincts. Yes, we humans certainly have the potential to modify and even override our instincts. This does not mean that we always choose to do so. Animals that hibernate, care for their young, migrate, and mate, do not have the potential to control their instinctual behavior. When we are behaving in an automatic, preprogrammed way, we are closer to our animal nature than our human nature. Being able to take control and modify our human instincts requires us to have deliberate intention and take deliberate action. To what extent our human instincts govern, motivate and drive our actual behavior depends to a large degree on how awake we are and our ability to separate from our automaticities and observe ourselves from a distance.

THREE INSTINCTS

We have hundreds of instincts such as our instinct to sleep, communicate, eat, and seek shelter. They can succinctly be categorized into three groups. We all have the predisposition to a) stay alive and be safe, secure, comfortable, b) affiliate and bond with others, and c) reproduce and transmit our genetic material. We do not need to use conscious effort for these instincts to function. If a wild boar were chasing us in the jungle, we would run away instinctively. Similarly, a hungry baby does not need to think about swallowing. Our instincts have a basic intelligence of their own that orients us to do what we need to do to survive, get along in a group, and reproduce.

In their natural state, our instincts respond to immediate needs. If, for example, our resources were wiped out by a massive fire, how would our animal instincts respond? With no food or shelter, we would migrate and search for food, band together to find new shelter, and continue on. We would not make up stories, get into dramas, or be tempted to give up. Such reactions would be distortions caused by our egos.

It is when our personality and ego come on stage that the expression of our instincts can get jumbled. Then our personality wants to have something to say about what we eat, when we eat, how much we eat. When our personalities are fixated and tight, the smooth expression of our instincts becomes increasingly hampered. Rather than attend to our instinctual needs, we can get twisted up about how much money we need, how to fit in, and how to attract a mate.

SELF-PRESERVATION INSTINCT (SP)

The Self-Preservation instinct is the instinct to be safe, secure, and comfortable. This instinct operates in our oldest, root, reptilian brain. It is the most basic instinct. The Self-Preservation instinct in us enables us to know what we need, and continually regulates us to drink, eat, and rest in order to be well. It is the instinct to do what is needed in the moment to survive. This instinct is particularly sensitive to life's instability. It motivates us to seek structure, stability, and safety nets. The Self-Preservation instinct is not interested in excitement and change. Nor is it interested in attuning to group interests and social norms.

This instinct is all about stability, comfort, and well-being. It is our instinct to have food, warmth, a pleasant place to sleep. This instinct wants to prevent disruption and stimulates us to plan for contingencies. Self-preservation is also about conserving energy and using time wisely. And it is very sensitive to potential dangers – food safety, home safety, environmental safety are important to the Self-Preservation instinct because threats to our safety threaten our stability and well-being.   The Self-Preservation instinct will try to do whatever it takes to prevent physical danger, suffering, or discomfort.

SOCIAL INSTINCT (SO)

The Social instinct is the instinct that enables us to fit into a group, and enables the group to survive from generation to generation. The Social instinct operates in our limbic system which affects our ability to affiliate, bond, and play, and is the source of our emotions. The Social instinct includes the instinct to nurture and take care of others, to understand reciprocity, and to adapt and modify habitual patterns to the needs of the group. It is also about the instinct to collaborate and cooperate. It is an instinct developed for mutual survival. For example, if I have a good hunt, I will share what I have with the whole group. When I don't have a good hunt, I trust that someone else will share with me.

The Social instinct is all about fitting in, bonding with, and supporting others. It causes us to focus on our interactions with other people, to understand "place" within social hierarchies, to enjoy participating in collective activities, and to avoid being ostracized. The Social instinct leads us to enjoy the social aspects of work, family, hobbies, and clubs. This instinct is not about stimulation or well-being. It is not about personal advancement or personal survival. Rather, it is the instinct that enables us to be focused on the survival of the group.

SEXUAL INSTINCT (SX)

The Sexual instinct is the instinct that enables us to transmit our genetic material. This instinct seems to be regulated by our root brain – the part of our brain that regulates the autonomic nervous system. This is the instinct to expend energy to do something intensely creative. This sexual energy is about the attraction, repulsion, and magnetic forces that propel us to reproduce. There is nothing rational about it. From nature's point of view, what matters is that certain combinations come together.

The Sexual instinct is about disruptive energy. It is about the willingness to go after what you want, invest fully, create something new, and not care about the consequences. If something attractive comes along, we take our chances. The thrill of the chase and the hit of the hunt are worth it. Creating new life and transmitting genetic material is not ordinary or stable. This instinct is about putting oneself on display so that others notice and are attracted to you. This is also the instinct of strong likes and dislikes, to be strongly attracted as well as strongly repelled. The Sexual instinct is curious, and wants to go deeply and intensely towards the object of attraction, to discover and create. It is an optimistic energy that generates excitement and conveys charge to others. The Sexual instinct is daring, bold, aggressive, and competitive, fueled by the hope that something great will happen. It is the instinct that enables us to go towards something that may cause us to die, literally or figuratively, with a come-what-may attitude. But the Sexual instinct also gives us our resiliency and perseverance. When an attraction does not work out and we fail, we need to have the ability to come back and try again. It is not about the survival of the group or even our own survival, but about the survival of our genetic material.

Figure 1: Different Instinctual Energies

Self-Preservation Instinct – Stable, Linear, Forward Moving

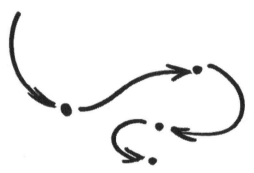

Social Instinct – Circulatory, Organic, Spatially Oriented

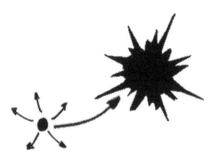

Sexual Instinct – Exploring, Intense, Disruptive

For each question, circle the answer that fits you best.

	WHAT'S MY DOMINANT INSTINCT?
1	a. Being adaptable is more important than sticking to my own routines. b. I want my life to be stable so that I can meet the needs of everyday living. c. A predictable, stable life would be boring. I crave stimulation and intensity.
2	a. I am willing to band together with others to bet big on a new venture. b. I believe in diversifying risk, so that I won't be vulnerable to one bad turn. c. When I want something, I am willing to put myself into it completely.
3	a. I love to indulge myself, but I balance that with being generous to others as well. b. I tend to spend on things that are functional, purposeful, and good value. c. I spend on things that give me a charge. I like to spend on my body, looks, art, music, clothing, and experiences.
4	a. I am likely to spend more than I planned when I am out with friends and everyone is having a good time. b. I try to be frugal and not spend more than I have. c. I spend spontaneously when something captures my heart.
5	a. I trust that I will land on my feet, because I have so many supporting me. b. I live constantly with anxiety about my ability to make money. c. When I am in my mojo, I am confident about my ability to make money.
6	a. I don't want to make money just to make money. I want my work to be of value to others. b. If I have to make ends meet, I'll do whatever I need to do. c. I couldn't do something just to make money. I have to love my work.
7	a. I love money for the contributions I can make with it. b. I love money for the security and independence that it gives me. c. I love money for the freedom and experiences it allows me to have.
8	a. Life may be unpredictable, but if we band together, we can weather it. b. I am averse to intensity, sudden, dramatic change because it is too disruptive. c. Life is unpredictable. You never know what might hit you. So enjoy life today.
9	a. I am optimistic that things will work out fine as long as we band together. b. I tend to be more realistic: If I work hard and plan ahead, things will work. c. I am optimistic that things will be work out fine. Possibilities trump problems.
10	a. What supports me are my friends and social bonds. b. What supports me is a warm, cozy home, and some savings in the bank. c. What supports me is my health and a strong, intimate relationship.
11	a. I tend to let things unfold organically, and respond to what is going on around me. b. I plan ahead and prepare for contingencies to avoid discomfort and disruptions. c. I can get so focused on what I am doing in the moment that it is difficult to plan ahead.

WHAT'S MY DOMINANT INSTINCT?

12	a. It is difficult for me to think too far ahead, but collectively we are moving in some direction and it is important to try to read the social trends that will affect all of us. b. It may be difficult to think too far ahead, but I try to do the best that I can with the limited information that I have. c. It is difficult for me to think too far ahead because who knows what the future will hold.
13	a. I trust that together we can manage the ups and downs of life. b. I think it is important to plan ahead so that I can avoid being taken by surprise. c. I trust that I will be able to handle what comes up.
14	a. I am willing to take risks if others are making the same bets. b. I am averse to loss and am more concerned about the downside than I am about the upside. c. I am willing to take big risks for a potentially great outcome.
15	a. I am not so motivated to save for myself, but if it will help my family and is the right thing to do, I will get on board. b. I am motivated to save for my own well-being and my own future. c. Savings for its own sake has no resonance for me. I prefer to invest in something that gives me a charge, like real estate or art.
16	a. If we're all doing something, it can't be too bad. We rise and fall together. b. The last thing I want to do is live a life of risk and uncertainty. c. Living on the edge has a certain appeal to me, even if it adds to my stress.
17	a. If I run into problems, I will go to my friends for support. b. If I run into problems, I can get really down and feel isolated. c. If I run into problems or get derailed, I am not deterred. I am very resilient.
18	a. I may make a job move to be closer to my social network. I need the support of a community to be at my best. b. I will only make a job move if I know that it will be good for me, money-wise, time-wise, and personally. c. I have made many job moves without guarantees of success. I work on intuition.

Interpretation:

If you had more than 14 "a" answers, your dominant instinct is most likely SO.
If you had more than 14 "b" answers, your dominant instinct is most likely SP.
If you had more than 14 "c" answers, your dominant instinct is most likely SX.

If you had fewer than 4 "a" answers, your blindspot instinct is most likely SO.
If you had fewer than 4 "b" answers, your blindspot instinct is most likely SP.
If you had fewer than 4 "c" answers, your blindspot instinct is most likely SX.

INSTINCTUAL STACK

Our instinctual stack is the order of the instincts we pay attention to and place energy towards, from most to least. The **dominant instinct** is the instinct we put most of our focus, energy, and effort on. It is what we believe keeps us alive. The focus on the dominant instinct becomes a distortion when I put almost all my energy here and little energy towards the other instincts. The benefits of directing my attention and energy towards this instinct are obvious. I am purposeful and planful about this instinct, and I believe that the time spent cultivating this instinct is well-spent. I can sustain interest in this area. I have a sense of agency, self-reliance and confidence about this area. I feel responsible for things in this arena, and do not rely on others to take care of things for me here. This dominant instinct is my gift to a relationship. It is how I tend to "serve" in my close relationships.

The **blindspot instinct** is the instinct that I put almost no focus or energy on. It is like an unused muscle that I don't remember having. This arena feels irrelevant to my well-being. I am not planful in this arena, mostly because I have no sense of agency or confidence toward this instinct. I don't feel like I have any control over what happens in this sphere. I have a feeling that my time is better spent elsewhere, and I rely on others to help me address the issues of this area. I cannot sustain interest in this area for long. The only way I can pay attention to this area is if the concern is immediate, and in front of me, visual. Otherwise, it easily slips into my unconsciousness. I always find other things more interesting to put my time and energy towards. I convince myself that it is not important to pay attention to this area. I convince myself it is boring and will take time away from more important things. But the truth is that I feel a great deal of anxiety and shame because I feel deficient and inadequate in this arena. I hope someone else will come to my rescue.

The **middle instinct** is the one we neither put too much weight on nor completely ignore. We tend to reference this middle instinct when we are more relaxed, or as a way to support our dominant instinct. We refer to it in a pinch, but we don't have a great deal of confidence in our abilities in this area. It is usually referenced either as a support or a relaxation. Though we are not as facile in expressing this instinct, we do not worry about it so much either.

Figure 2: The Instinctual Stack

Dominant instinct:
- Almost all my focus and energy go here
- This instinct keeps me alive
- It is the air I breathe
- Sense of agency, self-reliance, confidence
- The benefits are obvious
- Time spent cultivating instinct is well-spent
- Purposeful and planful about this instinct
- Can sustain interest in this area

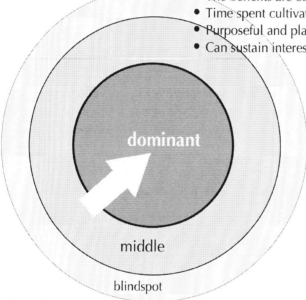

Blindspot instinct:
- Almost none of my focus or energy goes here
- This instinct feels random and irrelevant to my well-being
- I have no sense of agency or confidence in this arena
- I don't recognize patterns or feel there is a way to control this area
- I have a feeling that my time is better spent elsewhere
- I rely on others to help me address this area
- I cannot sustain interest in this area for long
- In order to pay attention to this area, I need it to be immediate, concrete, visual

From childhood, we tend to be unbalanced in these three categories of instincts. Shortly after birth, we develop ego structures that help us to survive and know ourselves as separate individuals. From this early concern about surviving, our bodies are already in stress. When we are in stress, concerned about our survival, our brains release hormones that put our bodies into heightened states of alert and increase the level of glucose in our body to provide our muscles with a burst of energy. It also shuts down nonessential bodily processes such as digestion and the immune response. In the same way, when we are stressed and overly concerned about our survival, we tend to shut down certain areas of focus while paying greater attention to the area that has traditionally worked best for us. Rather than spread our energies thin over three categories of instincts, we focus on one instinct if we are highly stressed, and two instincts if we are only mildly stressed.

When we are in survival mode, it is essentially impossible for us to pay attention to all three categories of instincts simultaneously. It just seems to take too much energy and presence to be able to multitask this way. If we are focusing on our Sexual instinct to keep us alive, any break to the charge and intensity feels like death. If we are focusing on our Self-Preservation instinct to keep us alive, we cannot afford to be disrupted from our stability. And if we are focusing on our Social instinct, any break to our social connection feels like a threat to our survival. In survival mode, our instincts are imbalanced, and we cannot thrive. We must learn to regulate and balance our instincts as we mature so that we can transition from survival mode to thriving mode.

Our instincts are very deeply programmed in us. We tend to relate to our instincts in a particular way throughout our lives. We may have periods when Self-Preservation is more salient and we put more attention there, for example, but overall, the way that we reference the various instincts is basically consistent over our lives. Our instincts and their balance/imbalance are the medium through which our personality types have an impact on our relationship to money. When our egos are running the show, we reflexively operate from fear and it is very difficult to balance these instincts. This creates many different problems for us with money. Only when our instincts become more balanced can our relationship to money become healthy. That is why balancing these three categories of instincts is so important.

What we have to do is become aware of our level of discomfort with the blindspot instinct. We must learn to accept that energy and integrate it through new actions into our lives. When we are in thriving mode, we feel more alive, more connected, more abundant. When something bad happens, we have the resilience to bounce back knowing that other possibilities await us, that we are and will be fine, and that there is nothing to fear. We are not ashamed of taking care of ourselves, interacting and participating, or exploring our passions. When we are in thriving mode, we experience less stress and are able to pay attention to more things, and broaden our attention across the three disparate categories of instincts, with their very different kinds of energy.

SELF-PRESERVATION INSTINCT – DOMINANT

The Self-Preservation instinct for well-being also brings along with it the possibility of discomfort, pain, and other suffering. This potential can motivate us to focus our energy on trying to protect ourselves. When we over-focus our energy on the Self-Preservation instinct, we become terrorized by the possibility that we might encounter disruption, discomfort, and danger. Rather than responding as needed, we can get overly obsessed with preventing "bad" things from ever happening. When Self-Preservation is our dominant focus, we believe that material resources help us survive. We tend to be very logical and analytical about what we need to survive.[3] This emphasis on material well-being can create a tendency to become selfish and cause us to experience self-imagined scarcity.

STABLE • PRAGMATIC • GROUNDED

We become protective of our resources, our safety, our time, and do not wish to jeopardize these things. We become energetically constricted. The energy gets locked in without a way to rejuvenate or replenish the energy. The preference is for linear progress, reliability, stability. I want to have a lifestyle where I can enjoy myself and be comfortable. I do not stop to consider what my passion might be, or how my social connections are doing. I go it alone, and am determined to keep my fortress strong and well-fortified. I like my

---

[3] For this reason, Type 1, 3, 5 energies, which are logical and analytical as well, reinforce the SP instinct, while Type 2, 7, 9 energies, which are optimistic and easy-going, move counter to the SP instinct.

routines and do not appreciate change. I sense that it would be dangerous to fully invest myself in something and follow a passion. I prefer to take the safe route where things are more certain to promote security. What I forget is that while this Self-Preservation instinct grounds me, I must continue to keep the energy flowing by connecting with others and finding my passion.

> **DISCIPLINED:** "I operate within parameters and am pretty frugal. I use my budget as a device for discipline. I reconcile expenses to the penny, on a monthly basis. Everything is methodical in my life, including my exercise, work, bill-paying, record keeping, savings. When we save up enough, we move it into a higher interest savings account. All receipts go into original envelopes."

> **SELF-RELIANT:** "I've been planning for retirement for years because I don't have a rich uncle. If you want it, you've got to work for it. No one is going to do it for you. I have no excuses. If I want something, I've got to work for it. No one is going to give it to me for free."

There are money strengths and weaknesses associated with a dominant Self-Preservation instinct. A person with a dominant Self-Preservation instinct will focus on taking care of the basics by spending money on physical necessities, earning enough to cover expenses, and staying roughly within budget. Money will be deployed in a pragmatic, functional way to ensure basic safety, comfort, and self-sufficiency. The purpose of money is to have a life that is comfortable and pleasant, with minimal disruptions.

SELF-PRESERVATION INSTINCT – BLINDSPOT

When I ignore my Self-Preservation instinct, I tend to have no foundation. I worry that I will never grow up and be able to function well in the world and take care of myself. At the same time, I fear that attending to Self-Preservation matters will divert my attention from my passion and my social engagements. I am not so pragmatic about life. I don't pay much attention to resource constraints, nor do I worry about planning ahead to maintain stability. I don't worry about what might go wrong, and I make things up as I go along. I don't pay much attention to material comfort. I only get motivated for money when it connects to something my lover or my group needs.

I am more focused on how people feel and whether there is energy. My clothing looks good and signifies status and image. My house is for socializing. I am willing to go out of my way for excitement or social connections. I am willing to take risks that might lead to big successes. All my energy goes towards fueling my juice and connecting with others. I rely on my social network and personal health and energy to get me through problems.

NOT FOCUSED ON MONEY: "I don't spend any time and energy focusing on money. When I was younger, my drawer was full of unpaid bills, and I just kept the drawer closed. I have been in positions of skipping meals and not having enough money to meet my basic needs. I went years without health insurance. I have never thought about retirement, not even once."

NOT MOTIVATED BY MONEY: "I measure my day based on how much I helped people. Money as a motivator does not seem right. It feels like people who are working for money are selling out from their higher aspirations. If I have money, I immediately use it for the family or for social gatherings."

LACK OF FINANCIAL GOALS: "I have no problem spending money. I like to treat myself well. If I have money, I spend it. I am in debt right now because I was using my credit card too much. I wish I had more money to be more secure. But I simply don't have goals about money."

LACK OF MONEY STRUCTURES: "I would be so unorganized around money without my partner. I am just happy that the rent gets paid. My interest in money is more around fitting in and not being embarrassed. Planning and savings seem difficult. Things always come up. I know I should save more, but I never seem to make it a priority. I spend for immediate gratification."

My relationship to money is very basic. I don't expect to operate optimally around finances. I am not able to create or maintain order, nor do I have a sense of how my well-being could support a larger purpose. I resist knowing about my money situation because that way I won't be responsible for it. I use money when I have it. I pay minimal attention to paying bills and budgeting. I have little orientation towards building a strong financial foundation with saving, safety nets, and wealth. I don't worry about having a large emergency stash. I hate insurance and thinking about downside risk. I don't feel I can be competent about money management. Instead, I rely on a spouse or friend to help me. As you can see in Figure 3 on the next page, when I have a Self-Preservation blindspot, my energy is mostly circulatory and intense. Because I lack stable, linear, forward-moving energy, my relationship to money will be difficult and my life will lack stability, planning, and grounding. When I put more attention on my Self-Preservation instinct, my life will be more balanced and satisfying.

Figure 3: Energy of Individual with Self-Preservation Blindspot

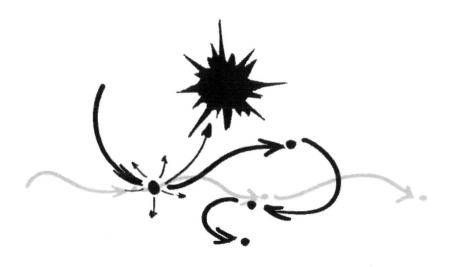

SP Blindspot – *Absence* of stable, linear, forward-moving energy

Means lack of:

stability

planning

grounding

If Self-Preservation is my blindspot:

1. How can I bring awareness to my Self-Preservation instinct?

2. What is the Self-Preservation instinct in me trying to serve?

3. What sensations do I experience in my body when my Self-Preservation instinct expresses itself?

4. What story do I tell myself about the Self-Preservation instinct?

5. How do I resist the natural operation of the Self-Preservation instinct?

6. What one thing could I do to exercise my Self-Preservation "muscle"?

Table 1: Contrasting Attitudes and Behaviors (SP)

Self-Preservation Instinct – DOMINANT	Self-Preservation Instinct – BLINDSPOT
DOMAIN 1: BUDGETING • Prioritize practical needs • Emphasize regularity • Interested in making ends meet	• Don't prioritize practical needs • No sense of regularity • No sense of grounding
DOMAIN 2: SPENDING • Pragmatic: food, shelter, comfort • Take care of practical matters	• Don't focus on physical well-being • Focus on social and energetic matters
DOMAIN 3: EARNING • Work hard to ensure material necessities • Responsive to material rewards	• Work is motivated by passion/contribution • Responsive to non-material rewards
DOMAIN 4: MONEY BELIEFS • Money is for security and well-being • Money enables me to be self-sufficient • I fear taking my attention off SP matters	• Security is not that important • No man is an island • I don't want to put my attention on SP
DOMAIN 5: MONEY KNOWLEDGE • There are ways to be smart about money	• I don't make the effort to be smart about it
DOMAIN 6: RISK MANAGEMENT • Safety is important • Need to consider contingencies • I am averse to change	• I do not worry much about safety • I don't think about what might go wrong • I am not averse to change
DOMAIN 7: PLANNING • Planning ahead makes sense • Planning ensures fewer disruptions	• Planning ahead doesn't make much sense • I live in the moment
DOMAIN 8: WEALTH-BUILDING • I believe in diversifying risk • I want to build wealth in a way that enables me to maintain my stable life	• Not taking risks can be risky • I am not averse to playing big
DOMAIN 9: BALANCE • Money is for having a good lifestyle • I will be more careful as things get tighter, because I don't want to be disrupted • A good lifestyle is one with routines, stability, and consistency	• Money is for connection, stimulation • Safety and security are boring • I don't mind expending energy if the upside might be really great

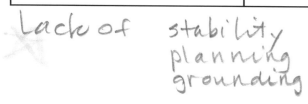

Lack of   stability
            planning
            grounding

SOCIAL INSTINCT – DOMINANT

The Social instinct for belonging also brings along with it the possibility of humiliation and ostracization. This potential can motivate me to focus my energy on trying to prevent social disapproval or rejection. My motivation for making money, working, spending and saving will all be driven by my quest for social approval. With a dominant Social instinct, my main focus will be on cultivating social bonds, fitting in, and contributing. I spend time and effort bonding and connecting with others. I like to be involved in community affairs, and like to donate generously to political, community and social causes. I want the support of my community and work to garner the approval and acceptance of others. I also like to host celebrations and social gatherings. I want people to feel good in my company and cultivate a sense of community amongst my friends. I tend to be optimistic and easy-going and want to cultivate positive experiences as a way to enhance the social experience and the social bonding.[4]

GENEROUS   •   COOPERATIVE   •   RECIPROCAL

My dominant Social instinct keeps me highly attuned to the needs of others. It feels obvious to me that we rise and fall together as a community. Often, I feel compelled to put the group's interests ahead of my own. It can feel difficult to spend on myself and stand up for myself in terms of higher pay. My dominant Social instinct instills in me a strong sense of the importance of reciprocity. I trust that those in my social group with whom I share a bond will be fair and abide by an honor code where we will all contribute our fair share, take what we need, and not take advantage of one another. We will not do strict accounting about individual contributions and takings, because we want to emphasize our common bond, affiliation of trust and goodwill, and cultivate a spirit of cooperation and collaboration. With money, the Social instinct prefers to navigate by implicit social norms rather than explicit and direct enforcement of rules and regulations. For example, when splitting a bill at a restaurant after a shared meal, the Social instinct would dictate that everyone should split the bill equally, though the implicit

---

[4] For this reason, Type 2, 7, 9 energies, which are optimistic and easy-going as well, reinforce the SO instinct, while Type 4, 6, 8 energies, which are intense and emotionally real move counter to the SO instinct.

social expectation would be to pay more if you ordered more because that's the fair thing to do.

To me, money is something to be spread around, not hoarded. To hoard resources and money feels wrong, and may be reason for expulsion from the group. The more I indulge myself with comforts and luxuries, the more important it is that I be generous to others. Not only do I enhance my social reputation as a team player, but I also cultivate a social safety net in case things go bad for me and my family. I tend not to have much fear about my own material well-being. As long as I have food, shelter, clothing, the basics, I will be fine and the group will take care of me. At the same time, I do work to enhance my standing in the group. I want to be recognized, validated, respected, and embraced. I temper my aggression around money and status in order to be socially appropriate. One way I do this is by being generous. My generosity not only helps others in need, but also cultivates people's good opinion of me and enhances my social standing in the group. My Social instinct wires me to believe that generosity will be rewarded.

FITTING IN: "Where I live, there are microclimates of social groups and I feel I need to fit in with all of these different groups. That means the proper brand names for the proper situations. All my brain power goes towards groups and finding the group I fit into. I do a lot of comparing. It drives my spending. I want to look as good as the next person. My spending depends on who I socialize with."

SUPPORTED: "For me, it's never been about the money. I trust that the money stuff will be okay. When I have been my most successful, it's been the community helping me. When I am not being supported by and giving to the community, or fitting in to the community, then I am not as successful. My social relationships are resources for me. They are dependable and something for me to rely on. I prefer being part of something bigger. I give to various charities."

My social network is more valuable to me than money, and I try not to do anything that would jeopardize my social standing. Because my energy is responsive to and moves organically with the group's energy, I can have difficulty directing my energy inward to ground myself and focus on my own well-being. I fear that moving inward will cut me off from others. I have the sense that it would be dangerous to be too self-oriented lest I seem selfish. I also sense that I cannot afford to invest myself fully in something and follow my passion, as that would divert my attention from the group. I prefer to stay in the loop, connected to others, taking the collaborative and cooperative route. I am more interested in being socially appropriate than I am in my own material well-being, or finding intensity. What I forget is that while this Social instinct serves to connect me to others, I must continue to keep the energy flowing. I am also meant to nurture my personal well-being and thrive.

There are money strengths and weaknesses associated with a dominant Social instinct. A person with a dominant Social instinct will focus some attention on the basics in terms of spending money on personal needs, making money to cover expenses, and staying roughly within budget, motivated by social responsibility to the family and group. Money is mainly for sharing and deploying for the benefit of others, and enables me to have a life of solid social affiliations, reciprocity, and harmony, where I support others and they support me.

SOCIAL INSTINCT – BLINDSPOT

When my Social instinct is my blindspot, I do not put my attention or energy into cultivating my social connections. Instead, I am preoccupied with my Self-Preservation and Sexual instincts. I do not have a sense of the patterns of social dynamics or a sense of the implicit rules and social conventions. Why get involved with a large organization where you will be an unknown or make only a small difference? It never occurs to me that generosity could have payoffs. Making anonymous donations seems even more puzzling. I do not take into consideration the benefits of being supported and cherished by the group, nor do I work to be a part of or attuned to the group. It would never occur to me to spend money to buy a status symbol, just for the social approval or recognition of the group, especially if I don't have the money to make this purchase. Much of the unwritten rules of this social game are a puzzle to me. I feel inadequate, but don't try to improve my social skills or learn how to navigate in this world. The blindspot creates both a lack of interest and a resigned attitude.

I don't really have a sense of the rules of the game, and I don't know how I would go about learning the rules of the game. It feels that I am doomed to stay an outsider. It feels like everyone else somehow got the secret code and I was passed by. I am aware that I am not able to enjoy the perks of information exchange that people on the "inside" enjoy. The cost of cooperating and collaborating, however, seems too high because of the sacrifice of time, money, and resources. Instead, I rely on gossip and information from others who are more plugged in than I am. I am not able to maintain social connections that do not have an immediate payoff. One person with a Social instinct blindspot explains: "I don't understand why it matters. I am a good people observer at the individual level, but I am not as astute about social group dynamics. I am good at reading non-verbal cues and deciding which person I am interested in, but social interactions don't interest me so much." There will be money weaknesses associated with a Social instinct blindspot. Whereas those with a dominant Social instinct intuitively understand the value of generosity, those with a Social instinct blindspot are cut off from the benefits of networking and collaboration. As you can see in Figure 4 on the next page, when I have a Social instinct blindspot, my energy is mostly linear and intense. Because I lack circulatory, organic, spatial energy, my relationship to money will be difficult and my life will lack social support, an understanding of trends, and the creative input of the group. When I put more attention on my Social instinct, my life will be more balanced and satisfying.

Figure 4: Energy of Individual with Social Blindspot

SO Blindspot – *Absence* of circulatory, organic, spatial energy

means

<u>lack of:</u>

social support

understanding trends

creative energy of the group

If the Social instinct is my blindspot:

1. How can I bring awareness to my Social instinct?
2. What sensations do I experience in my body when my Social instinct expresses itself?
3. What is true about how my Social instinct operates in me?
4. What story do I tell myself about the Social instinct?
5. How do I resist the natural operation of the Social instinct in me?
6. What one thing could I do to exercise my Social instinct "muscle"?

Table 2: Contrasting Attitudes and Behaviors (SO)

Social Instinct -DOMINANT	Social Instinct -BLINDSPOT
DOMAIN 1: BUDGETING • Being adaptable is important • I want to be responsible socially, and pay my obligations and not owe others	• I do what's best for me. I don't concern myself with social obligations or what's good for the group • I go my own way. I don't follow the herd
DOMAIN 2: SPENDING • My instinct to share is powerful • I like to be generous, give to charity and help others out	• I have very little instinct to share • I don't like to be asked to give money
DOMAIN 3: EARNING • I want to make a living doing something that has social value • I care about what people think about me	• I tend to make my job decisions based on pay, work conditions, hours • I do not have a large social network base
DOMAIN 4: MONEY BELIEFS • I am not so interested in material stuff • I feel that money should be shared and spread around to be helpful	• I feel anxious about giving money away • I want to be self-sufficient so that I am autonomous, independent
DOMAIN 5: MONEY KNOWLEDGE • I don't want to have to think about money • I learn a lot from people in my network • I trust my social network to keep me plugged in and informed, educated	• I don't have a good sense of the social trends or what's hot and what's not • I potentially miss out on key pieces of information that could be vital • I get my news from media sources
DOMAIN 6: RISK MANAGEMENT • I support my friends and they support me. • I will be generous to people, and they will be generous back to me. • My social network is my safety net	• I have to rely on myself to get things done, because I do not have a large social net to cast when I want to mobilize a project • My health and my money are my safety net
DOMAIN 7: PLANNING • I live in the present. I don't want to worry about the future • I do not do a lot of future planning or goal setting with money	• My vision of what is possible is constrained • I do not draw upon the larger social imagination & creative energy of groups
DOMAIN 8: WEALTH BUILDING • The power of money is in the spending of money, not saving money for myself • It feels that hoarding money for myself is selfish and inappropriate	• I do not have a social network base to call upon to pool resources • I don't mind driving a hard bargain, because it's transactional
DOMAIN 9: BALANCE • We rise and fall together • I don't have a lot of fear about my material well-being. I believe things will work out • I trust that I will be okay	• It's every man for himself • I am anxious about surviving, making it alone in this world • I worry about my own material well-being

lack of social support
understanding trends

SEXUAL INSTINCT – DOMINANT

The Sexual instinct for charge, juice, electricity also brings with it the possibility for boredom – the absence of charge, juice, stimulation. This potential can motivate us to focus our energy on trying to prevent this boredom. We can become terrorized by the possibility that we might be out of the chase and under-stimulated. Often, we end up unconsciously creating disruptions that force us to be challenged and stimulated.

> **SEEKING CHARGE:** "I enjoy the rush of being able to make a lot of money fast. I like putting together deals and working the system – that gets my juices flowing. I have a crisis orientation, having grown up with a lot of stress and drama. There is something metabolically in me that cannot tolerate a slow, stable pace. It's not exciting enough."

> **RESILIENT:** "I invest in my own businesses. It doesn't scare me at all. If there is a setback and things don't work out, I just keep going. Instead of getting bummed out, I move on and wait for another opportunity to come my way. It is hard to get me down. What happened in the past doesn't really register. I don't really worry or second guess things. I have no trouble pulling the trigger. I go for the juice rather than for security."

When my dominant instinct is the Sexual instinct, I am focused on the juice. I have very strong likes and dislikes. I want to be emotionally real and go deep as a way to have a more intense connection with my passion.[5] My radar is always up, seeking the juice and transmitting interest. I could never imagine doing something that I was not passionate about. I would never forsake my passion for the sake of stability or social approval. To me, that would be absolutely ludicrous. My life might be dramatic and stressful, but I am resilient and roll with the punches. I never assume stability. I don't have the attention span for stability. I have no interest in hedging my bets and diversifying risk. I am not at all interested in stability or hoarding resources. What I care about is being in my mojo, with the energetic confidence and charisma to do whatever I want. My mojo is my sex appeal, self confidence, sense of invincibility and virility, my ability to bounce back if something bad happens to me.

When the right opportunity strikes, I respond. It might be interpreted as impulsive, but I know what I am doing. It's about striking when the time is right. There is no planning for this type of thing. Opportunity comes when it

---

[5] For this reason, Type 4, 6, 8 energies, which are intense and emotionally real as well, reinforce the SX instinct, while Type 1, 3, 5 energies, which are logical and analytical move counter to the SX instinct.

does. And when it does, I will expend whatever energy is necessary to pursue it. I don't want to be restricted in any way from pursuing what interests me. I'm like a lion on the hunt. Don't stop me. I am willing to deplete my energy and let the hunt take me where it will. The bigger the challenge, the bigger the charge. I use my resources to find and nurture my next hit. I relish competition for its own sake. Competition helps me to hone my skills, be more confident and attractive.

CHARISMATIC • INTENSE • OPPORTUNISTIC

When the Sexual instinct is my dominant energy, I have little patience for routines, details, and maintenance. I am curious, impetuous, experimental. I am willing to go headfirst, deep, hard, intensely, without any concern for pulling back or burning out. I have little fear of material failure or death. I can get so tunnel-focused on what attracts me that nothing else and no one else matters. I won't hold back out of fear of being hurt. If I am going to fight to the death, then I will take down my opponent and we may both go down in flames. If I come out the victor, I will survive and go on to dominate (and reproduce).

This instinctual energy is not about surviving a storm by being prepared or huddling together. Rather, this energy is about the ability to survive by infusing my passion, coming back from the ashes, rising again. It is the instinct to take advantage of any opportunity, small though it may be, and make the most and best of it. It is is this resiliency that makes up a necessary third leg to this triad of instincts, without which we would never have survived as a species. When all else fails, and we cannot maintain the security of shelter, and even the banding together with our fellow mates does not work, we must rely on our own fire and passion to live and carry on, and this is what this Sexual instinct gives us.

There are money strengths and weaknesses associated with a dominant Sexual instinct. A person with a dominant Sexual instinct will be open to new opportunities and willing to take big risks for potentially big rewards. They have confidence and optimism and are bold, resilient and not easily deterred. Their lives feel meaningful, stimulating, interesting, and passionate.

SEXUAL INSTINCT – BLINDSPOT

When the Sexual instinct is the blindspot Instinct, there tends to be an avoidance, subversion, or procrastination about fueling the fire. I know that I have fire and passion, but it is locked up and I don't know how to let it out. I might ocassionally worry about being boring, unattractive, and uninteresting. But mostly, I just ignore this concern and focus on my well-being and my social connections. I do not have any sense of the benefits of being intense and passionate. In fact, it seems completely at odds with the things I care about. I do not see the logic of living a life full of disruptions, challenge, intensity, going into the flame, going down in flames, and coming back again. The sexual energy only seems risky, disruptive and destructive. What I miss out on is the charge that comes from a strong passion for a person or interest. I cannot access the pulsating excitement of living from my deep belly energy. I cannot access the fire that fuels me, energizes me, makes me feel utterly alive. Something feels missing in me, but I am too scared to open up this Pandora's box of sexual energy. As you can see in Figure 5 on the next page, when I have a Sexual blindspot, my energy is mostly circulatory and linear. Because I lack passionate, intense, exploring energy, my relationship to money will be difficult and my life will lack risk-taking, passion, and fire. When I put more attention on my Sexual instinct, my life will be more balanced and satisfying.

Figure 5: Energy of Individual with Sexual Blindspot

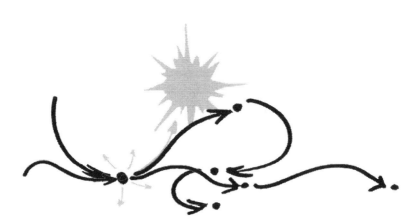

SX Blindspot – *Absence* of exploring, intense, disruptive energy means
<u>lack of:</u>
risk taking
passion and commitment
seizing opportunities that strike

<u>If the Sexual instinct is my blindspot:</u>

1. How can I bring awareness to my Sexual instinct?

2. What is the Sexual instinct in me trying to serve?

3. What sensations do I experience in my body when my Sexual instinct expresses itself?

4. What story do I tell myself about the Sexual instinct?

5. How do I resist the natural operation of the Sexual instinct in me?

6. What one thing could I do to exercise my Sexual instinct "muscle"?

Table 3: Contrasting Attitudes and Behaviors (SX)

SX DOMINANT	SX BLINDSPOT
DOMAIN 1: BUDGETING • I will bite off more than I can chew, work wise or money wise, and then figure out how to make it work. I enjoy the challenge • Balancing the budget is not interesting	• I do not crave stimulation or intensity • It would never occur to me to disrupt my life just for the excitement of it • I tend to be practical about my material and social obligations
DOMAIN 2: SPENDING • I am drawn to things that are beautiful, and pique my curiosity. I love sensory stimulation • If I have money, I spend it	• My spending is driven more by my personal needs and social responsibilities than whim or strong and electric attraction
DOMAIN 3: EARNING • I want to make money doing what I love • I get a big charge out of challenges • I have a great deal of confidence about making money when I am in my mojo	• It is acceptable to me to make money doing something I don't have a passion for • Moving into something I really care about with all my energy seems really risky
DOMAIN 4: MONEY BELIEFS • I am more interested in getting a charge and energy from what I am doing • Money is not a big motivator for me. But I love the freedom it gives me	• Money for me is not about intensity and charge • Money is for security
DOMAIN 5: MONEY KNOWLEDGE • You can't take the money with you when you die. Go for it, don't hold back • I live for today. Death could be right around the corner. Life is unpredictable	• I try to maintain stability and social connection and harmony • I try to pace myself and be reasonable about things
DOMAIN 6: RISK MANAGEMENT • For me, the possibilities and upside trumps potential problems or downside • What supports me is my health and energy, and good relationships.	• I try to plan ahead for social and financial contingencies • I try not to jeopardize my physical or social well-being, if at all possible
DOMAIN 7: • I am a survivor, not a planner • The future feels so abstract • I will meet what comes up	• I do not have confidence that I can meet what comes up • I try to create safety structures in my life
DOMAIN 8: • I am willing to take big risks for a potentially great outcome • I am oriented towards investing vs savings	• I get pushed off center if things go wrong • It is difficult to be resilient in the face of a social or financial setback
DOMAIN 9: • Living on the edge has a certain appeal to me, even if it adds to my stress. • I have an optimism that things work out	• I am anxious about scarcity, and that anxiety motivates me • Things may work out, but they might not

Lack of risk-taking, passion & commitment

BALANCING THE THREE INSTINCTS

Balancing our three instincts has the powerful effect of relaxing the ego's iron grip on our personalities. When we balance our three instincts, we cannot help but experience strong grounding, strong interconnections with others, and strong passion. When we are balanced, our ego-driven personality simply cannot have the pull and influence that it had when we were imbalanced. When our instincts are imbalanced, our ego exacerbates this imbalance. When we balance our instincts, putting even attention and energy on all three instincts, we become highly functioning and highly effective on our own. Our personalities have little room to maneuver and wreak havoc. Balancing our three instincts – Self-Preservation, Social, and Sexual – heals our head, heart, and belly centers, and enables us to be less fixated in our personalities.

The more effectively I meet my Self-Preservation instinct needs, the more clear-headed I am, and the less anxious I am about safety and security, which is healing for my head center. The more effectively I meet my Self-Preservation instinct needs, the more attuned I am to myself, and the less ashamed I feel about my value and worth, which is healing for my heart center. And the more effectively I meet my Self-Preservation instinct needs, the more self-reliant and autonomous I am, and the less constricted and tight I feel, which is healing for my belly center.

The more effectively I meet my Social instinct needs, the more clear-headed I am, and the less anxious I am about being rejected or ostracized, which is healing for my head center. The more effectively I meet my Social instinct needs, the more attuned I am to myself and others, and the less ashamed I feel about my image, contribution, and status, which is healing for my heart center. And the more effectively I meet my Social instinct needs, the more connected I am, and the less separate I feel, which is healing for my belly center.

The more effectively I meet my Sexual instinct needs, the more clear-headed I am, and the less anxious I am about finding the intensity and juice, which is healing for my head center. The more effectively I meet my Sexual instinct needs, the more attuned I am to myself, and the less ashamed I feel about not being impassioned and attractive, which is healing for my heart center. And the more effectively I meet my Sexual instinct needs, the more energized I am, and the less enervated and more vital I feel, which is healing for my belly center.

By bringing spaciousness to our three centers – head, heart, and belly – through the balancing of our three instincts, our Outer Work complements our Inner Work. Outer Work is the work we do to live in balance in our lives, while Inner Work is the work we do on the inside to connect to our true nature beyond our personality masks. When we are present and we cultivate a healthy relationship to ourselves, to money, and to one another, our Outer Work and Inner Work feel like a tight dance interweaving us with the larger universe.

Table 4: Balancing the Instincts in the Nine Domains

	Self-Preservation	Social	Sexual
1	I respect my budget, but I am not ruled by it. I take care of business, but I also make sure to take care of others and honor my own fire.	My responsibility to my family and community and my desire for respect motivate me to take care of personal financial matters.	I am excited to pay my bills and hit my budget. With a stable financial foundation, I can pursue my passion confidently.
2	I make sure that everyone is comfortable and well cared for.	I share my resources so that everyone can have a decent life.	I don't hesitate to buy what I love, but I also make sure to save some money and stay within budget.
3	I am willing to work hard, but insist on honoring my fire and making a difference to others.	Not only do I earn a living by serving others, I also honor my own fire.	I have confidence and energy to sell my services and earn a good living.
4	Money is for my well-being, but it is also to serve others and to energize and enliven me.	I do not have a problem earning a lot of money as long as I am earning in a way that serves. I always have the option to deploy my wealth generously.	Money enables me to live an intensely satisfying and joyful life. I do not have to create disruptions to live a vital life.
5	Money enables me to be self-sufficient, so that I can be a contributing member of society.	My social connections enable me to understand social trends. I take the time to learn how money works so that I can better serve.	I live for today, like I could die tomorrow, but I also plan ahead in case I do make it to tomorrow!
6	Once I prepare for what can go wrong, I relax and trust that things will be okay.	My social safety net is one form of support that I have. I also work to take care of myself, so that I can be self-reliant.	I throw caution to the wind when I am impassioned, and I also remember that my gifts serve the greater good.
7	I plan ahead, but also recognize that the best laid plans can be derailed, and I am willing to adapt my plan as needed.	I am adaptable, but I do not hesitate to envision where I would personally like to be in a few years and work to make it come true.	I focus on what I care about, but am willing to put attention and energy into certain critical routine maintenance areas, such as my diet, health, and money.
8	I save and invest and have resources in reserve so that I can live to my fullest potential as a contributing member of society.	Having wealth enables me to serve myself and others better.	My creative energy drives me to invest in the future. With successful saving and investing, I can continue creating.
9	I acknowledge and appreciate all the various forms of wealth in my life, and experience abundance.	We are each affected by others, and my participation really matters. I feel optimistic about our future.	There is no such thing as failure. We can learn from everything that happens to us in our lives.

CHAPTER 6

NINE MONEY TYPES

Some people hoard money while others spend liberally. Some people like to plan while others don't think about the future. Some people are determined to make a lot of money, while others are happy to make ends meet. Some people are greedy, while others are generous. Why are people so different with money? And why don't people do what they know they are supposed to do? These are big questions.

Without understanding the answers to these questions, we don't really have a way to help people address the root causes of their financial ailments. Without having answers to these questions, all we can do is to give them a bandage that heals the surface wound until the next set of problems crops up. Perhaps this is why when we go to a financial advisor, and they start reeling off a list of things we ought to do, like set up a 401K, pay down our credit cards, create an emergency savings fund, many people start to shudder and want to run away. They are telling us what we already know, but resist doing. It is like going to a doctor for an aching back, and the doctor telling us that we should take Tylenol, stretch daily, exercise more. Thanks. I know that! But why is my back aching? What's the root cause?

When it comes to money, the disciplines of economics and financial planning both over-emphasize our rational minds over our emotions and instincts. The discipline of economics, for example, has attempted to address the question of why we don't do what we are supposed to do in one of two ways. Either a) we are rational and know what we are doing, even when it doesn't seem to make sense, or b) we are irrational and can't help making mistakes. In the financial planning discipline, the basic wisdom around why we don't do what we are supposed to do is that a) we lack information and knowledge, or b) we lack self-discipline and need to be aided by an advisor who can keep us on track. So, we are rational and know what we're doing, or ill-informed, ill-behaved, or just plain dumb. Both disciplines acknowledge that there might be gender differences or cultural differences, but neither discipline has a satisfactory explanation of individual differences. We humans share certain similarities, but we also vary in distinct ways. Behavioral economists have recently begun to take more seriously emotions and the plausibility of decisions being "irrational" because of our human brain structures. For example, we over-emphasize recent events over past events. We prefer immediate payoffs to delayed gratification. We over-emphasize large results over incremental ones. We ignore data from large samples in favor of anecdotes, ignore new evidence that contradicts our beliefs, and interpret information in ways that confirm our preconceived notions.

But while it is interesting to contemplate all the ways we are not rational, we must also consider how we differ in the ways we are "irrational." Different personality types have rather distinct relationships to money. Rather than sorting people based on behavioral differences (for example, dividing people into savers and spenders), the following chapters begin from the inside out. We start from the inside out because superficial differences or similarities can be misleading. Two aggressive, risk-loving investors, for example, may look similar on the outside but be driven by very different things from the inside. Two compulsive spenders may look similar on the outside, but have very different motivations on the inside. Individuals with differing underlying motivations should not be lumped together based on superficial similarities.

This chapter provides an overview of the nine basic money personality types. Each of us expresses a dominant personality type, but we have all nine types in us to one degree or another. So we can benefit from each of the following nine chapters in understanding how these strategies work in ourselves and others.

WHICH DESCRIPTION RESONATES MOST?

A: *"I believe that money is meaningful up to a certain point. I need money to live, but I don't need a ton of it. I try to live within my means, not have debt, and not be overly greedy or excessive. I can become overly rigid in my beliefs and judgments about money, what is right and what is wrong, what is acceptable to have and what is not."*

B: *"Spending is how I show my love. I hope my generosity is appreciated. I hope others will return the favors I've lavished on them by loving me back. Spending on myself feels selfish."*

C: *"Money validates me. I want to make a lot of it and use it in a way that displays my success. My ambitions around money are unfettered. I invest in myself and my personal development so that I can be more successful. I put forth great effort for the sake of money."*

D: *"Money is rather mundane and doesn't have much to do with who I am. I don't want to be bothered by things that are not personally meaningful to me. I am an exception to the rule and cannot be bound by ordinary constraints. I am reluctant to put forth great effort for the sake of money because I don't believe that money is intrinsically meaningful or can fulfill me."*

E: *"I minimize my need for money. I need very little money to survive. By minimizing my needs, I can remain detached and safe. I am reluctant to put forth great effort for the sake of money. I value money mainly for the self-sufficiency it brings me."*

F: *"Sometimes I am frugal, but sometimes I find myself splurging. I am a bit back and forth when it comes to money. I care about making good money because money brings me security. But sometimes I doubt the value of money. Even though I think it will bring me security, I don't seem to feel any less anxious."*

G: *"Money is very meaningful and important to me. I perceive all the possibilities that money can bring. Money gives me options and freedom. I hate to be boxed in, restricted, or trapped. I don't like to limit my spending or feel that I have to stay within budget. But I value savings for the options that it gives me."*

H: *"I want what I want. I believe that through hard work, I can get what I want. Rather than pull back my spending, I'd rather go out and make more. I am proud of my role as a provider. I may make a lot, but I spend a lot as well."*

I   *"Money is for comfort. Money doesn't validate me. I don't want to strive too hard, or get too worked up about investing, managing, and making money. Having money is fine, but I don't want to stress about it."*

THE NINE MONEY TYPES

A: *"I believe that money is meaningful up to a certain point. I need money to live, but I don't need a ton of it. I try to live within my means, not have debt, and not be overly greedy or excessive. I can become overly rigid in my beliefs and judgments about money, what is right and what is wrong, what is acceptable to have and what is not."*

If statement A resonates most for you, then you are most likely a **Type 1** on the Enneagram, with a money strategy of ***Ordering***. You are a belly-center type who is gifted at self-regulating and being orderly.   You do things properly to feel aligned to your internal sense of what is right and good. You are <u>idealistic</u> in the sense that there is an ideal you aim for. You want to create order and and live in an orderly world. You try your best to stay within your means, not have debt, and not be overly greedy or excessive. *Ordering* is not about trying to have more or less. It is about having the right amount. Your appetite for money and the best that life has to offer is therefore constrained. You can become overly rigid in your beliefs and judgments about money and what is acceptable to have and what is not. Articulating your belly center would enable you to distinguish between being in alignment with your core self and trying to be perfect. Growth occurs when you move past superficial rules and black-and-white thinking to play in the gray zone where there are no clear boundaries of good and bad, right and wrong. But the gray zone is difficult for you. Afraid of the wild, messy, potentially disruptive instinctual energy that might arise unbidden, you stifle your instinctual energy, creating constriction and tightness. Resentment keeps your ego engine oiled. If resentment doesn't work, your superego will make you feel guilty that you are not working hard enough to fix things.

B: *"Spending is how I show my love. I hope my generosity is appreciated. I hope others will return the favors I've lavished on them by loving me back. Spending on myself feels selfish."*

If statement B resonates most for you, then you are most likely a **Type 2** on the Enneagram, with a money strategy of ***Giving***. You are a heart-center type who is gifted at empathizing with and nurturing others.

You are generous and thoughtful because you want to be loved. You are willful in the sense that you believe that you can create the conditions to receive love by being generous to others. You are determined to get your needs met, though not directly. You believe that by being generous, you can gain the appreciation and love that you desire. With money, as with love, you believe that you must work hard for it. You do not believe that money, or love, can come easily to you. You find it difficult to speak up directly for what you need, emotionally or money-wise. In spending, you are torn between meeting your own needs and meeting others' needs, which can generate guilt and shame about spending money on yourself. Money is intrinsically difficult for you because you cannot admit that you need it, even though you know you do. Underlying all your *Giving* is a deep envy. You want what others have, but don't want to be selfish. You desire connection more than anything else but your *Giving* can leave you feeling unappreciated and hurt. Developing your heart center would enable you to distinguish between being unconditionally loving and being loving to get something in return. Growth occurs when you feed your heart directly, rather than indirectly, by recognizing what you need for yourself. But listening to your own heart is difficult because you don't want to be selfish. You must cultivate your own self-reliance and the self-reliance of others. Pride keeps your ego engine oiled. If pride doesn't work, your superego will make you feel guilty for being selfish, and ashamed that you don't deserve things.

C: *"Money validates me. I want to make a lot of it and use it in a way that displays my success. My ambitions around money are unfettered. I invest in myself and my personal development so that I can be more successful. I put forth great effort for the sake of money."*

If statement C resonates most for you, then you are most likely a **Type 3** on the Enneagram, with a money strategy of ***Striving***. You are a heart-center type who is gifted at achieving and working to your full potential. The more you succeed and achieve, the more you feel valued and validated. You are hopeful in the sense that you hope success will bring validation. With money, you want to make a lot of it and use it in a way that displays your success. Your ambitions around money are unfettered. You invest in yourself and your personal development so that you can be more successful. You are not concerned about being selfish or greedy. You are not concerned about compromises that might be required. You try very hard to shine. Underlying all your *Striving*, however, is a deep anxiety that you lack value. You think you know what you should strive for, but you have difficulty connecting to who you really are. You can become a workaholic without any other personally meaningful hobbies or activities in your life. Bringing fruition to your heart center requires honoring what your heart craves and getting in touch with a deeper sense of who you are and what really matters for you. This would enable you to distinguish between being intrinsically of value and being externally successful. Growth occurs when you move past all the doing and *Striving* to relax and integrate all that is good in your life. But relaxing is difficult for you. Afraid of losing kudos, you do not allow yourself to relax, and this creates exhaustion and constricts your heart. Vanity keeps your ego engine oiled. If vanity doesn't work, your superego will make you feel ashamed that you are not good enough.

D: *"Money is rather mundane and doesn't have much to do with who I am. I don't want to be bothered by things that are not personally meaningful to me. I am an exception to the rule and cannot be bound by ordinary constraints. I am reluctant to put forth great effort for the sake of money because I don't believe that money is intrinsically meaningful or can fulfill me."*

If statement D resonates most for you, then you are most likely a **Type 4** on the Enneagram, with a money strategy of *Personalizing*. You are a heart-center type who is gifted at connecting to your true self and knowing who you are. You want to express yourself uniquely to align with your internal sense of who you really are. You are idealistic in the sense that you have an ideal concept of your authentic self that you aim to express. But you feel that you lack something that would enable you to enjoy life fully. You like to buy things that are personally meaningful and express who you are. You want to make money in a way that is in alignment with your special talents and skills. You want to invest in projects and stocks that are unique to your interests. You don't want to manage money in a mundane and ordinary way like everyone else, out of a sense of inadequacy or superiority or both. You feel that you are an exception to the rule and as such should not have to be bound by ordinary physical rules and fiscal constraints. You are reluctant to put forth effort for the sake of money because you don't believe that money is intrinsically meaningful or will fulfill you. Discipline, self-control, and staying on track with money can be great challenges. You desire self-expression, but your beliefs about being an exception to the rule can wreak havoc with your money. Articulating your heart center would enable you to distinguish between being in alignment with your true identity and doing things uniquely to seem special. Growth occurs when you move past your sense of inadequacy to acknowledge that you are special and loved. Afraid to leave behind your victimhood, you do not allow yourself to own your full adequacy, agency, and power – which creates a feeling of shame and constriction in your heart. Envy keeps your ego engine oiled. If envy doesn't work, your superego will make you feel ashamed of being like everyone else.

E: *"I minimize my need for money. I need very little money to survive. By minimizing my needs, I can remain detached and safe. I am reluctant to put forth great effort for the sake of money. I value money mainly for the self-sufficiency it brings me."*

If statement E resonates most for you, then you are most likely a **Type 5** on the Enneagram, with a money strategy of ***Minimizing***. You are a head-center type who is gifted at observing and making sense of the world around you. You prefer not to get pulled into the general hubbub of things, but to stay a bit distanced and withdrawn. You don't like to get too excited, and you don't like to need or want anything too much. You minimize your need for money because you don't want to be vulnerable. You are <u>willful</u> in the sense that you believe that you can create the conditions to be invulnerable by minimizing your need for money, people, and love. You believe that by minimizing your needs, you can remain detached and safe. With money, as with love, you believe that it is almost impossible to get what you want, so you are reluctant to put forth effort for the sake of money. Because you tend to be an expert in something, making money tends not to be difficult for you. You can be a good investor in the stock market because you are unemotional and logical. However, you are not willing to exert yourself beyond what you find interesting for the sake of money. You value money mostly for the sufficiency it buys you. Underlying your *Minimizing* is a deep desire to have what you want, but you refuse to expose yourself to this vulnerability. You don't want to get sucked in so much that you lose your objectivity. You can be overly willful in your *Minimizing* which makes you feel dry and without resources. Developing your head center requires you to participate in the world that you wish to know. Growth occurs when you can feed your mind directly, rather than indirectly, by putting some skin on the line. But investing yourself fully can be difficult because you don't want to be vulnerable. Avarice and holding back keeps your ego engine oiled. If avarice doesn't work, your superego will make you afraid of being in the line of fire and being a part of life.

F: *"Sometimes I am frugal, but sometimes I find myself splurging. I am a bit back and forth when it comes to money. I care about making good money because money brings me security. But sometimes I doubt the value of money. Even though I think it will bring me security, I don't seem to feel any less anxious."*

If statement F resonates most for you, then you are most likely a **Type 6** on the Enneagram, with a money strategy of ***Securing***. You are a head-center type who is gifted at being prepared, responsible, and planning for worst-case scenarios. You provide needed direction and leadership in emergencies, and you desire to be courageous, awake, and bold at *all* times. You are <u>hopeful</u> that being security-oriented will allow you to find your orientation and guidance in regular life. When you feel unsupported, you become anxious and reactive, and swing from one extreme to another. You hope that money will enable you to be more secure, and for this reason, you are frugal and have emergency plans. But at the same time, you fear that money will not support you, and you may give up on money as a form of support. When you do this, you splurge and try to be supported in other ways, socially or relationally. Spending, savings, budgeting, staying on track tend to be very back and forth for you. You want to trust money as a form of support, but then you distrust it.

So your efforts towards money are limited. You do not let yourself venture too far towards your full potential for fear of the consequences. You fear that being outstanding might invoke the jealousy of others, would set the bar too high, or drain your energy. Whatever the reason, you try up to a certain point, but then sabotage your own efforts. It can seem puzzling to both outsiders and yourself. You seem to be on a path to success, and then you suddenly slam on the brakes, without knowing why. Underlying all your anxiety and *Securing* is a deep desire to be grounded and relaxed. You assume you know how to be secure, but you have difficulty connecting to your sense of trust and faith. Bringing fruition to your head center enables you to distinguish between real security and false security. Anxiety keeps your ego engine oiled. If anxiety doesn't work, your superego will make you feel scared that you are not up to it and not brave enough.

G: *"Money is very meaningful and important to me. I perceive all the possibilities that money can bring. Money gives me options and freedom. I hate to be boxed in, restricted, or trapped. I don't like to limit my spending or feel that I have to stay within budget. But I value savings for the options that it gives me."*

If statement G resonates most for you, then you are most likely a **Type 7** on the Enneagram, with a money strategy of ***Optimizing***. You are a head-center type who is gifted at seeing the larger possibilities for how to make life great. You desire to align things to your internal sense of what is best, most fun, fulfilling and satisfying. You are idealistic in the sense that there is an optimum that you aim for. You can be visionary in seeing how to make things work better, and be more enjoyable, efficient, convenient, interesting. You tend to focus on how to make things the best that they can be rather than on maintaining order or simplicity. You don't mind complexity, either wading through it or generating it, if you can create a better situation for yourself. You have an intuitive understanding of the value of leverage, and have no problem wheeling, dealing, and taking advantage of opportunities that present themselves. You hate to be boxed in, restricted, or trapped. You don't like to limit your spending or feel that you must stay within budget. On the other hand, you value having savings for the options it gives you. The best way out of this bind is to make more money, so you can have your cake and eat it too! You don't mind putting forth great effort for the sake of money. Underlying all your *Optimizing*, however, is a deep desire to appreciate what is right here in front of you rather than always thinking that the grass is greener on the other side. But this is difficult. As a result, you feel compelled to have more money to feed your hungry soul. Articulating your head center enables you to be in alignment with your vision of an optimal world as it unfolds. Growth occurs when you learn that there can be freedom within boundaries and constraints. But accepting this wisdom is difficult for you. Afraid that you will be boxed in and deprived, you do not allow yourself to experience the freedom that can come with boundaries and constraints, and this keeps you feeling hungry and restless. Gluttony and an overactive appetite keep your ego engine oiled. If gluttony doesn't work, your superego will make you afraid that you are going to be trapped forever.

H: *"I want what I want. I believe that through hard work, I can get what I want. Rather than pull back my spending, I'd rather go out and make more. I am proud of my role as a provider. I may make a lot, but I spend a lot as well."*

If statement H resonates most for you, then you are most likely a **Type 8** on the Enneagram, with a money strategy of ***Exerting***. You are a belly-center type who is gifted at taking action and making things happen. You are forceful, big-picture oriented, not detail-oriented. You are <u>willful</u> in the sense that you believe that you can create the conditions to receive the love you want. You are determined to get your needs met directly. You believe that by exerting yourself, you can get whatever you want. With money, as with love, you believe that you must work hard for it. But you do not doubt that it can be yours. In spending, you are determined to buy whatever you want. You have difficulty distinguishing want from need. Anything you want feels like a need. You have no shame or guilt about going after all that you want. Rather than limit yourself, you would rather go out and make more money. Your ability to make money gives you a role as provider for the family, which you are proud of. You tend to live big. You can make a lot, but you can also spend a lot. You tend to be skilled at building wealth because you don't let barriers keep you out, and are willing to put in the effort to make things happen. Underlying all your *Exerting* and toughness, however, is a deep desire to be sensitive and attuned. You assume you know how to be tough, but you have difficulty connecting to your vulnerable side. Developing your belly center requires you to get in touch with what you really crave, which is vitality and aliveness. Growth occurs when you don't have to push against life so much. But you fear that pulling back may cause you to be weak. Lust keeps your ego engine oiled. If lust doesn't work, your superego will make you feel angry for not getting what you want.

I   *"Money is for comfort. Money doesn't validate me. I don't want to strive too hard, or get too worked up about investing, managing, and making money. Having money is fine, but I don't want to stress about it."*

If statement I resonates most for you, then you are most likely a **Type 9** on the Enneagram, with a money strategy of ***Settling***. You are a belly-center type who is gifted at being steady and grounded, seeing the bright side of things, and being at peace. You desire to be relaxed and undisturbed. You are <u>hopeful</u> in the sense that you hope *Settling* will bring peace and harmony, and are attached to *Settling* (not *Exerting*) for this reason. You do not strive too hard for the sake of making or having money. You are more concerned about having no money than having more money. You don't want to get too worked up about investing or managing money. You like the idea of automating bill paying and savings so that you don't have to make the extra effort. Money is more for functionality and getting by than showing off. Your ambitions around money are limited. You fear being bothered and troubled by money and desire peace with money above all else. Underlying all your *Settling*, however, is a deep desire to shine and really be in the dynamic flow of life. You assume you know how to be undisturbed, but you have difficulty connecting to your sense of heldness and wholeness. You can become zoned out and almost irresponsible for the sake of being undisturbed. Bringing fruition to your belly center requires honoring what your body craves and getting in touch with a deeper sense of what wholeness and connection really mean for you. This would enable you to distinguish between being relaxed and a stagnant false peace. Growth occurs when you move past your *Settling* to be bold and awake. But being truly bold and awake is difficult. Afraid of how awakening will disturb you, you do not allow yourself to fully wake up, which creates a body that is blocked in its flow. Sloth keeps your ego engine oiled. If sloth doesn't work, your superego will make you feel angry that you are being disturbed.

NINE TYPES and THEIR MONEY STRATEGIES

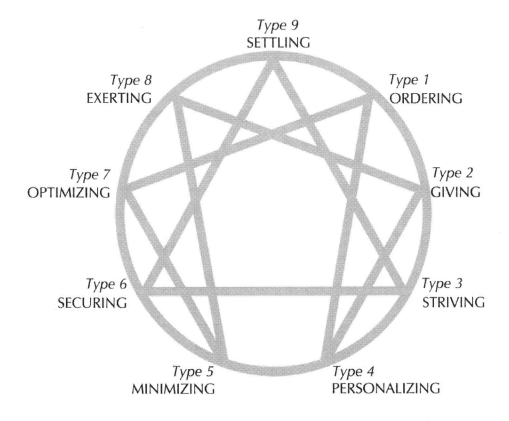

Note: Although we have the capacity for all nine strategies in us, our personalities cause us to focus on one strategy in particular. You may find that you also reference a neighboring "wing" (adjacent to your primary strategy) as a secondary strategy.

TYPE STRATEGIES

Each type starts out with a bad feeling, then embraces a defensive strategy to compensate for that feeling. But the strategy works to reinforce the bad feeling and block love out. Each type needs to learn to move in the opposite direction to let love in.

Bad Feeling	Strategy	Defending against	Need to integrate this	Will enable you to
1: I am Corrupt	1: **Ordering** *(to make things right)*	Being gluttonous, satisfied	Embrace pleasure and joy (7)	Be special with/despite my flaws (4)
2: I'm weak and I must earn my place to get love	2: **Giving** *(to get love and appreciation)*	Being needy and inadequate	Embrace your neediness and not hold it at bay (4)	Be here with vitality. Own your power (8)
3: It's up to me	3: **Striving** *(to achieve and be successful as a hero)*	Being supported	Support and be supported, act in service beyond yourself (6)	Relax and go with the flow (9)
4: I'm flawed, something Is missing	4: **Personalizing** *(to express who I am)*	How I am ordinary & universal – aligned to goodness	Align to your internal knowing of what is universally right & good (1)	Love yourself just the way you are (2)
5: I am rejected	5 **Minimizing** *(to restrict my needs and desires)*	Taking up space/ going after what I want	Embrace your real desires (8)	Participate in life (7)
6: I have no support	6 **Securing** *(to have support)*	Being okay	Relax and be okay (9)	Step into your full potential (3)
7: I have been deprived	7 **Optimizing** *(to have good times, grand vistas)*	Being without resources	Savor what you do have (5)	Accept and be grateful for life as it is (1)
8: I am bad and sinful	8 **Exerting** *(to be strong and prove self)*	Being sweet and loving	Be kind and Empathetic (2)	Pull back and be detached (5)
9: I am unseen	9 **Settling** *(to be okay and at ease)*	Striving to be seen	Embrace your full potential (3)	Be awake and engaged (6)

The underlying patterns of the types are the key to understanding not only why people do what they do, but also why they don't do what they know they should do. We rarely venture out of our comfort zones to do things that may be good for us, but are not familiar to our personalities.

This 3x3 matrix captures the fundamental distinctions of the 9 money types. The rows describe our motivations, while the columns describe our behavior. Each of the nine types has a gift vis a vis money, but also has weaknesses. We must do a balancing act to harness our strengths while not being hindered by our weaknesses. By understanding the perspectives and orientations of each of these nine basic money styles, we can better appreciate and integrate the wisdom of each type.

NINE MONEY TYPES	ASSERTIVE Put forth maximal effort for sake of money	DUTIFUL Put forth limited effort for sake of money	WITHDRAWN Put forth minimal effort for sake of money
IDEALISTIC	7 *Optimizing*	1 *Ordering*	4 *Personalizing*
WILLFUL	8 *Exerting*	2 *Giving*	5 *Minimizing*
HOPEFUL	3 *Striving*	6 *Securing*	9 *Settling*

First, let's examine the three rows of the 3x3 matrix. For Types 1,4,7 in the first row of the matrix, their money motivations are most connected to what is meaningful and matters for them, and less about what they feel they need or how money validates them. 1s are motivated to be orderly with money because this helps them to be better aligned to their internal sense of what is right and good, which is the thing that is most meaningful to them. 4s are motivated to be expressive with money because this helps them to better align to their internal sense of who they are and their uniqueness, which is the thing that is most meaningful to them. 7s are motivated to envision the possibilities around money because this helps them to feel less boxed in and more free, which is the thing that is most meaningful to them. Types 1,4,7 can get stuck in their superficial beliefs about what money means and forget to articulate what really matters for them in their belly, heart, and head centers, respectively. For example, 1s can get stuck in their superficial beliefs about money as good or evil, 4s can stuck in their superficial beliefs about money as mundane and ordinary, and 7s can get stuck in their superficial beliefs about what money can buy. When this happens, they can be overly repelled by or hungry for money, which creates imbalance. When 1s are repelled by the evilness of money, they cannot have a relationship to money that enables them to align with what is right and good, because they are taking an extreme stance that is out of balance vis a vis money. When 4s believe that money requires them to be ordinary, they are unable to have a relationship to money that enables them to feel and express their uniqueness, because they get attached to a victim mentality. When 7s believe that money can buy happiness, they cannot have a relationship to money that enables them to perceive spaciousness and joy because the joy gets overly tied up with the stuff money can buy rather than the experience itself. For this reason, Types 1,4,7 are **idealistic types** that tend to get frustrated by their superficial beliefs and attributions of money. What 1s in fact want is to have a relationship to money that enables them to align with what is right and good, but their superficial beliefs about money prevent them from doing so. What 4s in fact want is to have a relationship to money that enables them to feel and express their unique identity, but their superficial beliefs about money get in the way. What 7s in fact want is to have a relationship to money that enables them to perceive spaciousness and joy, but their superficial beliefs about the power of money to satisfy and fulfill get in the way of the experience itself.

For Types 2,5,8 in the second row of the matrix above, their money motivations are most connected to what they feel they need and desire in terms of resources, and less so about what is meaningful about money or how money validates them. 2s are motivated to be generous with money because this helps them to be connected to others and get love back from others, which is the thing that they feel they most need. 5s are motivated to minimize their need for money because this helps them to be detached, objective, and less vulnerable, which is the thing that they feel they most need. 8s are motivated to exert themselves for the sake of money because this helps them to feel strong and powerful, which is the thing that they feel they most need. Types 2,5,8 try to feed their needs indirectly rather than listening deeply to what they really need in their heart, mind, and belly centers, respectively, and addressing their needs directly. For example, 2s try to give their energy and money in order to get love in return. 5s try to withhold their energy and money in order to be detached, safe, and invulnerable. 8s try to exert their energy and money in order to be strong and get love. When they try to get their needs met indirectly rather than directly, though, they are left feeling rejected and bereft, rather than embraced and loved, which leaves them feeling ashamed, cynical, and angry. When 2s are overly giving with their money, they cannot have a relationship to money that enables them to feel included and attuned to, because they over-focus on others and leave themselves out of the equation. When 5s are overly minimizing about money and deny their need for money, they cannot have a relationship to money that enables them to feel a part of life, because they over-focus on their subsistence needs and leave their joy and other human needs out of the equation. When 8s are overly exerting about money, they cannot have a relationship to money that enables them to feel strong and powerful, because they over-focus on being defended and invulnerable and leave their receptivity, vulnerability, and innocence out of the equation. For this reason, Types 2,5,8 are **willful types** that believe they can assert their will to get what they want, but tend to feel rejected by the world. What 2s in fact want is to have a relationship to money that enables them attune to others and be attuned to by the universe, but their indirect *Giving* strategy prevents them from experiencing this. What 5s in fact want is to have a relationship to money that enables them to understand and know the universe directly, but their detached, minimizing, cynical orientation towards money can get in the way. What 8s in fact want is to have a relationship to money that enables them to feel vital and alive, but their over exertion for the sake of money can get in the way.

For Types 3,6,9 in the bottom row of the matrix, money is interesting to the extent that money gives value to, secures, and harmonizes their existence. 3s are motivated to strive vis a vis money because this helps them to achieve, and be acknowledged and rewarded, which is the thing that best validates their existence. 6s are motivated to gain security with money because this helps them to feel loyal and oriented to home base, which is the thing that they feel best validates their existence. 9s, in contrast, are motivated to settle with money, not get overly activated about money one way or another, because this helps them to feel at peace, which is the thing that they feel best validates their existence. Types 3,6,9 try to bring fruition to their hopes of being heros, but try to do so without honoring what their hearts, minds, and belly centers, respectively, crave. For example, 3s try to be successes to be worthy and heroic. 6s try to be prepared for worst-case scenarios to be responsible and awake. 9s try to be relaxed and okay to be whole and connected. When they try to bring fruition to their hopes and dreams without honoring what they really crave, though, they are left feeling unworthy, disoriented, disengaged. When 3s are overly striving about money, they cannot have a relationship to money that enables them to feel validated and worthy, because they assume that they must prove their worth. When 6s are overly anxious about security, they cannot have a relationship to money that enables them to feel secure and safe, because they assume there is danger lurking everywhere. When 9s are overly settled and zoned out about money, they cannot have a relationship to money that enables them to connected and whole, because they assume money is a disturbance. For this reason, Types 3,6,9 are **hopeful types** that tend to feel attached to money and what money can give them in terms of validation, security, and peace. What 3s in fact want is to have a relationship to money that enables them to feel worthy for who they are, but their over striving blocks this sense of value. What 6s in fact want is to have a relationship to money that enables them relax, trust, and step forward with courage, but their *Securing* strategy with money prevents them from experiencing this courage. What 9s in fact want is to have a relationship to money that enables them to be here, at one and in the flow with the universe, but their settling, non-disturbed, stubborn orientation towards money can block their sense of oneness and flow.

Now let's examine the three different columns of the 3x3 matrix. Types 3,7,8 in the first column are highly action oriented and willing to put forth **maximal effort** for the sake of money, believing that money is important, necessary, and validating. These assertive types are strong, bold, and do what is necessary to get the job done. They are more strategically planful about money than tactically or conceptually planful. They are more interested in looking at the big picture and figuring out how to get what they want in the most effective and straightforward manner. Where they suffer is in not being able to turn off the go-go machine to relax, recharge, and integrate. Types 3,7,8 have the greatest tendency to suffer from burnout and exhaustion. They are connected strongly to their belly and head centers, but lack solid connection to their heart center. They fear relaxing and becoming complacent, which would make them less effective. Because they have difficulty accessing their heart center, they lack the guidance that their emotions can give them about how to behave, communicate, and relate. They have difficulty sensing the real love and sweetness that already exist here for us. They could use the wisdom of the withdrawn group's natural gift of pulling back so that they can create space to open up and feel their hearts.

Types 1,2,6 in the second column are only willing to put forth **limited effort** for the sake of money, concerned respectively about the potentially corrupting, disconnecting, and destabilizing potential of money. These dutiful types are gifted at avoiding extremes. They are naturally skeptical about getting pulled too deeply in by the allure of money, but they are equally skeptical about forswearing money and resources, which they need for grounding, nourishment, and security. They desire to be in the natural balance of giving and getting: giving order, love, and allegiance, and getting back order, love and support. They appreciate the give-and-take logic of life better than any of the other types. They understand that neither extreme works. Too much assertion and self-interest leads to separation and disconnection. But so does too much withdrawal and detachment. The only solution is to be a part of the give-and-take of life. They tend to be more tactically planful around money than strategically or conceptually planful. They focus on implementing specific shorter-term action plans, arranging logistics, and managing tasks. Where they suffer is in not being able to put forth the requisite effort that would enable them to envision big possibilities, engage effectively, and shine. Types 1,2,6 have the greatest tendency to hold themselves back just when they are on the brink of success, joy, and power. They tend to hold themselves back because they are connected strongly to their belly and heart centers, but lack solid connection to their head center. They have greater difficulty accessing the clarity of their head center and the sense of trust, confidence, and perspective that comes from this clarity. They could use the wisdom of the assertive group's natural gift of stepping forth boldly.

Types 4,5,9 in the third column of the matrix are reluctant and only willing to put forth **minimal effort** for the sake of money, believing that money is neither meaningful, necessary or validating. These withdrawn types are gifted at looking inward for guidance and wisdom. This group is the most unwilling to get pulled into society's notions of what is meaningful or desirable, believing that they can only find this wisdom within themselves. They are more conceptually planful about money than tactically or strategically planful. They are more interested in thinking creatively and holding spacious intentions about the future, riding the wave of life to take them where it might. They are less inclined to use their energy to push life in some particular direction. Where they suffer is in not being able to balance their withdrawn energy with their engagement and action energy. Types 4,5,9 have the greatest difficulty in moving into action, following through on plans, and accomplishing goals. They tend to be withdrawn because they are connected strongly to their heart and head centers, but lack solid connection to their belly center. Because they have difficulty accessing the natural energy of their belly center, they lack the guidance about how to sense their bodies, engage and step forth into action. They have difficulty being grounded, noticing the tensions in their bodies, and physically adjusting and self-regulating in an intelligent and relaxed way. They could use the wisdom of the dutiful group's natural gift of balancing extremes so that they can learn to sense, engage, and flow with their bodies.

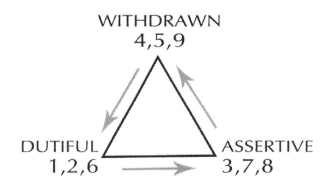

We're all on a journey to discover Love, what it means to be fully human, who and what we really are. Because we were born weak and vulnerable, we develop strategies for getting our needs met. The withdrawn types are most curious about Who am I? The dutiful types are most curious about How am I to be? And the assertive types are most curious about What am I to do? The problem with our personalities is that we are only able to perceive a portion of reality that supports our physical survival. So the personality asks and resolves questions from a limited vantage point. The personality understands these three fundamental questions Who am I? How am I to be? What am I to do? to be self-referential questions. The personality assumes that its agenda is limited to knowing itself as a solid, separate, being. We must work through several layers of our ego structure in order to access the abundance and love that is always here, but we are habitually blind to.

You will see in the following chapters how the overall framework of this book comes together. In order to understand our personal relationships to money, we must understand not only that there are nine different aspects of money (the Nine Money Domains), but that our nine personality types and instincts come together to impact how we interact with the Nine Domains of Money. For each personality type, we will explore how our type interacts with our Self-Preservation, Social, and Sexual instincts in each of the Nine Money Domains to generate vicious cycles that keep us blocked from prosperity and love. It is only by recognizing that we are blocked by fear, and working to unblock those fears, that we can move forward towards completely fulfilling lives.

MONEY: FROM FEAR TO LOVE FRAMEWORK

Nine Money Domains

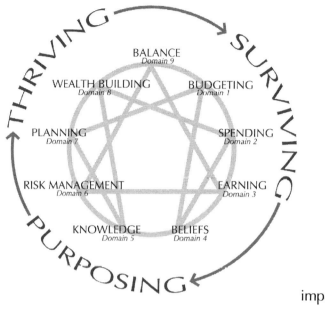

impacted by our...

Three Human Instincts

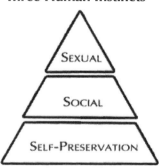

+ Nine Money Strategies

TYPES	ASSERTIVE	DUTIFUL	WITHDRAWN
IDEALISTIC	*7* *Optimizing*	*1* *Ordering*	*4* *Personalizing*
WILLFUL	*8* *Exerting*	*2* *Giving*	*5* *Minimizing*
HOPEFUL	*3* *Striving*	*6* *Securing*	*9* *Settling*

TYPES AND INSTINCTS

SP	SO	SX
DISCIPLINED 1: *Ordering* in SP * I make up for my corruptness by being self-disciplined/ordered in SP	**PRINCIPLED** 1: *Ordering* in SO I make up for my corruptness by being correct and ordered in SO	**CORRECTIVE** 1: *Ordering* in SX † I make up for my corruptness by being correct and ordered in SX
CARETAKING 2: *Giving* in SP † I compensate for my neediness by being attuned to others' SP needs	**CONNECTING** 2: *Giving* in SO * I compensate for my neediness by being attuned to others' SO needs	**CAPTIVATING** 2: *Giving* in SX I compensate for my neediness by being attuned to others' SX needs
ACHIEVING 3: *Striving* in SP * It's up to me to be a hero in the SP arena	**HEROIC** 3: *Striving* in SO It's up to me to be a hero in the SO arena	**DAZZLING** 3: *Striving* in SX † It's up to me to be a hero in the SX arena
AESTHETE 4: *Personalizing* in SP My way of doing SP is unique	**OUTSIDER** 4: *Personalizing* in SO † My way of fitting in is unique	**DRAMATIST** 4: *Personalizing* in SX * My way of intimacy is unique
ASCETIC 5: *Minimizing* in SP * I minimize my SP needs and hold on to what I have	**EXPERT** 5: *Minimizing* in SO I minimize my SO needs and hold on to what I have	**LOW ROLLER** 5: *Minimizing* in SX † I minimize my SX needs and hold on to what I have
GUARD 6: *Securing* in SP When I do find SP support, I've got to make sure about it	**ALLY** 6: *Securing* in SO † When I do find SO support, I've got to make sure about it	**PARTNER** 6: *Securing* in SX * When I do find SX support, I've got to make sure about it
OPTIONEE 7: *Optimizing* in SP † I can't be deprived in SP, so I am going to make it better	**PLAYBOY** 7: *Optimizing* in SO * I can't be deprived in SO, so I am going to make it better	**JUGGLER** 7: *Optimizing* in SX I can't be deprived in SX, so I am going to make it better
HEAVYWEIGHT 8: *Exerting* in SP I've got to be strong and exert myself to make sure my SP needs are met	**BIG BOSS** 8: *Exerting* in SO † I've got to be strong and exert myself to make sure my SO needs are met	**HIGH ROLLER** 8: *Exerting* in SX * I've got to be strong and exert myself to make sure my SX needs are met
STEADY 9: *Settling* in SP † I'm going to be okay with what I have in SP	**UNSUNG HERO** 9: *Settling* in SO * I'm going to be okay with what I have in SO	**GROOVING** 9: *Settling* in SX I'm going to be okay with what I have in SX

denotes double whammies, where the Type energy reinforces the dominant instinct energy

†*denotes countertypes, where the Type energy moves against the dominant instinct energy*

CHAPTER 7

ORDERING

Type 1

1. GIFT

My internal compass comes from my core intelligence aligning me to my intuitive sense of what is right and good. I know from deep inside that it is right and good to have order and structure. Order and structure enable me to be balanced and self-regulating. My core intelligence is that I am utterly meant to be here as a dignified and fully articulated being. I respect myself and I want others to respect themselves because I know that life begins with self-respect. Self-respect motivates me to stand tall, value my existence, and do the right thing. Because I have a strong sense of what is right, I can be very decisive. I prioritize what's important and organize myself accordingly. The solidity of my core enables me to persevere, do the right thing, and stay the course. I don't need others to tell me what to do. I govern myself.

2. STRATEGY

My life and money strategies grows out of my sense of the critical importance of order. At the unconscious level, I register the world as corrupt and wild, though I repress this feeling at the conscious level. At the conscious level, my belief is simply that I must do what's right. *Ordering* is about putting things in their right place and fixing what's wrong so that I can be beyond reproach. Others think that I am a perfectionist. That's what they see on the surface – my attention to detail and my desire to do things properly. What they miss is my desire to live from a place of integrity. For me, *Ordering* is about aligning with my integrity and making the world a better place. It is about focusing on what is here right in front of me and trying to fix the things that are wrong. This is my gift and my service to the world, but it can block my experience of spaciousness and joy.

Ordering is a defense against chaos and is opposite of *Optimizing*. I am not interested in making things the best that they could be. I am more interested in having things function orderly and simply. *Ordering* is not about trying to have more or less. It is about having the right amount. My appetite for money and the best that life has to offer is therefore constrained. I am always in the process of checking in with my inner core and discerning what is appropriate, balanced, and correct. I don't mind the trouble it takes to attend to details. For me, it's not about getting somewhere faster, with more stuff. It's about living in alignment to my core intelligence, and governing myself in a way that is self-respecting.

I do not trust that there is an inherent intelligence that prevents the universe from spiraling out of control. In looking to create order out of the intrinsic chaos all around us, I apply my definitions to both tangible and intangible things, be they people, places, things, or be they ideas, principles, laws. Whether these structures are tangible or intangible, bringing order to them provides me with a sense of goodness that I would feel uncivilized without. I deeply fear a life that is chaotic, wild, and corrupt. Making things better, not just locally, but globally as well, requires looking ahead. The difficulty, however, is that the territory ahead is unknown and therefore messier, wilder, and more chaotic. I am not so comfortable with this space. I prefer staying closer to what needs fixing right here. My values feel objective, universal, fundamental, and fixed. Not only do I not venture ahead, but I also never think to explore the idea of being in alignment with my authentic self. Connecting to my authentic self and discovering what is personally meaningful is difficult for me because it would push me into a place that is unbounded, unfamiliar, and potentially flawed. But if I do not connect to what matters personally, life is somewhat dry and dull. But I just don't know if

I am ready to bear the cost of moving beyond *Ordering* into the messy unknown.

3. THE VICIOUS CYCLE

If I were to look at my life objectively, I would notice that I have essentially been trapped in a vicious cycle of fear and scarcity. Because of this, my relationship to love and prosperity is constrained. *Ordering* is fundamentally about putting back in order that which is out of order, that which is wrong and needs fixing. In focusing on this, I reinforce the idea that things are not right. This orientation makes me uptight, frustrated, and resentful. But my ego enthusiastically keeps this vicious cycle going. I get addicted to *Ordering*. Even though I think I am moving along, I am merely moving in place.

When we are caught in a vicious cycle where our actions validate our beliefs, it can be very difficult to extricate ourselves. When we are stuck at a certain point along the scarcity-to-abundance spectrum, it is impossible to improve our position until we get out of the vicious cycle. If we are suddenly showered with new wealth, we will most likely dissipate it so that we can get back to our old set point. So in order to create new wealth, we must first become aware of the vicious cycle we are caught in. Once we become aware, we will be in a better position to consciously unblock what blocks us, and welcome new wealth into our lives.

My underlying assumption is that life is wild and chaotic, both on the inside and on the outside, and I must hold the line to prevent this wild chaos from getting the best of me. The potential chaos can be found both outside in the world, and also inside myself in the form of inchoate emotions, feelings, and animal instincts. Order exists in the realm of form, structure, facts, reality. Order exists in the realm of black and white, right and wrong. I do not want to admit that there may be several right ways to think or do things, or that things might have different meanings or interpretations depending on the context. I prefer black-and-white thinking so that things are clear one way or the other. I believe in the power of order to keep the wild, chaotic mess of life at bay.

Chaos exists in the realm of imagination, feelings, dreams, and the future, so I stay away from abstract and potentially chaotic thoughts. I tend to take things at face value rather than interpret or imagine alternative possibilities. To me, imagination and big dreams are fantasies that have nothing to do with what I am supposed to be doing to make things better. I focus my attention on things that I can control. I am grounded in everyday physical reality. I am logical and concrete, not dreamy. I find it a challenge to go beyond what is literally true in the here and now. For example, if in my mind, debt is bad, then I should pay it off as soon as possible. Having a mortgage could benefit me financially, but what is literally true feels more compelling than what might be theoretically true. I am compelled to pay off the debt because that is something concrete I can do to make a bad situation good. Stocks, in contrast, feel almost symbolic. It is much easier to relate to cold hard cash in a safe under my bed or to a house that I own than to stocks whose prices are based on a vision of what is possible and guesses about the future.

The world is intrinsically chaotic and uncivilized. The way I can be of value is by improving things and doing things properly. Whatever I pay attention to, I have to control and do well. But since I can only pay attention to and control so many things in my life, I focus on certain areas and disregard others. If I can't do something well, I would prefer to not do it at all. What I do focus on though, I need to do properly. For the things that I do pay attention to, I am organized and careful.   I like to do one job at a time, properly. I am details-oriented. I am not so much a big picture planner. Possibilities, theories, abstract thinking don't interest me as much as what can be done in the here and now. I can get tunnel vision about doing things properly.

I don't want to leave things to chance and I don't trust others to do it better than I can. It puts a lot on my shoulders. I often feel like a martyr, doing things that are not appreciated, but doing them anyway, for the good of everyone. I can be exacting, for myself and others, and I often feel resentful that I have to do everything myself. At the same time, if I left it to others, things wouldn't get done right, and I'd have to do it anyways. I cannot give up on the world, even when I am tired and feel that the world is hopelessly incorrigible.

I feel that I am better than others and superior to them because I know what is right and wrong and they don't. I resent that it's up to me to do things right, but who else will? If I don't keep trying to fix things, everything will fall apart. I feel frustrated by the huge job in front of me that never seems to end. I want to relax and have fun, but it is difficult. I feel like a man in a straitjacket trying to contain my impulses and messy emotions. I obsessively focus on what is wrong rather than right. My resentment fuels my ego engine.

I judge myself harshly, and I judge others harshly. My superiority disconnects me from others and cuts me off from myself, because I can never be as good as I think I should be. If I were to embrace the world as intelligently ordered, I would have to give up my beliefs about the chaos, corruption, and messiness. I can't do this because it would unravel my personality, and then who would I be? The dynamic of the ego structure keeps my ego employed and keeps me perpetually fixated on right and wrong. I can never find serenity for then I would have no excuse for *Ordering*. We are each caught in a vicious cycle of our personality and instincts until we decide to break free. This takes deliberate energy and momentum because the cycle is a compelling vortex. In order to create new wealth, we must see clearly the vicious cycle that blocks us from abundance. Then we must fight our way out of the vortex.

4. OPERATIONALLY

If my instincts are balanced, I will be able to attend to money in each of the Nine Money Domains in a healthy manner. If, however, my instincts are not in balance, then I will get stuck in my type fixation and I cannot be optimally effective. My motivation to be good and perfect manifests in different ways depending on my dominant instinct. Instead of addressing areas I don't do well, I will tend to focus on the things I can control and do correctly. As a SP 1, my *Ordering* energy reinforces my Self-Preservation energy, and I focus on being orderly about my physical life, my eating, my environment, and often my money, so that I can be secure. In contrast, as a SO 1, my *Ordering* energy combines with my Social instinct to focus me on making things right in the social arena. Personal money matters may not be a large focus of my attention. And as a SX 1, my *Ordering* energy combines with my Sexual instinct to focus me on being at my correct best to meet whatever opportunities come my way. How my instincts are imbalanced will therefore impact how I relate to the Nine Money Domains – where I put my attention and energy and where I don't.

"DISCIPLINED" SP 1	"PRINCIPLED" SO 1	"CORRECTIVE" SX 1

Domain 1 – Budgeting

When I am operating in a healthy way, my self-respect motivates me to take care of myself, be self-disciplined and hold myself accountable. I manage my affairs so that things operate properly without lack or excess. *Ordering* is about being aligned to my innate sense of what is right and good, and not being tempted by excess. When I am operating at an average to less healthy level, I only hold myself accountable in certain areas. But in those areas, I expect high performance, even perfection. Other areas I let fall by the wayside.

As a "Disciplined" SP 1, the value of being within budget is to have greater security. It is important for me to do my bookkeeping correctly, file my financial papers correctly, and pay my bills on time. Whether I have an explicit budget or not, I am aware of my financial constraints, and work to stay within my means. I understand innately the freedom that exists within constraints. I almost never pay my bills late or make mistakes that cause me to pay penalty fees. With my accounts in order, I have time for work, family, and myself. I can relax. It feels right to me when the inflow and outflow of energy I expend is in balance, and when the inflow and outflow of money in my life is in balance. I mostly live within my means and may even have savings left over. I may resist formal budgeting, and operate based on my internal sense of limits because budgeting can create more stress. The feeling that things *have* to be done a certain way can be an extreme burden and undercut my sense of balance and well-being.

> Whatever I think I can control, I will pay attention to, but whatever I can't, I just don't care. It's a protective mechanism, because I can get fanatical about things. If I can't do it well, I don't want to do it. I want to be able to maintain balance and I know I can't attend to everything. So there are areas I let go of completely.

> Paying the bills on time is really important to me. I like to keep the chaos at bay. I don't want to bounce checks, be in arrears, etc. These things frighten me, they send me into a kind of horror. Having a bill collector coming after me is my idea of hell. Shame, horror and mortification of doing it wrong keeps me motivated. I want to be beyond reproach.

As a "Principled" SO 1, the purpose of being ordered and within budget is to be a better social model and have integrity. My black-and-white thinking and lack of consistent attention, however, can create problems for me in this Domain. My black-and-white thinking leads me to believe that focusing on money for myself is not right – that it is selfish, greedy and wrong to pay attention to my personal finances instead of larger social problems. I might live hand to mouth, miss paying bills on time, and be somewhat unorganized. On the other hand, if I want to go on a vacation or make something happen for the larger social good, I can be very meticulous about planning and staying within a budget.

As a "Corrective" SX 1, the value of being ordered and within budget is to create a solid foundation from which to meet whatever comes up from the best position that I can. However, my Sexual instinct is lustful, expansive, and wants to roam free. I want to be spontaneous and do what I have passion for. It can lead me to actively resist this Domain. Checks may get bounced, bills may not be paid on time, there may be little or no savings, and possibly high credit card balances. I would rather pay attention to what I can control and be perfect at, and ignore the things that I cannot control. I can be extreme in denying my accountability about budgeting which can lead to more mess and less order in my life. Even though I like order, I may have trouble overriding my instinct to be spontaneous and expansive. This can create a vicious cycle where I continue to live hand to mouth and do not plan ahead.

Domain 2 – Spending

I want to do the right thing with my money. I don't want to spend incorrectly or frivolously, but sometimes I can be impulsive and splurge. As a "Disciplined" SP 1, I spend on things that reflect my Self-Preservation values and provide me with comfort, security, and well-being: vitamins, eating well, exercise, conveniences for the home. Experiences and fancy clothing tend to be lower priority than health and well-being. I don't want to be excessive or wild with money. I feel I need to control my money and time, because once it's gone, it's gone. I try to be practical, properly generous, and appropriately frugal. I don't want to be ostentatious about money. I try to plan ahead and be efficient. I may let myself splurge in a controlled way, I try not to let my gluttony drive me to be irresponsible. Sometimes, I feel like I have to personally make up for all the excessive consumerism and waste in the world by being frugal myself.

If something feels irresponsible, I get "freaked out." If something feels frivolous, I won't do it. I operate within parameters. That is my discipline. I make a rule that's kind of arbitrary to keep myself disciplined.

As a "Principled" SO 1, my spending tends to be directed more towards the group or family. I want to create space for social gatherings and celebration. I want to be generous to my family and to charities that could really benefit from the money. I believe that those who have a lot of money should contribute back to the society that supported them in making that money. People should not hoard money. The power is in the spending. My image of being generous and good is important to me. I can easily spend money and not save much. If I get a late fee, I will feel shame. But I can be stymied from asking for help around money because I feel so much self-criticism for not being competent about it.

As a "Corrective" SX 1, my spending tends to follow the charge. I spend to attract interest from others, make things happen, and fuel my passion. I love to spend on beautiful clothes, books, music, fancy foods and wines, and things that really speak to me. I appreciate visual art. I love new experiences. I consider these expenditures discretionary. In contrast, I consider my physical health and well-being a necessity and will continue to spend on things such as gym membership, vitamins, exercise equipment, and personal development even when money is tighter. My spending tends to be more impulsive than controlled as I take opportunities that come my way. I am more relational than calculating about money. If something feels right in the moment, I want to do it, especially when it is with someone else. My splurges tend to be less contained or controlled. If I have a budget, I may exceed my budget in one month and then try to make up for it in other months.

Domain 3 – Earning

I am a responsible and hard worker, but I will not compromise myself for the sake of money. I sense that money can lead me astray. If I make what I need, that's good enough for me. I may have opportunities to make more money but turn them down because I don't want to sell myself out. I try to adhere to my values, beliefs, and guiding principles. Because I do not want to make any mistakes, it can be difficult to be creative. I tend to get stuck in my stories about money being bad, or that there are only certain right ways to make money.

> I always make sure that I don't have too much money. If I have too much, I just slow down and make less. Guilt about having more than my fair share enters into the picture, and so when I think I have enough, my interest in money drops off, because too much of a good thing does not seem good. I've internalized a lot of guilt about money and the unfairness of it all.

As a worker, I am self-disciplined and organized. I believe there is a right and wrong way to do things, am good at accomplishing concrete tasks, following rules, and organizing around procedures. I am not comfortable in an environment where rules are not clearly spelled out. I am not good at imagining possibilities, and can get in trouble for being too rigid, overly concerned about rules, and missing the bigger picture.

As a "Disciplined" SP 1, I believe I must work hard for what I earn. I prefer work that does not consume my life, but allows me to do something I am competent at so I can get paid a decent wage and have balance in my personal life. If I am an entrepreneur, I try to create organized structures for income generation and time management. I am more interested in doing the job in front of me well than I am in planning ahead, which seems like dreaming. I'm not a dreamer. There is something disturbing to me about extreme appetite and extreme ambition. I can be hindered earnings-wise by my beliefs about how much is enough. Extremes lead us down the road to excess and no good. We should live in balance individually and as a society. The tradeoffs between time and money are clear to me.

As a "Principled" SO 1, I believe that my work should help people in the physical, personal development, or spiritual realm. I am comfortable earning to meet my needs, but I don't necessarily want to stockpile money. My general confidence that I could make more if needed keeps me from wanting to make more now. I do believe that I must work to earn money. The idea that I could earn money passively is a foreign, abstract concept for me.

As a "Corrective" SX 1, when I am in my element, in the flow, in my passion, it feels like nothing can get in my way, and anything is possible. However, when I am stuck, I can be stuck for what seems like forever. When I am stuck in a place of scarcity thinking, I feel that money is not for me, and I just need to get by. This cuts off my flow of energy and puts me into a funk where I cannot work at my best. It can be difficult for me to appreciate that it is possible to be both passionate about my work and well paid.

Domain 4 – Beliefs

With certain things, I have a strong personal conviction and trust my inner knowing. Part of me rejects my appetite for money as something almost debased. On the other hand, I do need money, to be autonomous. My appetite for money is constrained by my strong aversion to greed and excess. I can be quite judgmental about money. I can easily harbor beliefs about money being the root of evil, money being vulgar, money disconnecting us from what is important. Because of these beliefs, I tend to feel it is best not to focus on money so I won't risk being corrupted by it.

As a "Disciplined" SP 1, I believe that money gives me the means to have a stable, secure life. A certain amount of money is okay, but too much is greedy. I have a pragmatic, materialistic, black-and-white orientation to money. It's not about expressing my personal uniqueness. It's not about chasing my dreams. It's simply about having enough right now, and being in balance. I feel I must constrain my appetite.

As a "Principled" SO 1, I believe that money is a tool that enables me to do good socially and contribute to the world. My Social instinct wants to be of value to the group. My type energy wants to fix what's wrong. Money can be a very charged topic for me. I can easily believe that money is evil and resent others who seem to be corrupted by money, spend it too freely. If I believe that money is evil, I will also believe that I must restrict my own personal needs so that I will not be corrupted by the need for money. I can easily believe that money creates power imbalance. I do not want to wield power over others, but I do not want to be subject to the power of others either. I believe that money should be used to serve people and used fairly. Money should be well-managed and put to good use. These can be rather severe black-and-white perspectives that limit my own experience of abundance. I can have difficulty seeing the intelligence and good in the world.

As a "Corrective" SX 1, I believe that money is a tool that enables me to experience the world, even though money is not an absolute requisite. It feels more important to be connected to my passion doing something meaningful than to compromise my integrity doing something I don't care about. What's most important to me is that I am living my life correctly. When I get stressed out, I feel like an outsider and victim reacting to what happens instead of being proactive. Since there's no money, there's nothing I can do. I can be resentful that the world doesn't pay me more for my important work, and I can feel under-appreciated. I am comfortable thinking that I am doing what is right, while others are selling their souls. I may not get paid properly, but what can I do about it? Secretly, it makes me feel superior. The truth is, I'd rather not fail than risk being less than perfect.

Domain 5 – Understanding

I am literal, fact-based, logical, and detail-oriented. I do not relate to money in an abstract, theoretical way. I do not think about dreams and possibilities. Money is an object to be contained and ordered like all objects, thoughts, and people are to be contained and ordered. I can feel like money is foreign to me and that I am in the dark about the more sophisticated aspects of money. I don't want to be crafty, calculating, or shrewd about money.

As a "Disciplined" SP 1, I desire security and stability and am motivated to save for the longer term. I want to be wise and not wasteful. I keep records and stay organized. I like to feel in control of my environment. I will not necessarily use the records to help me make decisions, but I want to understand my money in a concrete, factual way. Did the money go up or down? What were my big budget items? I will not consider questions like: How could I make more money? How could I use leverage and other possible financial strategies to grow my net worth? I would rather get a mortgage from a local bank that I am familiar with, even if it has a slightly higher rate, than a lower cost loan from a mortgage broker. I am more motivated to do things cleanly than to get the best possible deal, especially if it is messier and more complex.

As a "Principled" SO 1, I am less interested in learning about how money works and how to grow money than I am in using money immediately to address current social needs in the world. I want to teach people how to provide for themselves and be responsible. I can be turned off by stocks that feel like rolling dices. I think money should come from hard work and sweat, not from gambling and doing things the "easy" way. If you can pay your bills, and invest, that's okay. Raising capital to build a new company is okay. But I want things to be on the up and up. Often I prefer to delegate money management to a financial advisor so I don't have to understand too much about money that is potentially "dirty."

> I personally felt money could be used for evil if not used for good, so I had to educate myself about it. I saw how others did good with money and they

inspired me to learn about it. It was huge when I could move from a view of money as evil to a view of money as good.

As a "Corrective" SX 1, I can be happy to use money without understanding much about how it works, as long as I am able to meet my needs and follow my passion. I might be interested enough to read my statements, make educated decisions, choose an expert, but I have a limit to how much I want to know. If Self-Preservation is my blindspot, I have difficulty understanding how money fits into the context of my life. I do not make the connection between money and well-being. Like a child, I do not really want to learn how things work, for fear that if I learn, I will become overly burdened with details. I therefore resist tracking, record-keeping, monitoring, and analyzing the financial facts of my life. It almost feels painful to do because I am so afraid of discovering a truth that may require me to pull back from my current way of living. Therefore, my awareness and understanding of the actual facts of my financial situation can be very low.

Domain 6 – Risk Management

I don't want to be reliant on others if something goes wrong. As a "Disciplined" SP 1, I try to manage money and risk in a way that prevents disruptions. I try to have some emergency savings to serve as a cushion and buffer in case something goes awry. I want to have life insurance for the primary breadwinner, auto insurance, and health care. In contrast, if I am inattentive about Self-Preservation matters, I will not worry as much about disruptions to my life or try to manage my life and my money to avoid downside risks. I will not purposely court problems and risks, but I will not actively try to avoid them either. I will not think so much about having emergency savings. I prefer to live my life and spend when I want to spend. As a "Principled" SO 1, my social network can often be more of a safety net for me than money is. As a "Corrective" SX 1, the most important thing for me in getting through an unexpected financial crisis is my health and intimate relationship with my lover or spouse. Without my juice and mojo, I have difficulty being effective, whether there has been an emergency or not.

Domain 7 – Planning

I can create goals but my attention tends to be more focused on the here and now. I scan my environment for what needs to be improved and if it is clear what should be done, I can be very proactive. But I lack the vision and appetite for more. I have a sense of agency that I can make things happen if I want to, but I lack a desire to optimize. Being successful or too goal oriented about money feels a bit dirty, even sleazy.

I am also aware that there are only so many things I can control. The things that I believe I cannot control move out of my responsibility zone and I can ignore them without too much guilt. If something is in my zone of "responsibility," I must deal with it responsibly. For example, for debt that I believe is "bad," I am disciplined about getting rid of it.

> I don't trust debt, don't feel safe with it, and want freedom not to have to pay it.

I don't get too excited about future possibilities and I am not oriented towards getting more for less, a greater bang for the buck. Rather, I want to do what is proper right now. Planning ahead requires imagination, wanting what I don't have, and trying to figure out how to get those things. This is hard for me because it goes against my literal, black-and-white way of thinking and my sense of what is right. I do not want to make my life revolve around money goals. Other things like my family, time, and values are higher priorities. The stakes I put in the ground have more to do with things that I can control like my diet, health, and behavior. If I am planful, it may be more about creating an orderly calendar and bounded pockets of time where I can relax, be spontaneous, and recharge.

Domain 8 – Wealth Building

Investing can be difficult for me because it challenges my beliefs about being able to control things and not being greedy. I may avoid investments altogether and stick with cash in my bank account. If I do invest in stocks, I choose funds that are more conservative and pay dividends that I understand. I am willing to take risks, but I would like to understand the risks and try to make sure things are not too wild. I try to do my due diligence, understand my options, and get the right advice. I don't want to invest in companies that are unethical.

I want to make the right decision. But I know that no one really knows which stocks are going to go up, and that is difficult for me. There is an inherent lack of control that bothers me. Investing in bonds or CDs or real estate can be a bit easier because it is more concrete and straightforward. It seems rather abstract. I can't get too excited when stocks go up. But when stocks go down, I feel disappointed in myself because I didn't make the right decisions. So it can be difficult for me to be happy about my investment choices either way.

As a "Disciplined" SP 1, I don't have a problem prioritizing retirement savings, debt reduction, and mortgage payments, over spending. A priority is a priority. My priority is to be self-reliant and take care of things that need to be taken care of. It is more important to me to be self-sufficient than it is to be wealthy. As a "Principled" SO 1, I have a quality of not giving up on making the world a better place but I hold myself back because it feels a bit corrupt to be "too big." If I believe that money is evil and bad, then I may not have any savings. I am intrigued by power and what it could achieve, but too much power or wealth repels me. I think everyone should contribute in some way, and the wealthier ought to contribute more. As "Corrective" SX 1, I feel there are some things that I can control, and there are some things that I cannot control. If I have a Self-Preservation blindspot, money feels like something I cannot control. So I just try to get by and don't pay much attention to building wealth.

Domain 9 – Balance

I try hard. I want to be a good person. But I can also be very critical and judgmental. I understand that abundance is about having what I need, and being in alignment with my sense of what is right and good. But the more I fear that things are disorderly and out of control, the less I can relax, and the more perfectionistic, obsessive, and uptight I become. I end up being a martyr, overdoing things, and then feeling resentful and unappreciated. I want so badly to do things right that I end up making things worse. All of this makes it very difficult to integrate what is sweet and good in my life, be joyful and grateful for all the people who do support and love me. This makes it difficult to appreciate my good health, my good work, my good intentions, my good deeds. By not being able to harmonize my relationship to money with my life, I cannot go with the flow and feel prosperous.

> I diminish the flow when I "should" myself. I grew up with intense "shoulds." I learned I could live more freely. But the gravity of "shoulds" as a 1 has pulled me back. My sense of abundance is lower than it might be.

> My money pain comes from my judgments about people which has caused me to end relationships, distance myself from others, keep me from developing personal relationships. I didn't even give them a chance.

I must confront my superficial beliefs about money and entertain the possibility that I could be wrong in my beliefs. I must confront my need for order and control. By letting go of my fixation on what is wrong, I can participate with what is right in this moment, both sacred and profane. I must work towards being in the flow of life and wealth without blocking love out.

5. THE PARADOX

The fundamental paradox is that *Ordering* never leads to balance. It can only lead to imbalance and excess.   Not only is the actual outcome the opposite of my original intent, but it can never be otherwise. What is order? Can order be imposed on the world from outside? Or is it something that is intrinsic to the nature of things? *Ordering* is supposed to give me more balance. But when I overdo this strategy, I actually become imbalanced. My denial of my wild impulses and messy imperfections keeps me from connecting to my true nature, which would enable me to be relaxed and joyful. The defenses I've employed bring about the very imbalance that I fear.

The paradox is that *Ordering* causes me to disconnect from the thing I care most about, which is finding inner balance and serenity. I forget that my basic alignment and goodness do not come from order at all. There is a part of me that knows that I am not corrupt. But honoring this part of myself would create conflict with my ego structure, and that tension would be too much for me to bear. So instead, I continue fixing, ordering, perfecting. I sense that I am being blackmailed into *Ordering* and that this entire structure is built on fear, but I do not know how to move past the fear. The more I fear being corrupt, the more constricted and resentful I become.

The paradox is that in always paying attention to what is wrong, I become part of what's wrong. In always trying to fix things, I only see what's broken. In needing to be right, I become more wrong. In needing to control and contain what is chaotic, I can never stanch the chaos. In learning to be wrong, though, I can become more balanced. In surrendering to the chaos, the chaos no longer has power over me. When I let myself go to be more creative and joyful, I become more balanced.

6. BREAKING THE VICIOUS CYCLE

In order to break the vicious cycle of my personality, and move from Fear to Love, I must embrace and resolve the fundamental paradox of *Ordering*. I have spent my whole life denying my wildness and gluttony. This denial has cut me off from the true me. I have been crippled by needing to be perfect and correct. But what incredible possibilities could exist if I didn't deny a part of me? In keeping my wild, gluttonous side at bay, I have also held away love. As I throw off the shackles of my personality and orient to my true nature, I begin to own the whole me. I know that I am part of an intelligently ordered universe and that I don't need work hard for order. I see the mess, the paradoxes, the ambiguities, and know that there is an intelligence to it all. I know, without being reactive, what I should do and when I should act. In surrendering to my core nature, I stop resisting the truth. I become embodied Love, with compassion in my heart, wisdom in my head, and well-being in my body.

My journey with money is a journey to serenity. My journey to experiencing the implicit order and intelligence of the universe requires me to connect my body to my heart and head. By nurturing an accepting heart and appreciative mind that can be present with both the bad and the good, I can relax knowing that I participate in the implicit order of things, without having to fight against things from outside. Instead of trying to fix everything and do things right, I can relax, knowing that what needs to be done will get done. I no longer feel scarcity driven by my need to have more order. I no longer need to sort things into good and bad. I no longer believe that money is evil or that money is the answer. I can be with what is here right now, sensing the sacredness of the moment, sensing something beyond what is literally here. In this sacred space, all the bad and good, corrupt and virtuous, can co-exist and be held with compassion and appreciation, as I remember the truth and perfection of the universe. In embracing these truths, I can move past my old beliefs and patterns and welcome abundance, prosperity, and love into my life. I can begin to feel more spontaneous and free. But this is not comfortable or easy. I feel the pain as my ego resists losing its job. I feel remorseful about how I have lived my life and hurt myself and others. I am scared that I won't be able to survive on my own deeper knowing alone.

When I live abundantly, I am in integrity with myself and the universe. From this place, I can be of greatest service to others, without the heavy weight of my judgments and black-and-white thinking. I can be humble and not superior. I can be joyful not exacting. I do not give in to my ego's frustration and resentment. I hold myself accountable as the architect of my own wondrous life. I acknowledge that resentment only fuels the ego engine and does not serve my higher self. I meet each moment with appreciation. I can be with all of life, with its intrinsic messiness and wildness, and it doesn't really matter. I know there is an implicit order unfolding each moment before me. When I can connect to what really matters to me, I can attune to myself. When I can attune to myself, I can attune to others. When I can attune to myself and others, I can finally be of real service to the world. From a place of balance and inner serenity, there is nothing to do but love and serve. From here, I am able to teach others what Love really is, and how abundant the universe is both materially and spiritually.

	Brief Description
"Disciplined" SP 1	I focus on being orderly in my physical life. I want to have my finances in order, want to repay debt as soon as possible, be practical, properly generous, and appropriately frugal. I can only relax when I know things are in order. I am repelled by extreme appetite/ambition in earning and wealth building. I aim for balance.
"Principled" SO 1	I focus on making things right in the social arena. Focusing on money for myself instead of larger social issues feels selfish, greedy, and wrong. I earn to meet my needs, but don't want to stockpile money. I want to be generous, contribute back to society.
"Corrective" SX 1	I focus on being at my correct best to meet whatever opportunities come my way. I focus on the things I can do correctly and well. I love to spend on things that appeal to me. My spending is more impulsive than controlled. It can be difficult for me to believe that I can be both passionate about my work and well paid.

Type 1	Summary
Gift	Being aligned to what is right and good.
Unconscious Belief	The world is corrupt; I am corrupt.
Strategy	*Ordering* – putting things in their right place and fixing what is wrong to be beyond reproach.
Vicious Cycle	Because I must hold the line against corruption and chaos, I must stay away from the abstract, vague, and unknown, and focus on right and wrong. But because I judge myself and others harshly, and can never be as good as I think I should be, I feel even more flawed, imperfect, and corrupt.
Defended Against	Being gluttonous and satisfied.
Operationally	• It's up to me to fix what's wrong. • I must contain my impulses and messy emotions. • I focus only on the areas that I can control and do correctly.
Paradox	*Ordering* does not generate balance.
Breaking the Vicious Cycle	I must recognize that the universe is intelligently ordered. It is not up to me to fix what is wrong. My job is to be a part of the intelligent order.
Direction of Growth	Embracing my uniqueness allows me to attune to myself and others and be of real service to the world.

CHAPTER 8

GIVING
Type 2

1. GIFT

My heart is my guidance system. I am attuned to others and feel the need around me. When someone feels pain or sadness, I comfort them. When someone wants to celebrate, I celebrate with them. I've always been naturally attuned to what others need. It's my gift.

I feel powerful because I know that my love is healing and nourishing. Love validates, nurtures, and grows people. I know the power of love to triumph over evil. I know that people who feel loved will stay on a good path and do right by the world. The love I give is the foundation upon which people can be healthy, happy, and well-adjusted, and go into the larger world and be whoever they might be. I am the wind beneath their wings.

The world needs me to tend to it, nurture it, witness its progress, and validate its efforts. The world needs me to care about it and love it. I nurture people until they are ready to leave and live their big lives. Without me, they would not be who they are. The love inside me fuels my energy to nurture and care for others. Being responsive and helpful feeds my soul. I give my gift of love freely.

2. STRATEGY

My life and money strategy grow out of my sense of the critical importance of love. At the unconscious level, I believe that the world does not have enough love. At the conscious level, I believe that I can generate the love the world needs. I want to stay connected to those who need me, so that I will be validated, valued, and loved. Helping others by *Giving* of myself and my money is a way to stay connected. My fear of abandonment stimulates my strategy of *Giving*. *Giving* is about responding to need and creating more love in the world. But this strategy of *Giving* fills me with shame and sadness because I continue to feel unloved, even with all the *Giving* that I do.

Giving is a defense against my own neediness, and is opposite of the *Personalizing* strategy. As much as I can sense what others need, I deny my own needs. The truth is that I can only sense others' needs because I have needs myself. When I give with an expectation of something in return, the love I give is conditional. This *Giving* strategy creates a vicious cycle of having to misuse my gift of empathy to get my needs met indirectly, which leaves me unfulfilled and needing to try harder yet. Trading in love doesn't work, and keeps me locked into scarcity.

The *Giving* strategy is a distinctly indirect way of getting one's needs met. It is an attempt to have others need me and want me. It is an attempt to be indispensable in their lives, and to have a place at the table. Being direct and assertive is difficult because I am afraid that if I put myself on the line and am direct about what I want, I will be rejected. I am deathly afraid that I will be cut off from love if I own my power. But true love comes from strength not weakness. It is only when I can be fully here, confident and attuned, giving from a place of strength, that I can love unconditionally.

3. THE VICIOUS CYCLE

If I were to look at my life objectively, I would notice that I have essentially been trapped in a vicious cycle of fear and scarcity. Because of this, my relationship to love and prosperity is constrained. *Giving* is fundamentally about trying to get love because I do not feel loved already. This orientation makes me feel unappreciated and ashamed. But my ego enthusiastically keeps this vicious cycle going so that it can keep its job. I get addicted to *Giving*. Even though I think I am moving along, I am merely moving in place.

When we are caught in a vicious cycle where our actions validate our beliefs, it can be very difficult to extricate ourselves. When we are stuck at a certain point along the scarcity-to-abundance spectrum, it is impossible to improve our position until we get out of the vicious cycle. If we are suddenly showered with new wealth, we will most likely dissipate it so that we can get back to our old set point. So in order to create new wealth, we must first become aware of the vicious cycle we are caught in. Once we become aware, we will be in a better position to consciously unblock what blocks us, and welcome new wealth into our lives.

My underlying assumption is that in order to be loved, I must earn a place at the table by doing for others, giving to others, and being selfless. I fear being rejected, unneeded, unloved. I believe the best way to get love is to do for others. I assume that I must stay focused on others. To be attuned to my own needs is selfish. I cannot afford to invest in myself. It is difficult for me to see that we all have needs that we are trying to get met, and that it is okay to have my own needs. It never occurs to me that it is as loving an act to take care of myself as it is to take care of others.

I am confident that I am not selfish because I am generous to others. I am also confident that I can make others need and love me. I can be quite willful in getting others to like, need, and want me. I will flatter, pander, and sacrifice myself. In wanting to fit in, I will tell you how popular you are. In wanting to be desired, I will tell you how desirable you are. In wanting to be taken care of, I will take care of you. I pay close attention to whether my services are appreciated. I keep tabs on who "pays me back" and who doesn't. The love I understand is transactional – I give you love and you give me love back. It seems natural to me that the world works this way. I want to believe that I give without strings attached, but secretly I expect that all my care-taking and generosity will be reciprocated.

Because I can't be selfish, I must get my needs met in a roundabout way. I like relationships where I provide certain services and the other person provides different but complementary services. That way, I can feel generous but also be taken care of. I tend to rely on others to take care of money matters because I don't want to be thought of as selfish or money grubbing. The love I give is conditional: I will give you love as long as my needs continue to be met. This negates my ability to truly understand the nature of love and also negates my ability to be self-reliant and independent.   I   a m ashamed of how much I need your validation, but I do it anyways. I can get carried away with trying to be liked, to fit in, be desirable, and wanted. Often I spend a lot of money on gifts instead of taking care of myself directly. I work hard to earn my place at the table. If I have to give myself away to be needed, then I'll do it. I trade in love. I give to get. In order to get love, I give my services, my attention, my nurturance. This makes my giving obligatory rather than choiceful. I am ashamed that I do this, but this is the only way I know to get love.

I spend most of my energy on family and friends. I play the role of caretaker, and use my time, money, and energy to make sure their needs are met. Sometimes I can become a martyr. I get tired and exhausted from all the care-taking, but I do not really feel that I have a choice. Without me, those who depend on me would crumble. It is my ego that makes me believe this, and makes me feel that the care-taking is required. I resent this, but I am not sure why. In subordinating myself to others, I put myself in a powerful position in one sense, but in a vulnerable position in another sense. I am powerful because I am needed. But I am vulnerable because I need appreciation and validation to feel good about myself.

I can become quite intrusive in other people's affairs, believing that I know what others need, even if they themselves don't know. I don't mind playing the supporting role, as long as they know that I am absolutely indispensable to them. I may give money to family members in need, pay for a niece to go to college, support others in their dreams, but then not feel sufficiently appreciated, and become resentful. I can also feel superior to others, believing that I am more competent than those that depend on me. I may even undermine people or tear them down so they won't leave me, creating unhealthy co-dependencies. I can become abusive towards those I take care of, and strip them of their power. I want to work for the angels but cannot see the devil inside me. Because I do not include myself in my care-taking, I can get resentful about how much I do for others and how little gratitude I get back. When I can't be honest about my needs, and can't be honest about my strategies, I have to engage in deception, both of myself and of others. This lack of honesty makes my relationship with others manipulative and less than clean.

When I get stressed, I can become irate and angry. I may spend lavishly on myself in secret to punish my spouse. I can become uncooperative and passive aggressive about money, while at the same time feel deeply guilty and ashamed. I become more cut off from those I most want to be loved by. My assumptions lead to thoughts, actions, and consequences that validate my assumptions. In this case, the more I ingratiate myself to get love, the more I turn others off, and the less love there is for me. This dynamic keeps my ego employed and keeps me perpetually fixated on giving and getting love. I can never find love for then I would have no excuse for my *Giving* strategy. We are each caught in a vicious cycle of our personality and instincts until we decide to break free. This takes deliberate energy and momentum because the cycle is a compelling vortex. In order to create new wealth, we must see clearly the vicious cycle that blocks us from abundance. Then we must fight our way out of the vortex.

4. OPERATIONALLY

If my instincts are balanced, I will be able to attend to money in each of the Nine Money Domains in a healthy manner. If, however, my instincts are not in balance, then I will get stuck in my type fixation and I cannot be optimally effective. My motivation to be giving and loving manifests in different ways depending on my dominant instinct. I will tend to focus on the areas where I can be most helpful. As a SP 2, my *Giving* energy is focused on being helpful about self-preservation aspects of life such as making food, cleaning, earning and giving money for comfort and well-being. As a SO 2, my *Giving* energy reinforces with my Social instinct, causing me to focus on being generous and connected to others to enhance my social image. As a SX 2, I focus on being generous with my compliments, charming others, and giving my passion, energy, and attention to others. How my instincts are imbalanced will therefore impact how I relate to the Nine Money Domains – where I put my attention and energy and where I don't.

"CARETAKING" SP 2	"CONNECTING" SO 2	"CAPTIVATING" SX 2

Domain 1 – Budgeting

I can adhere to budget constraints, but I may choose to ignore them. As a heart-based type, I am more connected to what I want than to my fear. I prefer to spend what I spend and do what I do without having to justify my behavior. I resist budgeting, which would force me to look at my spending patterns and might bring shame and guilt. My identity is being helpful, so I resist looking at facts that might suggest I am selfish. I am more intuitive than logical about money and I tend to be optimistic that things will work out. I just try to do the best I can, and don't naturally worry much about a budget.

My reluctance to budget stems partly from a fear of my own power. If I did a budget, I might be able to control the path of my life, get what I want, and get too big. I'm afraid that would disconnect me from others. It feels uncomfortable to take a leadership role around money. There is also a way that I don't feel confident about my abilities. If I did the budgeting, maybe I'd do it wrong. I often enter into implicit arrangements with my partner. He takes care of me in certain ways while I take care of him in other ways. We both get our needs met without having to be explicit about it. Being too self-reliant and independent feels scary and undesirable.

Budgeting can also be difficult for me because it challenges my pride, either because I feel ignorant about money, or because I'd have to see explicitly how I spend money on my own needs. Perhaps I don't deserve spending money. My shame keeps me away from engaging in an honest appraisal of the financial situation. If my partner can help me to be honest and supports my being vulnerable, this can help a lot. If, however, I feel unappreciated, despite all the care-taking that I do for the family, then I may use money to soothe myself and even be passive aggressive in spending too much to get back at my unappreciative partner.

I have the potential to do budgeting, especially if it makes me helpful or even indispensable. I can put my energy towards this endeavor if it will make the relationship stronger and bring me closer to my partner. I can leverage my willfulness to make things happen. Even if it weren't my strength, I could make myself do budgeting, simply to have a place at the table. I could find it within myself to be quite effective at tracking, organizing, filing, budgeting, saving. But if I feel that I have little to contribute, then my attention and energy will gravitate to other areas. I tend to slip into the role that complements my partner's role.

As a "Caretaking" SP 2, my Self-Preservation instinct drives me to be more concerned about security and stability than a typical 2, and more concerned about having enough to make ends meet. I may even put aside money for emergencies and retirement. However, I tend to be pulled more towards the needs of today than I am towards the needs of tomorrow, focusing on helping people now. If there are kids involved, I feel that it is important to focus on them now, and that many expenses are unavoidable. When things are tight, I want to do what I can to be helpful, hoping that I'll be loved and supported in return.

> I never talked about budgeting. Till my late 30s, I struggled and resisted looking at the facts. I really had to apply my logic and head to budgeting. This required friends to help me out. I don't want to appear unsuccessful. But a system of budgeting that was specific was hard for me. I felt the shame of somebody questioning my accuracy, questioning my values and right to this or that. If we have to talk about the budget, it might suggest that I haven't earned it. I can feel wounded and get really reactive.

As a "Connecting" SO 2, I want to be well thought of, and like to circulate and connect. Budgeting does not factor in much. As a "Captivating" SX 2, I can be an extravagant spender. I have relatively little concern about stability or budgeting, and can find numbers and details tedious. I tend to guesstimate the numbers in my head, but not put anything on paper. Budgeting feels like a commitment that could lead to bigger possibilities. I resist empowering myself this way. When I don't do a budget, I don't have to be accountable and can blame others if things go wrong.

Domain 2 – Spending

I don't have a lot of fear around money. Spending on others makes me feel good about myself. I can go overboard taking care of others, paying for their education, their debt, their physical care, while depriving myself of those same luxuries. Sometimes, though, I can be self-indulgent, especially if I am feeling a bit down. In general, I spend money easily on myself and others, but with the hope that I will indirectly get appreciation and love in return. When I spend from a place of lack rather than a place of abundance, I am not nurtured by it.

When I am in a good place, feeling loved and appreciated, I can be very organized, responsible, and controlled in my spending. I can be very resourceful and goal-oriented for the sake of others and the family, and can figure out how to make things work. I can be a good saver, planner and budgeter. I can be quite task-oriented, paying bills, prioritizing. In contrast, when I am not feeling loved and appreciated, my spending can get out of control. I can get angry, uncooperative, and passive aggressive. I may engage in covert spending to soothe myself. I may spend frivolously and irresponsibly as a way to get back at my spouse who is not appreciating me. My spending is strongly affected by my mood.

As a "Caretaking" SP 2, I am a bit tighter and less generous than a typical 2 because my Self-Preservation instinct tells me to be frugal and careful. I spend more on practical matters to keep things grounded and secure. I am not as interested in conspicuous consumption. I can be generous though if things are secure for me and there is a purpose to it. Buying clothes, paying for education, or helping someone get back on their feet would be legitimate things to support, but paying for luxuries would not. I can easily believe that without me, my family would fall apart. My imbalance, as I find myself enmeshed in taking care of other people's needs, is not paying attention in a direct way to my own needs, interests, and passions.

As a "Connecting" SO 2, I like to spend in a way that connects me to others, by contributing my time, energy, and money so that I am of value. I want to say yes all the time and get over-involved in other people's affairs. If others drop $150 for dinner and a show, it will probably be difficult for me to say no. I have a comparative mind and I want to fit in, and that often requires spending on name brand things that are in fashion. I need to look good socially. I've even been told that I can be inappropriate in my rush to pay for others, and not giving them a choice about whether to pay for themselves. I can get competitive about being the most generous. If I feel poor, I might go find people even needier than me and bring them to my home. I set myself up to be needed and to provide for others. Much of my brain power goes towards finding groups that I can belong to. Looking at my expenses can induce a lot of guilt and difficult feelings, because I don't want to have to justify how I spend money. My imbalance is in not pursuing my own goals and gifts.

> I am oblivious to my own needs. I want to personalize gifts to people. I feel an urgency in wanting to give something from me. I want to give myself as a gift. I would love to spend a lot of money on gifts for others and for a lover. It is hard *not* to spend on them during the Christmas season. I want to shower gifts on people.

As a "Captivating" SX 2, I buy what appeals to me, energizes me, and makes me look good. I like to spend to make myself look attractive and pleasing to my lover. I can be spontaneous about my spending because I can think of plenty justifications for what I want. I am not ashamed of my spending. I also like to travel and have fun. I can get energized by putting my energies behind someone else's agenda. I love to be absolutely fabulous and indispensable to them. I like to lavish attention, money, and gifts on them and make them feel unbelievably showered with love. I live life intensely and like it that way. My imbalance, as I find myself intensely enmeshed in supporting a special person, will be in not putting energy towards nurturing my own gifts.

Domain 3 – Earning

As someone who understands other people's feelings and needs intuitively, I can be very effective in the services industry and in jobs that require empathy and emotional intelligence, like nursing, social work, facilitator, executive secretary, coaching, or customer service. When I am in my power, I can be quite effective at making money. I have a lot of energy for helping others, and my services can be well remunerated. Being sociable and good at reading people, I can rise in a job quickly. I can be decisive and a quick study. Unconsciously, I like to leave a bit of value on the table so that my services are fully appreciated. I also like the idea of being irreplaceable, because I offer so much value to my employer.

Typically, I don't earn to my full potential. Often I will subordinate myself to someone more powerful.   I can put my goals on hold for my partner, child, or boss, and limit my earning potential. I don't really know how to share power in a relationship. I believe that either I am in power or they are in power. Typically, I am more comfortable being the supporter and I am willing to stay small to keep the relationship going. My shame about having needs makes me reluctant to step forth and own my power. It seems easier to stay small, limit my ambitions, be self-sacrificing, and get my needs met indirectly.

> I am trying to let go of my idea that I must make money by doing and giving. I have not believed before that making money could be easy. I always believed it was a difficult thing. I am trying to make things easier for myself now. I am trying to charge more for my services. I am learning to put a good price on my work. Before I would sell my work too cheaply. I wouldn't value my services enough.

There are moments in my life when my energetic services may be dismissed or even rejected by someone. It can take months to recover emotionally from this rejection. Because I am already vulnerable to feeling ashamed of not being loved, rejection can have huge reverberations for my earnings when I lose my confidence and feel inadequate. There is a way that I cheapen myself and feel undeserving which makes earning money difficult. Because love feels conditional, I believe that I need to work hard for money and love. As hard as I work to help and support others, I find it difficult to receive, which makes it hard to charge appropriately for my services. I must learn the give-and-take nature of real love. If I believed I was loved, others would pay me a fair price.

As a "Caretaking" SP 2, I am less image-oriented than a typical 2. If people depend on my income, I may work long hours, difficult shifts, extra jobs, in order to make extra money. I tend to gravitate towards jobs that enable me to help others in their well-being and comfort, such as nursing. As a "Connecting" SO 2, I am very sensitive to my social image. I like to be acknowledged for my service to the group, and I tend to gravitate towards jobs where I can be a gatekeeper at the center of things. As a "Captivating" SX 2, I am bolder than a typical 2, and more willing to put myself on the line to shine. I tend to gravitate towards jobs where I can be indispensable. I can, though, get distracted from earning directly for myself, lavishing my attention on another.

Domain 4 – Beliefs

I believe that I have to work really hard to get love. I am ashamed that my need for love has not yet been met. What is wrong with me? I feel that I should hold myself small and subservient to others to stay close to them and get love in this indirect way. I have a similar feeling about money. I have to work really hard to get it and I am ashamed that my need for money has not yet been met. I feel that it is safer to stay small, indirect, and not take up too much space. If I owned my own power and claimed what I need directly, I would risk rejection. So with money, I am willing to play the martyr. My needs are not so important. Don't worry about me. I don't need a lot of money.

> Money is difficult for me. I've realized that what is difficult for me is that I don't feel that I deserve money. I feel I need to work for the money. If I am to have love, it must come from hard work and serving others.

> Money is not important. I just need enough to get by. It's not important to be super wealthy.

I just want someone else to do it for me. I want to be loved.

Money can connect me to others, but it can also disconnect me from others. My empathy of others makes me highly attuned to the divide that money can create between people. I also interpret money as a medium of power. There is a power in making money, but there is also a power in giving money. I am both attracted to and repelled by money. I know that in making money for myself, with my own capabilities and skills, I can feel more confident about my gifts. But I often feel that there is more power in spending to support others than in investing in myself. It can be difficult for me to strike a balance between money for myself and money for others. I associate having money or making money with selfishness, and that drives me to not keep money for myself. If I could be more confident about other ways that I provide service, I would not have to judge myself so harshly.

Unfortunately, when I allow my critic to drive my beliefs, I am unable to connect money to what really matters for me. What I really want is to be accepted, loved and cared for. How can I do this for myself? Allowing myself to earn a good living and save for myself would enable me to address my day-to-day needs, and enable me to have time for myself. It would provide me with the grounding I need to take care of myself. Money can be for me too.

Domain 5 – Understanding

Because I am empathetic, nurturing, and oriented to *Giving*, I do not relate to money as something to be hoarded, to dream about or build up. To me, money is about making and spending, giving and taking. It is about spreading around and circulating. When I don't make enough money, I unconsciously feel that others should help me, the way I would help them.

> I have low understanding about money. I lack interest in it. I trust my money with others to manage. I don't take the time to research investing options because it is too boring. Money is one of the pedestrian things we need to live. My interest is in energy, deep things, chocolate.

As a "Caretaking" SP 2, my Self-Preservation instinct makes me more organized about my papers and records, but not perfectly so. My organization is sufficient for me to find what I am looking for, but not meticulous. I may track the inflows and outflows of money, but more likely than not, it will be more intuitive than rigorous. I understand the relationship between spending less and having more, and can be frugal about my own needs. As a "Connecting" SO 2, I am more interested in my image and my contribution. If I feel I can be of contribution, I will be more motivated to understand finances and be the one to manage the household. If, however, I feel that I cannot be of service, then I focus my energy on other areas. As a "Captivating" SX 2, I am less interested in meticulous filing and organization and more interested in pursuing the charge. I really need a visual system to stay organized. I need something concrete to be able to focus on, for example, tidy envelopes for different expenses. I like to know what I have in the bank so I know what is available for spending. It is a lot more fun for me to stay on top of the finances when I do it with someone else. As a part of a team, where we are cooperating, I can really put my helpful energy towards this endeavor. The relational juice is what motivates me to stay on task with money.

Domain 6 – Risk Management

I do not consider how money can support me, or how I might need support in general. I tend to be pretty optimistic about life and I don't have a strong orientation towards risk management or emergency savings. It's not that I can't do it, but I am not strongly pulled that way. I am generally less concerned about preparing for emergencies than I am about helping in the present. Unconsciously, I assume that my support of people creates a safety net that I can count on in my own times of need. I might make a real estate investment that helps a friend in need. I trust that I will be supported in return. As a "Caretaking" SP 2, I am more susceptible to worrying about downside risk and instability than a typical 2. As a "Connecting" SO 2, my Social instinct reinforces my optimistic energy and makes it difficult to feel afraid for myself. I have a strong trust that I will be okay because of the strong social network that I have cultivated all my life. As a "Captivating" SX 2, my Sexual instinct makes me less afraid of potential risks. Rather than planning directly for my own well-being in case of an emergency, I focus on cultivating relationships.

Domain 7 – Planning

I can be goal oriented for the sake of a relationship, but I am not very goal-oriented on my own. When I can be honest about my desire for money, I can plan more effectively for my financial future. Otherwise, there is a way in which I feel ashamed about wanting or needing money, and am resistant to planning and being attentive about money. My optimism further constrains my desire for planning. There is also a way that I secretly prefer someone else to figure out future stuff. I prefer to concern myself with nurturing people now.

As a "Caretaking" SP 2, I am more fearful about instability and insecurity than a typical 2. For this reason, I have a slightly stronger tendency to plan ahead and want an emergency cushion. I am not strongly goal-oriented, but I do worry about what might happen. As a "Connecting" SO 2, my Social instinct reinforces my type energy and makes me optimistic that things will be okay. I find it very difficult to worry about, much less do anything about, the future. As a "Captivating" SX 2, my Sexual instinct motivates me to invest in myself, in my passions, and in my relationships, and motivates me to think ahead from this perspective. But planning related to security is not very interesting to me.

Domain 8 – Wealth Building

This is my weakest Domain, and the Domain that I most need to pay attention to. I am resistant to saving and wealth building because saving feels selfish and wealth building feels empowering. My aversion to saving keeps me stuck in a uni-directional flow of money where I cannot enrichen and develop myself. I am reluctant to be big and powerful because I am afraid that this will disconnect me from others, and prevent me from being loved. It is so much easier for me to be over-responsible and over-enmeshed in the affairs of others and not put myself first.

> I've been careless with money. I haven't been good at saving it – feeling that I don't deserve to have it. I've spent it, given it away, etc. We've been generous to the kids. Lately, I've been better though, and I have tried to pay more attention to the issue of money and how to make it and keep it.

> When I compare myself to others, it's very painful. I feel I've shrunk so small. I need to claim my own power. I want to be in a healthy relationship with my value.

I am not connected to the potential power of money in my life and how money could be used directly to meet my needs and make things happen. I am more oriented towards believing that I am already okay and can afford to be generous. I am not very good at negotiating and bargaining for myself. I'd rather be connected and interdependent. I must recognize my vulnerability to having my confidence rocked by mistakes, setbacks, and rejection. I am more susceptible than other types to getting emotionally hurt and not wanting to try again. We all make mistakes with investments and financial decisions, but I tend to take it harder than most. When I get hurt, I can feel so inadequate and small. And then I find it even more difficult to take care of myself, to save and build wealth for my empowerment and future.

> I rejected money and wealth in my life because I didn't want to be like my siblings. They created separation with loved ones because of money. I don't need the wealth. There is a self-sacrificing nobility about being poor. I can do without. If I did need money, I might pretend I don't need it. Now, I am beginning to see the virtues of having wealth.

My direction of growth is to step into my own power. With money, that means being more self-reliant and independent. This can feel difficult because it threatens my self-image as someone who is close to and connected to others. I am reluctant to be selfish and admit that I have needs that I might have to address directly. Saying yes to wealth is saying yes to my power and vitality. It is saying yes to taking care of myself and my own needs directly. At the core, saying yes to wealth is saying yes to Love. It is about dropping my story about conditonal love and my story that I can only get love if I keep myself small. The work of this Domain is big work for me.

Domain 9 – Balance

Of all the types, I think I understand the give-and-take of life the best. I have an abundant and optimistic orientation. When I am at my best, I know that money comes and goes, just as love is given and taken. I don't worry about money much. I recognize that there is a natural ebb and flow that I do not need to stress about. When I am in this flow, I attend to money in an organic way, going with the flow. I have satisfying relationships, good balance in my life, and feel content. I own my own power, welcome and harness wealth in my life, and experience life as abundant and loving.

Scarcity for me comes from my belief that love is conditional. When I believe that I must give to get, then I get very anxious about not being appreciated. When this happens, I feel I must try harder, ingratiate myself further, and give of myself more. Scarcity for me means having to earn my love and having to keep myself small. Scarcity means not being able to be honest and forthright about my needs. Scarcity means having to hold back my own power and vitality, and being weak. Abundance comes to me when

I know and live the truth of the fact that I can go for what I want, that I can assert myself directly, and that my personal power connects me to a greater power that is Love.

I must directly confront my fear of my own neediness, my own strength, and my own loveability. I must be willing to confront my own neediness and be willing to look at how my beliefs about money block me from loving myself. I must confront my unwillingness to step into my own power and harness wealth in my life. And I must look at how my spending patterns belie my *Giving* strategy and keep me impoverished, both materially and spiritually. By admitting my own needs and being honest with myself, I can have the love I want. I must work towards being in the flow of life and wealth without blocking out Love.

5. THE PARADOX

The fundamental paradox is that *Giving* never leads to the Love I am looking for. It can only lead to feeling unappreciated and disconnected. Not only is the actual outcome the opposite of my original intent, but it can never be otherwise. What is Love? Is love what I get when I have been good and helpful? Is Love something that has to be earned? Is love a scarce commodity that can be traded? Or is Love something that exists here for all of us always and unconditionally? *Giving* is supposed to help me get Love. But when I overdo this strategy, I feel less connected and loved. My denial of my own human needs keeps me from connecting to my true nature and experiencing myself fully. The defenses I've employed bring about the very selfishness and separation I fear.

The paradox is that *Giving* causes me to disconnect from the thing I care most about, which is finding love and attunement. I forget that my being loved does not come from my doing and *Giving*. There is a part of me that knows that I am not selfish and conditionally loved. But honoring this part of myself would create conflict with my ego structure, and that tension would be too much for me to bear. I sense that I am being blackmailed into *Giving* and that this entire structure is built on fear, but I do not know how to move past the fear. The more I fear being unappreciated and unloved, the more I ingratiate. In continuing to search for love and acceptance, I can never actually feel it.

The paradox is that in always paying attention to how I can be helpful and appreciated, I forget that I am already appreciated. In always trying to help others, I do not leave room for others to help me. In always giving without receiving, I am actually being selfish. In willfully making things happen, I cannot avoid the shame. In learning to take care of my own needs, and in learning how to ask and receive directly, I can feel nurtured and connected to others. When I listen to my own needs, I am loved.

6. BREAKING THE VICIOUS CYCLE

In order to break the vicious cycle of my personality, and move from Fear to Love, I must embrace and resolve the fundamental paradox of *Giving*. I have spent my whole life hiding my shame and neediness. This hiding has cut me off from my own strength. I have been crippled by needing to be accepted and loved. How can I simply be here with what is? What incredible possibilities could exist if I spoke from my heart with honesty and openness? In keeping my neediness at bay, I have also held away the love. As I throw off the shackles of my personality and orient to my true nature, I begin to own the whole me. When I do this, I move past my story of being unloved.

My journey with money is a journey to humility. My journey to humbly nurturing my own needs and embracing my own messiness requires me to connect my heart to my body and head. By doing this, I begin to have a more spacious sense of my life. I can now participate in the love and know that my needs are not less or more important than others. By taking care of myself, I can be in relationships without needing to be repaid. This enables me to be fully present with others without conditions. Real love is patient, strong, and can embrace everything. I do not have to try hard to make others love me. I do not have to try hard to connect. I can relax, knowing that I am part of a loving and benevolent universe. Love is not about doing but being. Giving love is like trying to give someone the air we breathe. The air is not for me to give or get, for it is already mine to have. I cannot give to another what they already have, and I cannot get from another what I already am.

Love embraces everyone, and it is unconditional. My needs count just as much as others' needs. In surrendering to my core nature, I stop resisting the truth. I become embodied Love, with compassion in my heart, wisdom in my head, and well-being in my body. I now occupy a much vaster reality and feel unconditional love. I am attuned to each moment, confident that I will know what to do and how to be when that new moment arises. In embracing these truths, I can move past my old beliefs and patterns and welcome abundance, prosperity, and love into my life. I can begin to feel more powerful and vital. But this is not comfortable or easy. I feel the pain as my ego resists losing its job. I feel remorseful about how I have lived my life and hurt myself and others. I am scared that I won't be able to survive on my own deeper knowing alone.

When I live abundantly, I know that I am part of a loving universe. I am no longer reactive about getting or not getting feedback from others, because I am confident about my place in the universe. When I live abundantly, I can be humble and kind, without being prideful and reactive. When I see human need, whether it be in others or myself, I can be with it all, connected to my power. When I can be fully me, I become empowered to step forth and shine in my full potential.

	Brief Description
"Caretaking" SP 2	I focus on being helpful in the self-preservation realm of food, money, physical well-being. I am practical about spending for food, clothing, education. I am pulled towards the needs of today rather than the needs of tomorrow. I may work long hours, difficult shifts, extra jobs to make extra money for the sake of the family.
"Connecting" SO 2	I focus on being generous in connecting others. I spend to fit in, be connected and well-thought of. I am not very aware of my own needs. I want to shower gifts on others, be indispensable to others, and be the gatekeeper to real power.
"Captivating" SX 2	I focus on being a fabulous support to a special other, generous with my compliments, and captivating with my attention and energy to do things on their behalf. I can be an extravagant spender with little concern for details and budgeting, and enjoy the limelight a bit more than the average 2.

Type 2	Summary
Gift	Being nurturing and attuned to others' feelings.
Unconscious Belief	There is not enough love in this world
Strategy	*Giving* – doing for others, giving to others, being generous and helpful, so that I can earn love.
Vicious Cycle	Because I must earn love, I must stay close to others, focus on what others need, and be indispensable. I cannot be selfish and nurture myself. But because I cannot nurture myself, I feel even more unloved.
Defended Against	Having needs of my own.
Operationally	• It's up to me to create the love. • I must get my own needs met in an indirect way. • I focus only on the areas where I can be helpful and needed.
Paradox	*Giving* does not generate appreciation.
Breaking the Vicious Cycle	I must recognize that the universe is attuned to me. It is not up to me to create love. My job is simply to be a part of the attunement of the universe.
Direction of Growth	Owning my power and strength allows me to shine to my fullest potential.

CHAPTER 9

STRIVING

Type 3

1. GIFT

I am an exemplar of value. I know how to perform to give the world what it wants of me. I have an innate sense of what is valued by others and I believe it is up to me to shine. I am an excellent communicator and promoter. As an exemplar of excellence, I make my family, my community, my people proud. I represent the best of who they are and where I come from. I am energetic and action-oriented and I know how to get things done efficiently and effectively. I don't get mired in the details or lost in the what-ifs. I just get down to business and get things done. When I know the markers of success, I lock on to the task at hand and go for the gold. In being engaged with life and an exemplar of value, I am an embodiment of human potential. I live to be a winner.

2. STRATEGY

My life and money strategy grow out of my sense of the critical importance of being of value. At the unconscious level, the world does not fully and properly see me, though I repress this feeling at the conscious level and believe that I can generate validation. Others might think I am over earnest in my desire to be successful. What they miss is my desire to be valued and loved.

An aspect of *Striving* is the ability to adjust to what is valued by others. I push myself to achieve so that others will admire me. My approach to life is structured and defined. *Striving* radically differs from the strategy of *Securing*. In *Striving,* I reject my anxiety, lack of faith, and desire to be secure so that I can be bold and heroic. I am proactive about developing myself to become shinier and brighter. I am never satisfied to just be. I must do stuff, challenge and succeed, so that I can be a hero. I assume that my family and community need a star. Without my shining existence, the world would be a dimmer, less hopeful place. I take it upon myself give hope to my family and world. I deeply fear a life where I am not seen and valued.

But being validated is not really about being the hero. A need to be validated assumes that there is a lack of validation to begin with and that I would be a loser if I were not a winner. The reality is that we can be validated just by being who we are. We do not have to show only our "best" side to the world and hide our "lesser" selves. We are only truly seen when we can be comfortable with our whole selves. But it is hard to be okay with who I am, as I am, and put aside my never-ending *Striving* to be a winner. I prefer winning to relaxing. I prefer to stay in doing mode. For me, being in action is about winning. I never think to explore the possibility of doing as a part of being. Just being okay as I am is difficult for me because I would have to trust that I can just be.

3. THE VICIOUS CYCLE

If I were to look at my life objectively, I would notice that I have essentially been trapped in a vicious cycle of fear and scarcity. Because of this, my relationship to love and prosperity is constrained. *Striving* is about trying to be a success and look good. This *Striving* reinforces the fact that I have not won yet and makes me more competitive and determined to succeed. My ego enthusiastically keeps this vicious cycle going. I get addicted to *Striving*.

When we are caught in a vicious cycle where our actions validate our beliefs, it can be very difficult to extricate ourselves. When we are stuck at a certain point along the scarcity-to-abundance spectrum, it is impossible to improve our position until we get out of the vicious cycle. If we are suddenly showered with new wealth, we will most likely dissipate it so that we can get back to our old set point. So in order to create new wealth, we must first become aware of the vicious cycle we are caught in. Once we become aware, we will be in a better position to consciously unblock what blocks us, and welcome new wealth into our lives.

My underlying assumption is that I am not intrinsically worthy and must prove myself to be loved. By working harder, and being better, smarter, and shinier than others, I will achieve the validation that I crave. Having money shows that I am "successful." How much money I make and have are part and parcel of the success metrics I use to measure myself. I use money to buy nice clothes, houses, and cars. Everything in my world, including money, will be a reflection of my winner status. I am hooked on accomplishing more to get more praise, acknowledgement, recognition. I will be the hero and others will know just how valuable I am. Nothing is more important than being productive and achieving success. If I am a loser, I am a nobody, a nothing, a big fat zero.

I believe that my value comes from how others perceive me. I know how to dress appropriately, present well, make a good impression, be a "success." The more I fear being worthless, the more I strive. My compulsive *Striving* is driven by a scarcity feeling that there is not enough validation. It causes me to be imbalanced. I don't have many hobbies. My life is my work. I shut down my heart and go for the gold. Work gives me my identity. I don't have any hesitation to spend money, time and effort on personal development that will reinforce my achievements.

What I don't know is how to fail. I avoid things I might fail at. I shut down the part of me that could go wrong. I cannot be my authentic self. I am ashamed that I must deny my authentic self, but I am so afraid of being exposed as a fraud and failure. This fear requires that I keep up a charade of success. It feels difficult to put my heart out for the world to see. I subsume anything about myself that is unattractive. I expend energy squashing the things that I am ashamed of but can't address – I tell lies, deceiving myself and others. I become disconnected from being "real" and define myself by my superficial qualities. I feel hollow inside, like I am an empty, shiny shell of a person, disconnected from my heart. I don't like the deception, but I don't feel I have any options. I want to be true to myself, but I don't have practice knowing who I am – for so long, I have defined myself by others' definition of success. I so naturally take on others' definition of success that I forget to look inside for what my own definition of success might me. I must learn, at some point, to define success on my own terms. When I can be more honest with myself, I will understand that my beauty comes from within. At some point, I might even realize that I can drop my need to be "successful." I won't have to choose between doing and being.

The defenses I've employed bring about the very worthlessness I fear. *Striving* generates uncertainty about who I really am. The dynamic of the ego structure keeps my ego employed and keeps me perpetually fixated on success and failure. I can never find success for then I would have no excuse for *Striving*. We are each caught in a vicious cycle of our personality and instincts until we decide to break free. This takes deliberate energy and momentum because the cycle is a compelling vortex. In order to create new wealth, we must see clearly the vicious cycle that blocks us from abundance. Then we must fight our way out of the vortex.

4. OPERATIONALLY

If my instincts are balanced, I will be able to attend to money in each of the Nine Money Domains in a healthy manner. If, however, my instincts are not in balance, then I will get stuck in my type fixation and I cannot be optimally effective. My motivation to be successful and validated manifests in different ways depending on my dominant instinct. Instead of addressing areas I won't be successful at, I tend to focus on the areas in which I can achieve. As a SP 3, my *Striving* energy complements my Self-Preservation instinct to be comfortable and at ease. As a SO 3, I am motivated to be a hero. As a SX 3, I focus on being the alluring, irresistible catch. How my instincts are imbalanced will impact how I relate to the Nine Money Domains, where I put my attention and energy, and which Domains I tend to ignore altogether.

"ACHIEVING" SP 3	"HEROIC" SO 3	"DAZZLING" SX 3

Domain 1 – Budgeting

There is a potential discrepancy between my actual behavior and my self-image. Depending on my dominant instinct and level of health, I may be more or less organized around record keeping, tracking, and budgeting. On the one hand, I may be very organized, and diligent about record keeping and budgeting, not because I like to do it, but because it is what successful people do and it allows me to measure my success. On the other hand, because this is an area that is mostly out of view of the outside world, I may be tempted to neglect it. Part of the difficulty with this Domain is that it forces me to look at my own behavior. The more I feel that I have not lived up to expectations, the more ashamed I feel, and the more I want to avoid dealing with budgeting.

As an "Achieving" SP 3, my Self-Preservation instinct wants to be secure and comfortable, and my type energy wants to be successful. I range from being anxious to perfunctory about tracking, budgeting, and categorizing expenses. I try to put away enough for taxes, pay credit card balances, know where I am with money. Budgeting is a way to relieve anxiety that comes from not knowing. It is also a way to track my progress and achievement. But I have a bit of resentment and resistance to this Domain. "Successful" people shouldn't have to worry about money. The more anxious I am about money and security, the more I am tempted to do this Domain "approximately" and get on with the business of earning money.

> I am efficient and data oriented about record keeping. I don't think I'm great at it, but I want to make sure it is done right. I don't balance the checkbook regularly. I do make sure to pay the credit card balance each month. I do make sure I put away enough for taxes. I do my own bookkeeping and know where I am at each moment. I obsess about it pretty much. Mostly I don't mind doing it, but sometimes it drives me crazy. I would never turn over my finances to someone else. I need to have a crystal clear sense of what's going on – that gives me a sense of independence.

> I am very efficient about record keeping, keeping all papers filed properly, being very on top of things, maintaining a good credit rating, never bouncing checks. It's about my image – having an internal image of character and responsibility and looking like I am "together".

> I am not meticulous with record keeping. I don't enjoy doing it, but like that it is done right. I do it "good enough." Bills get paid on time, and put in a folder and labeled paid, and filed sequentially, and I know where to get them. I don't like to make mistakes. I want to get it right.

> I've been tracking my budget for several years now so that I can have more security and options. I have different categories and allowances for different purposes. This gives me peace of mind, but also makes me feel like I am living hand to mouth in scarcity and tightness.

> I do very little tracking or record keeping or budgeting. I have a general idea what comes in and out, and pay a little attention at the end of each month, but I am not too nervous about it and so I don't pay much attention to it. I am more focused on my work.

As I become healthier and less fixated on being "successful," I will find it meaningful and refreshing to know what the facts are, while trusting that things will be alright.

> This year, the budget is becoming less important to me. It's not as crucial anymore. As my anxiety falls, my need to track money falls. Now I am trusting more that I have ability to create it when I need to and everything will be okay. All the money anxiety wasn't serving me well before, worrying about What if I won't have work next month? How am I going to afford this? Now I just figure it will work out some how. I'll figure out a way to make money.

As a "Heroic" SO 3, the degree to which I think about money will depend on whether Self-Preservation is my middle instinct or blindspot instinct. I tend to live more in the present and not be a big saver. I am not very organized around money. Things will not necessarily be at my finger tips, but I manage. I just throw my bills and receipts into a big box, year by year, and pull things out as needed. If Self-Preservation is my middle instinct, budgeting doesn't feel complicated. I will do basic record keeping to uphold my social image even if I don't love doing it. If that requires being decently organized and responsible about money, then I will attempt to do so. I can be efficient about budgeting, and make sure bills are paid on time, that I don't incur late fees, but I am not fastidious. I just want to get things done. If Self-Preservation is my blindspot though, I will tend to be terrible at bookkeeping, record keeping, tracking, and budgeting. I can get overwhelmed at tax time, and feel helpless, even though I don't want to admit how incompetent I feel.

As a "Dazzling" SX 3, I tend to resent having to deal with the tedium of a budget, but I can force myself to do things out of a sense of duty and wanting to get it right. I prefer to be out in the world *Striving* and shining. I like things to be in order, even if I don't enjoy doing the bills and filing. I can get organized, have files year by year, and category, and do financial statements. If Self-Preservation is my blindspot though, the budgeting Domain is very difficult for me. It feels like the tedium of budgeting drains my energy. I don't associate budgeting with anything that would contribute to my success. I want to focus on things that help make me more successful, like eating, exercising, sleeping, networking, traveling. Money doesn't feel like it fits into my picture. For example, I can go several weeks with a letter about being overdrawn on my checking account and I won't do anything about it. I might put entries into my checkbook perfunctorily, but immediately forget what they mean. I'm afraid that budgeting and setting up systems around money will cut off my spontaneity.

> I am terrible at record keeping. It is too detail-oriented for me. I have never been good at the small world of details. I dismiss it. Budgeting feels like I'd have to sit down and work out little stuff and that gives me no energy. In fact, it takes energy away from me. I just recently started entering information into a checkbook and it is not 100% accurate. It's boring, takes time and focus away from what I'm trying to accomplish. I am more disciplined about running than I am about money. I can be very disciplined about things that matter to me.

Domain 2 – Spending

Spending on myself validates me as a winner. The more effectively I play the part of winner, the more confident I feel. I believe I deserve the best that life has to offer because that's how successful people live. I want to look the part, and enhance my image as being together and successful. Depending on my dominant instinct, I am motivated to be successful in meeting my needs, fitting in, and being alluring. All these things require spending.

I would not describe myself as frugal. A better description would be tasteful, with high standards. But I'm adaptable. If the external environment shifts and the standards of "success" change, I can adapt. If conspicuous consumption were inappropriate, I would restrain my spending. In other settings where having a fancy car and fancy address is a sign of "success," I could play that game as well. I am more motivated to avoid shame than I am to avoid deprivation. I can get spooked once in a while by my own extravagant lifestyle, and get anxious about money. And my spending may exceed may income, putting me into a situation where I have to work hard to feed my spending habit.

As an "Achieving" SP 3, I am motivated to project an image of being a successful provider and breadwinner. I like to have nice cars, clothes, houses, personal grooming, and stay in fancy accommodations. My spending ranges from pragmatic to indulgent. On the pragmatic side, I try to get good values. I'd prefer to be frugal than go into debt. On the more indulgent side, I spend on nice clothes for work, cosmetics, and nice jewelry. I want people to think well of me, and my image matters. I don't want to look cheap or poor.

As a "Heroic" SO 3, I am motivated to project an image of being the perfect parent, coach, citizen, and play my social role appropriately and well. I dress appropriately, live appropriately, give appropriately. I like to be generous to show that I am successful, even if I have to borrow to do so. My spending tends to be more indulgent. I am driven to look good and prove my worth. I love to treat myself to luxuries – personal care, massages, haircuts, personal grooming. I drive a nice car, go to nice restaurants, and act like a winner. I also like to be generous, pick up the tab at dinner, take a friend to a spa. "Look what I can do for you." I am not a comparison shopper or haggler.

> When we were working and making a lot of money, we lived life to the limit. We always had credit card debt, but knew we could resolve it if we had to. We bought a huge house in the downtown area. Maybe that was not a good idea because it stretched our income. We tried to do a budget. We realized we were spending twice as much as we earned. I would overspend to compensate for my bad feelings. I have an image of myself as being successful, but it was not supported by the facts. I was very driven to make a good income and a good life for myself. I wanted to feel good about myself and view myself as a success.

As a "Dazzling" SX 3, looking hot, together and professional is my first priority. When I am in my groove, I feel confident about earning and fine about spending. With my kids and lovers, and people I want to impress, I can be very generous. I am attracted to expensive art, fine furniture, fine housing, fine automobiles, luxury landscaping. I tend to spend first, and worry later about how to pay for things. My assumption is that I can figure out how to make the money. When I am not in my groove, and I am more anxious about things, my spending alternates between being disciplined and spontaneous. I can be frugal, like taking a shuttle bus instead of a taxi, or not ordering appetizers, but this is not my general mode of operation. I do this mainly when I get anxious about things. In general, I tend to be spontaneous and impulsive – about things like clothing, personal grooming, and body work. And shopping serves as a pick-me-up when I am feeling down.

Domain 3 – Earning

When it comes to making money, I am very ambitious. I know that the more I adjust myself to external standards and values, the more I will be successful and rewarded. Money and pay validate my sense of worth, and I find it rewarding to be successful this way. I gravitate to work where there are immediate rewards and payoffs, such as sales and commission-based jobs.

As an "Achieving" SP 3, I am very determined to be successful in my work in order to garner company recognition, industry accolades, and good pay. I push myself to work hard to make money because a good standard of living is the most important thing to me. My Self-Preservation instinct drives my fear of scarcity and disruption. I get anxious if my bank account balance drops below some threshold. I feel great when I am earning money and making things happen. I can easily become a workaholic, pushing myself to the point of exhaustion to get stuff done and be successful at work. Work is where I have a firm identity and feel in my element. Commission-based income is even more addictive than working for a promotion. The rewards are so clear, and the correlation between input and output so obvious. My Self-Preservation instinct makes me reluctant to work 16+ hours a day on a sustained basis because that would not be a comfortable lifestyle. However, my ego might override my Self-Preservation instinct and force me to work beyond what is healthy for me. The more insecure I feel, the more compelled I am to overwork. But, in general, I prefer a job where I can work decent hours. I don't mind taking calculated risks for my career, but I don't crave risk. What I like to do is be in an environment where I am constantly busy and challenged to achieve. That keeps me occupied and focused. My Self-Preservation instinct causes me to be a private person who likes to work on my own. I do not naturally like to network and and beg for work. I'd rather focus on my own work. Working in a large corporation suits me well because I can earn a stable salary. I am not good at relaxing and taking time off. Idle time feels like wasted time which I could be using to be productive, and makes me edgy.

As a "Heroic" SO 3, I am motivated to be the family and community hero. I don't want to disappoint others. I know how to jump through hoops, but I question whether this is really what I want. I worry I've sold myself out, but my dilemma is how do I do fulfilling work that pays well.

Because the question of my worth is so emotionally charged, I struggle to know whether I am charging too much or too little. Typically, I end up either doing work where I undercharge, but can make a difference socially so that I feel like a hero, or I end up taking a job where I am paid well, but feel like I have sold my soul to do it. In either case, it feels difficult to earn money in a way that is aligned to my authentic self.

> I have difficulty in setting rates and holding myself to them. It is a dilemma. I have difficulty distinguishing my inherent value and my sense of myself as a coach, and the value of an hour of my time. Am I charging too much or not enough? Having a conversation about money is not natural for me. My superego punishes me for not making enough money.

> For me, the nature of the job has always been more important than what I made. I teach at church – I never felt like I wasn't making enough, but I always took on extra jobs if there were any. I do not choose my path or career based on money calculations. My orientation was always to work with people.

> I pushed myself hard to work a lot. But money has not been my main motivator. My sense of identity was more important to me. But I need to make money now. I have had a private business for six years, but I still can't support myself fully on it. I am trying to break through the denial and create more structure around money for myself now.

As a "Dazzling" SX 3, I've taken risks and haven't worried much about money. I generally follow what interests and juices me up. When I have my mojo, I have optimism and don't worry about money. If the money is not there, I know how to be a rainmaker because I'm a good salesperson. I'm very good at presenting, promoting, and marketing. I have an innate sense of how to work a room, make a good impression, and say what is needed to move things forward. I could be very rich because I get a kick out of hard work, and it is stimulating and exciting. When I am humming along though, I can get cocky and screw things up. Sometimes, I think I unconsciously bring myself down just so I have the challenge of coming back again. The rush of having to get into gear and fire up my brain really turns me on. I can get quite emotional about failure and success. But I am learning to be calmer. I am a hard worker by nature, a doer. But the downside is that I could have no real life and become the kind of person who steps on others.

When I am less confident, I become very competitive and hard working, wanting to be successful. I strive to impress others and I can become all bluster in trying to pump myself up. If a better job opportunity comes along, I wouldn't hesitate to take it. Because so much of my identity is linked to my work identity, being fired or laid off can be a huge blow. It is humiliating because it feels like I am valueless.

> I have a compulsive striving. I worked 60-70 hour weeks when I was younger. I was trying to get promoted quickly in my late 20s and 30s. Then, I hit a place where it didn't matter anymore. I was under stress and just disappeared. I was in a tenuous space. I knew I would get laid off and not make a big income and thought my husband wouldn't love me anymore. It was all crap. Layoffs were humiliating and it felt so shameful that I couldn't hold a job.

I need to learn to stop performing to please others so that I can please myself. I need to learn to honor my own heart. Even if I am not as successful in my new work, at least I will be doing what I enjoy doing. Ultimately, my journey is to learn that I do not have to strive to be worthy. I am inherently of value.

> I had to do something else. My work was crushing my spirit. But I was scared. I had no faith that I'd know what to do. I didn't doubt that I would succeed. But the question was – what am I going to do? What is the work going to be? I was terrified of letting go of my old identity. I had to learn to trust that things would work out. That was a gateway to the joy I'm experiencing now in my work. A level of joy that is not about performing to please others, but to serve. That's very gratifying and a big shift for me. I can slow down. I am becoming more balanced. I can work part time and be happy.

When I finally find work that I really love, I can be more fully who I am and trust that life will unfold the way it is supposed to. I will most likely work till the day I die because I enjoy my work so much.

> I will work till the day I die. I enjoy my work, it's fun, and I love it, but I am trying to do other things besides work. Work gives me my identity. It gives me a buzz. I took a look at the sacrifices I'd have to make to keep on performing for others, and I realized that I wanted to be my authentic self.

Domain 4 – Beliefs

My main belief about money is that money is a marker of success. It may not be my only marker of success, but it certainly validates my value in society. As an "Achieving" SP 3, I believe that I have to work hard to earn money, and that money gives me options and helps me control my destiny. It gives me security and stability. The more work I do and the more value I provide, the more money I will make.

> Money represents service I do in the world. The more service, the better service, the more money will come in. Money is a measure of success. The money I make helps me have confidence in the work I am doing. The money validates and feeds me.

As a "Heroic" SO 3, money may or may not be my currency of success. It depends on the social group I run in. My marker of success might be money, but it also might be innovation and creativity, academic achievement, doing social good, being a good mom. Whatever it is, I want people to think of me as together and successful. I don't want to seem incompetent or immature about money. If money is my currency of success, then I need to make money in order to prove my worth.

> Money represents my self-worth. If I'm not making money, how do I prove my worth? I stayed in my corporate career for as long as I did, because I was a somebody then. I liked the good title.

> I want to be competent about things, including money. I want to have the image that everything is fine and I have abundance and I have it all together. I don't want to feel immature, incompetent, or come off seeming this way.

> Money is not my metric of success. I think very little about money. I think more about my career. My values have very little to do with money. Money is an afterthought. My currency of success is innovation and creativity.

> I care that people think of me as successful. I do like being a perfect mom. I felt I had to justify my existence as a housewife by being productive, easy, and put together. The image is so important to me. I like having well groomed kids, and I am an incredible time manager. I have food ready, laundry done, I make everything look so easy, I have social energy. I have energy to project confidence and being well-organized. I don't feel I use money to keep up that image. I try to be economical.

As a "Dazzling" SX 3, I may or may not believe that money is the most important thing to focus on. I am motivated to follow my passion, and focus on my relationships and my health. I want to focus on what I want, and if other things are trying to drag me down, I have no problem throwing money at the problem to make it go away. I know that I can go and make more money. But money is important to me because it marks my value, worth, and status.

My least favorite topic is money because I hate that it is a marker of value and worth. I've had to learn to trust that I would not be abandoned when I didn't have money.

Money is important for my image. I am competitive. My friends are building their house on a mountain and I have a strong impulse to best them.

The focus on money has steered me to shallow, competitive terrain. My early conditioning rendered me to believe that money is all important. I've found it difficult to strike a balance between money and being normal.

Domain 5 – Understanding

By modern day social values, understanding money is part and parcel of being competent, effective and successful. I want to understand money so that I can feel competent and effective. As a hard-charging, determined type, I might deal with this is by being proactive at gaining knowledge and understanding. My comparative mind stimulates me to look at my competition and those who have "made it," and figure out how to be successful as well. If I don't feel competent at money myself, I might surround myself with people who know about money and try to soak up the knowledge by osmosis.

I figure knowledge is power, so I make it a point to meet regularly with my accountant so that I can try to get a better handle on the numbers from a broader perspective. I also try to read the Wall Street Journal every morning to stay on top of things.

On the other hand, money can be an emotionally charged topic for me, and I might be so embarrassed about my lack of competency that I have trouble reaching out for help. I might be able to force myself to get focused and energized about what I need to do, but I might also end up trying to cover up these feelings of inadequacy and procrastinating about learning and taking charge of money in my life. I am not used to feeling incompetent. I know that everyone has areas of incompetence, but I am particularly hard on myself about feeling inadequate. If I am insecure about money, then I try to compensate by working harder in other areas. I will let someone else manage my money, and I will muddle through.

I feel embarrassed about not having it together at this age. I fear being judged. That has prevented me from reaching out for help. It has prevented me from being serious about it. I am not kind to myself about this. I have an inner critic always in this area.

If Self-Preservation is my blindspot, learning and understanding money feels doubly difficult for me. I don't know how to deal with money, can't control it, and need someone to do it for me. I don't want to know much about what's going on with my money for fear that I'll have to do something about it. I am so afraid of being exposed as a fraud that I try to keep my feelings of inadequacy at bay. I don't want others to see that I've made bad decisions and am ignorant about things. I've spent my energy trying to look successful, have the right image, car, house, so that I could fit in. I've pushed myself to be the leader, but underneath I've been scared.

> I have difficulty putting attention on something that brings up so much charged emotions. When I had to track expenses more closely, I was shocked by how much I spend. I really don't want to go into the inner depths of my emotions and feel the pain. It felt easier just to keep the murky, conflicted stuff at bay, and not get clean about it. I did this till I could no longer keep it all at bay.

Domain 6 – Risk Management

This is not an area that I worry too much about. I try to be matter of fact about managing risk and move on with my life. As an "Achieving" SP 3, I worry about the downside of things, but try to be proactive in preventing bad things from happening. One way I manage risk is by playing it safe and being conservative with my investments and my career. I try to be planful for the short to medium term to avoid disruptions. It's easy for me to get worried and worked up about things. But I mainly push my feelings of anxiety away. I want to be self-reliant and not have to count on others. The fact that it's up to me to do things properly, but not all in my control, makes me anxious.

As a "Heroic" SO 3, I tend to range from conservative to moderate about risk. As an image-based type, the cost of failing spectacularly is much greater than the benefit of making a bit more money with my investments. I try to make sure I have financial resources in case something bad happens. I have an illusion of control. It may be in the form of savings, a line of credit, or simply a credit card. I prefer to be conservative and have a solid base rather than take a risk and lose. And I know that there are people who can help. For example, I have hired an investment advisor to manage my money and I trust him and things have gone pretty well.

As a "Dazzling" SX 3, I may be more daring with my career and my investments. I have an instinct for challenge and an appetite for big gains. I tend to rely on myself and not expect support from others. I try to put money away for emergencies, but mostly I rely on my own good health and energy to get me through life. I am pretty hopeful, optimistic about my future, and don't worry much about what might go wrong.

Domain 7 – Planning

I believe it is up to me to create the life I want for myself. But depending on my dominant instinct, I might not plan much. As an "Achieving" SP 3, I want to have a good life and be able to retire. A certain amount of planning is required for me to have the life I want. I don't necessarily aspire to optimizing my life; I'm more interested in the steps needed to be successful in the way I care about. It seems like a good idea to have different buckets set up for education, emergencies, retirement, vacations, etc. Planning for the near and medium term feels more concrete than the long-term. It's not always easy to afford everything at once, or have a fix on the actual numbers. I try my best, but things can feel tight. I expect to work for a long time. As a "Heroic" SO 3, I am not that goal-oriented around money. I've always wanted to do more saving but I defer it till later because, with all the spending demands today, it's difficult to have much left over. As a "Dazzling" SX 3, I am happy to let someone else do the planning. I assume the money will come as long as I am doing what I love. I am not that interested in money plans or goals because this feels too restrictive. I am more of a big picture person. I need to know what is going on, and I want to be in control. I might do what I need to do and put away some money, but not have a deep or rigorous relationship to money. I do find the vision and goal thing very interesting and going after it and the big picture quite engaging, but I have difficulty focusing on little goals and details. I tend to be more spontaneous than planful. I tend to bite off more than I can chew, challenge myself, and then figure out how to do it. I don't really plan ahead a lot.

Domain 8 – Wealth Building

In general, I base my validation on my income; my net worth and wealth are secondary signals of my success. As such, my focus tends to gravitate more towards current earnings than wealth building. When I force myself to save, it tends to be earmarked for various expenditures.

> I have to build wealth because I don't want to die a poor old man and I want to be secure and taken care of.

> I want to set aside money to buy and sell stocks and do some general investing. But right now, I don't have the funds for that. I'm just barely making ends meet right now.

If I feel competent and invest in the stock market, I tend to be the kind of investor who wants fast results. I track the performance of my investments carefully, and sell things that aren't doing well. I can be a very active trader. When stocks rise, I get very excited and get a high from it. When stocks fall, I want to sell and cut my losses. My overconfidence in my own abilities coupled with my emotionality can undermine my skills as an investor.

If I do not feel competent about investing, I will be more conservative. There is a part of me that doesn't trust things that I can't see or touch. I want to be able to understand what my money is invested in, and I will not try to time the market. I value my liquidity and flexibility more than the potential for larger returns. I might hire someone to manage my money for me, and only get involved once in a while to stay on top of things. I don't hate it, but I don't want to take the time to do it myself. I know there is a lot that I cannot control, and that makes me more anxious and conservative.

Domain 9 – Balance

I have a lot of difficulty feeling abundance and prosperity. Even if I have a large income or am wealthy, I am always striving for more. Even though I may project a confidence and optimism, inside I always harbor doubts. I feel I need to keep it all together, stay in control, be the doer. I put pressure on myself to succeed, and I also feel pressure from others to be the hero. I constantly push myself to try harder. It is difficult to feel supported by the universe. I feel that it is up to me to take care of myself.

> When I was young, the only thing that mattered for me were the levels above me – not where I was currently. I compared myself to external benchmarks that were always unattainable.

My pain is around trust and wondering where the money is going to come from – that can evoke anxiety in me. I don't want to deal with money. Maybe it has something to do with worth and value and what money represents.

The fear of not earning or having enough money stems from needing to prove myself. My sense of scarcity is right at the surface of my consciousness. I don't believe that abundance or love is my right. I believe that I must earn it. The moment I disguise my true emotions to avoid being a failure, I have given up on being loved. The more I try to be validated, the more it cancels out the validation that is already here. It is difficult for me not to get freaked out by downturns and ebbs because it feels like failure. When my confidence is shaken, I can get really unhinged because that's exactly what I have been trying to keep at bay. The dichotomy of success and failure keeps me anxious and edgy. It is hard to relax and trust.

5. THE PARADOX

The fundamental paradox is that *Striving* never leads to validation. It only leads to more *Striving*. Not only is the actual outcome the opposite of my original intent, but it can never be otherwise. What is value? Is value something I can create? Does value come from what I do? Is value a scarce commodity that some have and others do not? *Striving* is supposed to help me be of value. But when I overdo this strategy, I actually feel less valued. My denial of my basic support keeps me from connecting to my true nature, which would enable me to trust. The defenses I've employed bring about the very futility that I fear.

The paradox is that *Striving* causes me to disconnect from the thing I care most about, which is to be validated as valuable. I forget that my value does not come from doing and achieving. There is a part of me that knows that I am effortlessly radiant and glorious. But honoring this part of myself would create conflict with my ego structure, and that tension would be too much for me to bear. I sense that I am being blackmailed into *Striving* and that this entire structure is built on one of fear, but I do not know how to move past the fear. The more I fear being worthless, the more I perform. In continuing to strive, I can never reach an endpoint.

The paradox is that in always performing a role, I forget who I am. In always saying yes to life, I cannot relax and just experience myself as a radiant part of the universe. In *Striving*, I cannot avoid the shame. In learning to relax and stop doing, I can experience myself and feel my value. When I feel my value, I am validated.

6. BREAKING THE VICIOUS CYCLE

In order to break the vicious cycle of my personality, and move from Fear to Love, I must embrace and resolve the fundamental paradox of *Striving*. I have spend my whole life performing to please others, cut off from my own intrinsic value. I am ashamed that I must perform to prove my worth. How can I just be myself? What incredible possibilities could exist if I didn't have to hide my true feelings? In keeping the fear of failure at bay, I have also kept away the love. As I throw off the shackles of my personality and orient to my true nature, I begin to own the whole me. When I do this, I move past my story of being a winner and not a loser.

My journey with money is a journey to authenticity. My journey to my true self requires me to connect my heart to my head and body so that I can honor my authentic self. I don't need to perform to be of value. I do not have to pretend to be someone that I am not. In surrendering to my core nature, I become embodied Love, with compassion in my heart, wisdom in my head, and well-being in my body. I now occupy a much vaster reality. I experience my vaster identity, and feel effortlessly radiant. I trust that I am exactly as I am meant to be. In embracing these truths, I can move past my old beliefs and patterns and welcome abundance, prosperity, and love into my life. I can begin to feel more supported and relaxed. But this is not comfortable or easy. I feel the pain as my ego resists losing its job. I feel remorseful about how I have lived my life and hurt myself and others. I am scared that I won't be able to survive on my own deeper knowing alone.

When I live abundantly, I feel intrinsically valued. I no longer feel scarcity because of my need to have more validation and confirmation. I trust that the universe supports me and I can relax. I feel abundant because I know that I am part of the effortless functioning of the universe. I don't need to perform a role. When I am simply here, as myself, I will be doing what I need to be doing. I can accept my essential nature and trust that I am intrinsically of value. Because I am gloriously radiant just as I am, I can be authentically who I am, sourced from something much greater than I had ever imagined.

	Brief Description
"Achieving" SP 3	I focus on being successful in the self-preservation realm. I want stability, security, a good standard of living, and to be a good provider. Money is an important metric of how well I am doing. I don't want to look cheap. I am determined to be successful at work and garner recognition, accolades, and good pay. I can easily become a workaholic, thinking about work all the time. Work is where I have a firm identity and feel in my element.
"Heroic" SO 3	I am motivated to project an image of being the perfect parent, coach, citizen, and play my social role well. I dress appropriately, live appropriately, give appropriately. I am driven to look good and prove my worth. I like to be generous to show that I am a winner. I don't think the upside reward is as big as the potential loss of the downside, so I'd rather be more conservative with investments.
"Dazzling" SX 3	I want to dazzle and shine. Looking hot, together and professional is my first priority. I want to impress. When I am in my groove, I feel confident about making money and like to spend on the finer things of life. Tedious stuff in the background does not have juice for me. I tend to spend first, and worry later about how to pay for things. When I am not in my groove, I can get anxious, and my spending will alternate between disciplined and impulsive.

Type 3	Summary
Gift	Being an exemplar of value, an embodiment of human potential.
Unconscious Belief	I am not fully seen.
Strategy	*Striving* – achieving accolades, receiving admiration, being recognized and lauded, so that I can be fully seen and validated.
Vicious Cycle	Because I need to be seen and validated, I must continue to earn external recognition for my good work, achievements, and accomplishments. I must focus on winning. But because I cannot fail, I feel even less seen for who I really am.
Defended Against	Being supported.
Operationally	• It's up to me to be the hero. • I must be a winner. • I focus only on the areas that I can be successful at.
Paradox	*Striving* does not generate validation.
Breaking the Vicious Cycle	I must recognize that the universe supports me. It is not up to me to generate validation. I am intrinsically of value. My job is to be my glorious, radiant self.
Direction of Growth	Relaxing, not compulsively striving allows me to be authentic, real.

CHAPTER 10

PERSONALIZING

Type 4

1. GIFT

I am connected to the intangible magic of our existence – that which expresses the authentic nature of who we are. I care about having moments of real connection, real depth, real intimacy with who we are. By being my unique self, I contribute something special and important to the world. If we were all the same, life would be boring and dreary. Our individuality is at the foundation of our humanity. Out of my uniqueness, creations blossom that have never been seen by this world before.

Part of what makes me special is my particular life difficulties and personal flaws. I embrace my flaws, inadequacies, pain, and suffering as a part of who I am. My suffering allows me to feel life deeply, and experience both the lows and the highs. I intuitively understand that my suffering is never for naught. My pain and suffering not only fuel my creativity, but also help me to grow and heal. When I suffer through and through, I am humbled, my passions are conquered, and the world no longer has any further power over me. My suffering brings me to my knees, and I am forced to surrender and give up my will. I recognize that the worst suffering can bring the greatest renewal.

2. STRATEGY

My life and money strategy grow out of my sense of the critical importance of having a stable identity and knowing who I am. *Personalizing* is about being connected with my authenticity and recognizing the universal appeal of an authentic story. In *Personalizing,* I ascribe personal meaning to each of my experiences and want to express my unique nature. I like to surround myself with memories, treasures, and other meaningful momentos. I am attached to my history and my stories. Everything has personal meaning: my work, my spending, my home, my gifts. My outward identity reflects me back to myself, so that I can feel my stable identity. *Personalizing,* a strategy emphasizing my uniqueness, is distinct from *Ordering*. Though both strategies are idealistic, *Personalizing* emphasizes aligning to personal meaning, while *Ordering* emphasizes aligning to what is universally right and good.

Because ordinary equates to being without identity, I over-focus on how I am unique, different, and flawed. But in focusing on who I am and what makes me special, I fail to see how my humanity connects me to others and how I share much in common with others, including pain, inadequacies, neediness, and mortality. Denying the universality of my experience fills me with yearning and shame because I cannot honor what is ordinary and yet good in me, and I continue to feel that there is something missing. Without being able to connect to what is universal in me, I can never have what I long for.

Personalizing creates a vicious cycle of emphasizing my flaws and suffering to be unique, thereby generating a feeling that something is missing that I yearn for but cannot find. I need to embrace not just my uniqueness, but also my ordinariness. But this feels unnatural to me because if I were ordinary, I would not be special. What is unique about me does not feel fundamental, fixed, or universal. It feels determined by my emotions that are ever changing and subjective. I do not entertain the possibility that my personal uniqueness might be grounded in what is universally good. Connecting to my grounded, intelligent, dignified, knowing self and discovering what is good and perfect in me is difficult because it requires that I shift my perspective from flaws to features. True identity comes when we can own our whole nature, not just a portion of it. It embraces our flaws, but also our perfection and dignity. Only when I can embrace my true nature and true identity can I be attuned to the love that is here for us all.

3. THE VICIOUS CYCLE

If I were to look at my life objectively, I would notice that I have essentially been trapped in a vicious cycle of fear and scarcity. Because of this, my relationship to love and prosperity is constrained. *Personalizing* is fundamentally about trying to be unique and express my identity because I do not feel I have a true identity. This orientation makes me feel like something is missing in me. But my ego enthusiastically keeps this vicious cycle going so that it can keep its job. I get addicted to *Personalizing*. Even though I think I am moving along, I am merely moving in place.

When we are caught in a vicious cycle where our actions validate our beliefs, it can be very difficult to extricate ourselves. When we are stuck at a certain point along the scarcity-to-abundance spectrum, it is impossible to improve our position until we get out of the vicious cycle. If we are suddenly showered with new wealth, we will most likely dissipate it so that we can get back to our old set point. So in order to create new wealth, we must first become aware of the vicious cycle we are caught in. Once we become aware, we will be in a better position to consciously unblock what blocks us, and welcome new wealth into our lives.

My underlying assumption is that I am different. I yearn for belonging and satisfaction, but cannot expect it from this world. I long to be connected to a sense of home, a place where I am from, that would provide me with a stable identity. Home would be comfortable and easy, not a chore. But it feels like in this world, satisfaction is not mine to be had. Though I do not expect to be satisfied in this world, I do what I can to attune my environment to my personal sensibilities, and to what is beautiful and speaks to me.

Because I am an exception, I don't live by the same rules that others do. I don't try to be like others, hold myself to the same standards or compete on the same basis. I see what others have and how happy others seem, and I wonder why I can't have that. I am envious but do not feel that I could ever be like them. Truthfully, I'm kind of proud of it. But it's lonely. I try to celebrate being different. But, oh how I suffer. I struggle to be understood. I struggle to understand. I struggle to connect. I struggle to be comfortable in my own skin. No one understands how hard it is being me.

Who am I? I think that my feelings and how I express them define who I am. The more I suffer, the more unique and special I am. I am reluctant to get too pulled into life's demands for fear that I would lose myself in the world. I like to give myself time to be me. I yearn for that which is missing in me. I try to address my longing by connecting to the feelings that produce that longing. I think that I can get satisfaction by going deep into my internal world and whatever difficult feelings exist there. I have a sense that I am at the same time inferior and superior to others. I am broken, outcast, and a victim. And yet at the same time, I am above it all. I have more integrity, more class, more taste than other people. Being different is both a curse and a blessing. It is difficult being so different and I suffer from it. At the same time, my difference makes me special. I suffer more than most, but I also feel more deeply than most. I have always had the sense that I should not avoid my pain and suffering, and that my suffering would bring me closer to my freedom. I can't explain how I know this. If things were always good, then we would never yearn for anything beyond what is in front of us, and there would be no redemption and no salvation.

The "real" world feels like a dream, while my private world of books, secret tunnels, and tall trees feel more real. My private worlds enable me to fantasize about an alternative life, but hold me back from being an insider who belongs and feels invested here. I am convinced there must be an alternate world that is more vivid, more real and sensible. I am frustrated and disappointed that I can't seem to find this place. But I am convinced it exists. I can feel it in my bones. I bumble through this world, doing what is necessary to survive, but always believing that there is something more beckoning me. In this place, I am enveloped in love and welcomed. In this place, I finally know who I am because I am home. I often get mixed up between being in the "real" world and in the "dream" world. In the dream world, I am royalty and can have what I want. In the "real" world, I feel I ought to be able to have what I want as well. I forget the normal "rules" that apply in the real world. I tend to believe that my thoughts can have an effect on the world in a manner not governed by ordinary laws. It doesn't feel like I actually need to do anything to make things so. If I dream it, then it becomes real for me. This can lead to incredible denial, but also great creativity.

For someone who engages in wishful thinking, feels entitled, and struggles, one would not expect to find resilience. Yet, I have a strong belief that nothing can really keep me down. Material setbacks are nothing. I can bounce back from my difficulties and pain. Something inside me knows that through suffering, I can be renewed. I know that I can always be creative and resourceful if the chips are down. I may have troubles and problems, but things have always worked out. I may not be able to have everything, but I just have this feeling that things will be okay. I've had lots of money and been dead broke and everywhere in between. I am not afraid to be poor. I don't want to be poor, but I don't associate my value with how much money I have either. It's part of why I can't really get too excited about money. I just know I can do whatever it takes to make money if I need to.

I actually feel, inside, more competent than I probably let on. I know at some level that my playing the victim and sufferer is a sham, and that I am much more powerful than I can even admit to.   It may seem like a contradiction when I say that I feel like a victim, but know I can survive. When you are a victim and survive, you learn that you can bounce back, which gives you a tremendous sense of resilience.

I need to express myself and do what fits for me. Money in itself is not motivating for me. My ambition for money and material things is limited to what is personally meaningful to me. I prefer that someone else takes care of it for me. I am reluctant to participate in the material world because I fear it would block my creativity and authenticity. I refuse to be money hungry like others because that seems base and crude. I take the moral high ground, feeling defiant and superior. I am convinced that my creative juices would not flow if I were concerned about making a buck. I cannot imagine being able to straddle both worlds skillfully.

For me, fighting about money seems crass. I would much rather maintain a good relationship than fight about money. If a spouse or someone else becomes angry or aggressive with me, I would rather withdraw than stand up for myself. Feeling vulnerable, I tend to go along rather than push for a difficult conversation that may be necessary to establish healthy boundaries. I believe I can get emotional stability by pulling away from the world, but this pulls me back into the quagmire of my own emotions and takes energy away from my life in the real world.

I don't and can't do things in the normal way that others do. I don't relate to life in the same way that others do. I am skeptical and wary of the material world that seems banal, mundane, ordinary. Being different enables me to maintain the emotional charge around being misunderstood and keeps me away from feeling capable. This sense of wanting what is missing, but having minimal expectation of getting it, mires me in envy and holds me back from action. I am more apt to stay in my envy than to take action to make my dreams come true. I tend to work below my potential. I feel inertial when I think I ought to do something that has no emotional resonance for me. Everything that I do needs to have deep and resonant meaning for me. Learning to deal with mundane things in a skillful way without reactivity is a growing edge for me.

I take things personally. Everything has personal meanings and connections for me. But the sense that I am not home, that I do not belong, makes me feel that I can never be truly nourished. My sense of scarcity comes from my fear that I am a nobody. I try to navigate between how things are and how things ought to be. It always seems that there is something better out there, but I can't have it – a better job, a better relationship, more self-confidence. This longing keeps me away from the reality in front of me. I am resigned to be envious, instead of motivated to go after things. To the extent that I do participate in the material world, I struggle. Sometimes I live hand to mouth with high personal debt and late bill payments. I can feel stranded in a system that does not reward my talents or interests. I can't seem to hold on to money I do get. I always seem to be working against something. What I don't see is that my aversion to the material world creates struggles that I am secretly proud of. In my struggling, I can be more unique.

At the conscious level, I believe that my struggles are due to the fact that I am not competent and I am a victim because others prevent me from getting what I want. I tend to behave like a martyr and let others get what they want from me. I am willing to carry burdens, both emotionally and physically, and let myself be used, abused, and abandoned. I may also act irresponsibly towards myself. For example, I overspend on my credit card, and then spend years paying off my balance. Then right after I get out of my mess, the whole pattern repeats itself again. So even if I do get out of a hole, I just dig another hole. I am also vulnerable to being duped by service providers, contractors, and others who are paid to help me. These struggles are tiresome, but somehow keep repeating. The dynamic of the ego structure keeps my ego employed and keeps me perpetually fixated on what's meaningful and what's mundane. I can never find my identity for then I would have no excuse for *Personalizing*. We are each caught in a vicious cycle of our personality and instincts until we decide to break free. This takes deliberate energy and momentum because the cycle is a compelling vortex. In order to create new wealth, we must see clearly the vicious cycle that blocks us from abundance. Then we must fight our way out of the vortex.

4. OPERATIONALLY

If my instincts are balanced, I will be able to attend to money in each of the Nine Money Domains in a healthy manner. I understand what is universal about the personal and can nurture myself and others. I do not stay resigned in my suffering, but use my suffering as a catalyst for creativity and inspiration. This balance helps me engage without losing my connection to myself. If, however, my instincts are not in balance, then I get stuck in my type fixation and I cannot be optimally effective. My motivation to personalize things manifests in different ways depending on my dominant instinct. I tend to focus on areas that are most personally meaningful to me and ignore areas I deem mundane. As a SP 4, my *Personalizing* energy is focused on connecting my well-being and security to what is personally meaningful. As a SO 4, my *Personalizing* energy contradicts my Social instinct and I am torn between pulling in and going outwards. As a SX 4, my *Personalizing* energy reinforces my Sexual instinct and I focus on my personal drama and intensity of experience. How my instincts are imbalanced will therefore impact how I relate to the Nine Money Domains – where I put my attention and energy and where I don't.

"AESTHETE" SP 4	"OUTSIDER" SO 4	"DRAMATIST" SX 4

Domain 1 – Budgeting

The choices I make are driven by what makes sense for me personally, and how I can express who I am, even if they are not financially optimal. I don't naturally gravitate to having a structured budget in my life, and it can be difficult for me to keep my spending aligned with my income. Discipline and consistency can be very good for me, but it can be difficult to create this for myself. When I do make an effort to maintain a holding container around my finances, I feel proud. The sense of discipline gives me self-respect.

My spending tends to be driven by what feels right for me in the moment, and is inherently unconstrained. It doesn't generally occur to me that money should or could get in my way. I tend to feel free and unbounded by financial constraints, and carried by my emotions and feelings. Having to live by a budget can trigger feelings of being undeserving and denied, which I am very sensitive to. I would rather someone else hold me accountable than hold myself accountable. It's not that I explicitly try to break free of constraints. It's more that I simply imagine constraints away. I don't tend to think about money as a factor one way or the other. I don't want to be foolhardy, but I would rather others deal with it on my behalf.

As a "Aesthete" SP 4, I tend to have some internal sense of expenses, even if I don't track them concretely. I am more concerned with not having any money than getting more of it. I can manage the money and make sure there is enough to pay for what we need. I am willing to sacrifice and do a budget if there is something tangible that I want to buy with the savings. But saving for the future is a bit too abstract to motivate me. If I have enough, and don't have to think about it, that suits me fine. I'll have things like retirement contributions and insurance fees deducted automatically if I can, so that I don't have to think about it. I might be able to stay on a budget for a few days, weeks, or months if I had to, but don't generally feel the need to do so.

I tend not to be very organized or diligent about record keeping and tracking where the money goes. I may misplace papers, fail to file insurance claims, fail to pay bills on time, etc. The mundane tasks of life can get out of hand and overwhelm me. When I sit down to do it, I can do it well since I love to organize, sort, and get things done. My problem is that I don't want to do it regularly. For example, even though the rest of my house is beautiful, with candles, organized books, and a clean kitchen, my office might be a disaster with random piles of paper everywhere. Papers are always coming in and going out and I am not always in the mood to attend to things that require regular attention. When I am in a healthier place, I can manage mundane tasks. But when I am in my emotional stew, this part of my life simply falls apart.

If I am married, and if my spouse isn't inclined to be on a budget, I will happily go along. I don't really want to admit how much money I spend and am happy to abdicate responsibility. It's a way to share a special relationship with my partner, even if it isn't the healthiest behavior. If, however, my spouse is even less able than I am to do a budget, I can step up to the plate. The relational dynamics will tend to determine the role I play in the household finances.

As an "Outsider" SO 4, I feel inadequate around Self-Preservation matters like managing my finances. Often I don't know how much I earn in a year, or how much I spend, so budgeting can be a big challenge for me. I believe I deserve good things, and I can run up credit card debt with high interest rates, and not even realize it. Reality often doesn't cooperate with me. When money is scarce, I might be afraid to open a bill. I get depressed and begrudgingly pay the bill, but it is a horrible ordeal. It feels like "Poor pitiful me." I want to blame others for my financial troubles. It's easier to play the victim than to own up to my own responsibility.

As an outsider, I fantasize about a life where I am nourished and happy. I may use money to buy myself some self-care, but it doesn't really help because I am still in the longing mode. The truth is that I crave a holding container where I am supported in being who I am. Without boundaries, I am apt to get sucked into other people's agendas. Being more intentional about my spending, my work, my life, helps me to be more contained. And these boundaries enable me to take care of myself and rejuvenate. With a budget, I can really see how my spending and income support me and get me out of my story about not deserving and not being capable. The tracking of expenses and being more conscious of the budget helps me to feel more contained. It helps me not get lost in my feelings so much. I don't have to do more work processing emotions than I have to. I can allow myself material comforts without feeling guilty. I can also see that I am nurtured by my spending and am not really deprived. Being able to be contained and disciplined and do these normal things allows me to feel like I can belong, self-nurture, and participate in the real world.

As a "Dramatist" SX 4, I am more concerned with finding the charge and intensity. If Self-Preservation is my blindspot, money almost never crosses my mind. This can lead me into terrible debt. I use a lot of denial. My drawers can be full of unpaid bills and I just keep the drawers closed. I want to avoid feeling desperate even if my financial situation is not stable. I focus on my passion, and other things that are not as interesting fall by the wayside. I am terrible at record keeping. I try not to overspend, but there are certain things that I must spend on, including my looks and my body. These are not discretionary! I can be good with money if I force myself to pay attention. Having a tactile and visual record keeping system with folders and labels helps. Anything which makes money more concrete helps bring it to my attention. But generally speaking, managing the mundane matters of life don't interest me much. Money seems abstract and numbers feel like they have no relevancy to my daily life and concerns. I have to psyche myself out to do bill paying. I forget money that people owe me, forget to file for reimbursements, and forget to deposit checks, pay bills, etc. My Sexual instinct drives me to gravitate to challenges and the juicier parts of life.

Domain 2 – Spending

There's nothing consistent about my spending. I don't allow limits to keep me from living the life I believe I ought to be living. Even when someone tells me that money is short, it's hard for me to believe them. There must be a way to create and have what I want. I feel like royalty and like to treat myself as such. I love to live in glorious places, eat good food, drink fine wines, travel to exotic places. I have a taste for luxury and beauty.

I like to buy what inspires me. I want the freedom to go to a gallery and buy art that I like, buy gifts to make others happy, go to the movies, play, travel. I love beautiful things – art, jewelry, clocks, crystals, carvings, paintings, clothing, shoes. I buy clothes that reflect my style and personality. I buy jewelry and mementos that have sentimental value. I try to personalize my travel so that it will be meaningful and provide lasting memories. The place I choose to live in reflects my aesthetics and my temperament. If the experience or thing I buy is meaningful, then the money feels well spent.

My spending is also driven by my sense of image. I want to display my good taste and my sense of quality and beauty. For example, I love my hand-painted mosaics, my china pieces, and rare books. I have a closet full of jewelry and memorabilia. I have nostalgia for the past that connects me to who I am. Even if my acquisitions become almost unmanageable, I bring them with me when I move. I can't get rid of things that are a part of who I am. Some things really are priceless. If I am willing to buy it, then it must be worth it. On the other hand, ostentatiousness and pretentiousness make my blood boil because it insults those who have more fine-tuned sensibilities.

I am willing to live on very little, but when I do indulge, I want no limits. I want to be able to have a complete experience, with total indulgence in every aspect. I will consider my budget constraints, the amount of time I have, all the logistics, cover all the bases in advance. But whatever happens when I'm there, I will just have to figure out how to make it up later. I'm an emotional spender. I often use spending as a pick me up when I feel sorry for myself or lonely. I use spending as a way to distract myself, or as compensation for my suffering. If I can't spend the money, I feel resentful and constricted, so I just put blinders on so I can go ahead and do what I want to do. I may find myself eating out at an expensive restaurant and then complaining about not being able to pay the rent!

I like to buy special, heart-felt, gifts for others. I'm generous because I know what it's like to be down and out. I choose my charities emotionally. The ones that tug at my heart strings, seem under-funded or have some personal meaning get my dollars. How can you get a brochure from Smile Train and not want to help those precious children?   Guide Dogs for the Blind? Indians with Diabetes? I like to give to unique causes, not the big ones like United Way and Red Cross.

As a "Aesthete" SP 4, I particularly love to spend on my home, and decorate it in a way that suits me and expresses who I am. A beautiful home environment means a lot to me. I am very atmosphere oriented. I love to spend on aesthetically pleasing and sensory pleasing things that look good, smell good, taste good, and sound good, such as lotions, food, books, candles, and music. In a less healthy state, I simply spend, without thinking about how I will pay for it. It's the $20 here and $40 there that do me in. I don't save a lot. I just try not to get into any more debt. I lack follow through when it comes to sticking to a budget and restricting my spending.

As an "Outsider" SO 4, I want to be accepted, even if I don't feel like I fit in. I want to have a good lifestyle. I could spend in one week what the average 3-person family spends in a whole month. I like to shop at Whole Foods and other speciality stores. I do a lot of impulsive, self-indulgent, self-comforting spending for smaller items. For example, I might buy four or five scarves in different colors. I might buy dresses that I wear only once or twice, or shoes that I never wear at all. I don't think about saving when I am spending. I would rather buy something of high quality than buy something that looks cheap. I can easily spend more than I make.

As a "Dramatist" SX 4, I spend money on vibrant experiences. I love to travel, and have the best luxuries. I like to shower my lover with gifts. I hate to spend money on insurance and contingencies. I am willing to cut back on insurance, cable, gas, but I will let small things sneak through. For example, I love flowers and I have a passion for color. I try to be mindful of the money limits, but I have a bit of resentment around my money being limited and not being entitled to more. When I like something, I just feel that I must have it. That's where the debt comes from. The limits don't always hold me. I am trying to distinguish between want and need, and be more vigilant about my spending.

Domain 3 – Earning

I am able to create income streams in creative ways. When my creative enterprise is attuned to me, I can be incredibly engaged and hard working. I am most excited about work that is meaningful and enables me to express myself. It might be body work, jewelry design, writing, painting, curating, small bookstore owner, therapist. I can dream up ideas, music, poems, art, stories. I can make a good living in the creative world. I don't want to be a part of the 9-5 masses punching the clock. I need to personalize my work to suit me and who I am. I want to "earn" my money being creative, unique, special. I would rather get paid less and do something meaningful, than get paid for doing something that is not true to me.

I want a job that suits me, that is personally meaningful. But I've always assumed that such jobs don't pay well. It would be exciting if I actually made money doing something I love, but I don't really expect it. My fulfillment feels a bit out of my reach. I envy what others have, but something – perhaps my unwillingness to be ordinary – prevents me from having what others have. The pickier I am about what is acceptable, the more difficult it can be for me economically. I reject jobs that are ordinary, where the work feels demeaning or beneath me, does not support my "uniqueness" or does not have emotional resonance for me. When my work does not express who I am, it feels boring and it is easy to be distracted. I might leave a job after only 18 months because I learned the job, knew I could do it, but then didn't feel like doing it anymore. I need to give myself time and space to be me, and if I take a job that is too consuming, I will lose me. I might find myself doing odd jobs to make ends meet, dreaming that someday I will finally be doing what I am meant to be doing. Circumstances being what they are, I try to make do in the meantime.

I often let myself down. I might drop out of a graduate program two weeks before graduation. Or I might fail a training program at work. Or not make it to an interview on time. Large dramas often disrupt my life. I am more inclined to be a starving artist than a captain of industry. I may lack self-esteem and a sense of myself as capable, believing that others have it together, but I don't. I can have trouble "selling" myself. And part of my problem might be my lack of faith that others will understand my creativity and support and value it.

I respect success, but it can be difficult to create opportunities for success. The funny thing is that I am very resilient. I can feel inferior to others and that I can't do things in a "normal" way. But when I am up against the wall, I know that opportunities will present themselves and that I will bounce back. It's just that I have difficulty going out and making these opportunities for success happen when my back is not up against a wall. Recognizing that making money is not just about being cutthroat and competitive, but is a means to be creative and challenged with endless possibilities, could turn money making into something more meaningful for me.

As a "Aesthete" SP 4, I am resourceful and more willing to make money any way I can to make ends meet. I tend to be more practical and self-sufficient. I would rather take on a second job and have a little margin of error than play things too close. Comfort and convenience are a bit more important to me than living my passion, and I am willing to defer my heart's passion for the sake of stability and a reasonable lifestyle. I will have a lot of excuses for why I can't step into my heart's desire now. I get tied in knots about finding work that really suits me. I fantasize about the perfect job, but actually following through seems a big leap. The closer to personal work I do, the more difficult it feels to charge for my services. I put up barriers to impersonal transactions. I feel that selling myself for my best parts is almost like prostitution. I might also rationalize that I am not worth it, I don't deserve it, I'm not up to it, or that I should be able to give my best work without putting a price on it. The deeper truth is that my ego cannot tolerate the idea that I could be paid well for a job I love. Perhaps this is why it is easier for me to long for a perfect job than to go out and make it happen. As a "Dramatist" SX 4, I must do work that I have a passion for and can't stand the idea of a regular 9-5 job. I'm not willing to take a regular job just to make ends meet. The starving artist archetype fits me. I can easily feel that it is necessary to do work that I love, but impossible to be paid properly.

Domain 4 – Beliefs

I have some strong beliefs about money. First, the world of business is crass, competitive, and beneath me. Business and the making of money is a corrupt, cutthroat, hyper-competitive affair which causes people to lose their identity and soul. I resent the importance of money and am reluctant to buy into the system. I am repulsed by the greed and crassness embedded in the business ethos. It also seems that the focus on money is antithetical to being authentic. My stories would not have come if I had chosen the money route. My hard experiences have been invaluable to me. I don't shy away from difficult emotions. In fact, I am proud of being able to go deep. Had I put money and comfort front and center in my life, it would have taken me further away from my authentic self. As a starving artist, I believe money is not spiritual, and therefore is something to avoid. The world could never properly value me and my work. These crude people involved with making money could not possibly understand me or what I contribute.

It does not occur to me that money can be my friend. I feel that I am a victim of the system. Money is of the world. I am over here and money is over there. I might earn some and spend it, but I don't really have any control over it. Because I don't have any personal relationship to money, it is not fundamental to how I think of myself or my life. If I want something, I ought to have it even if I can't afford it. These beliefs about money create a large emotional charge for me.

Domain 5 – Understanding

Money feels mundane to me and I prefer not to think about it. I may be able to make ends meet, but beyond that, I don't tend to have a lot of curiosity or interest in it. I prefer to focus on what matters to me and have someone else take care of money matters. I don't think of myself as caring about or knowing a lot about money. I prefer to get professional advice that is tailored to me, from someone who is able to explain things to me effectively. With the big picture, I can be responsible, sensible, knowledgeable, even clever about investments and money. If I pay attention, I can understand what my financial options are and how my investments are doing. But for things closer to home and more personal, I tend to be emotional and reactive, and I can screw things up. I resist being careful with money because dealing with money makes me feel incompetent and inadequate. It's easy to feel humiliated, disrespected and not heard by financial advisors and others. It can be difficult to communicate with others around money because of this. My understanding about money is enhanced when I am in a safer, more contained environment where I can feel safe to say what I think.

Domain 6 – Risk Management

Because of my resilience and experience with pain and suffering, I am not as afraid of failure as other people are. I don't avoid risk the way others do. As a "Aesthete" SP 4, I want savings as a back stop against emergencies. I am not afraid of the lack of money, but would prefer to have some savings for security. It helps to protect me from life's ups and downs. The lack of health insurance and the unknowns about my coverage does scare me. It bothers me when I think about others who don't have health care coverage - it seems unfair and a bit arbitrary. There seems to be a lot of randomness and red tape. When you get sick, you need to fight for proper care, but who can do that when they are sick? I resonate with the emotional difficulty of managing in crisis times. As an "Outsider" SO 4, I am generous to others and believe that others would be generous to me if I needed help. Social relationships are more reliable protection than money. I don't cultivate savings for emergencies the way I cultivate social relationships. I don't plan ahead money-wise the way I plan ahead socially. As a "Dramatist" SX 4, I am not as concerned about what could go wrong. The "in case of an emergency" mentality is not compelling. I am okay with dental insurance but I don't like it. Money spent on insurance feels like money going down the drain. Planning for something to go wrong is difficult because fear does not motivate me and I figure I will be okay somehow. I might go years without health insurance or skip meals if I am broke. My support comes from my relationships and my health more than it does from money.

Domain 7 – Planning

Long-range planning seems a bit impossible. How can I know where I will be emotionally that far in the future? Goals and benchmarks seem arbitrary. I try to control what I can control, but some things are not in my control and there is a limit to what I can do. For me, it's more about the creative process than where things end up.

As a "Aesthete" SP 4, I do consider what I have to do to keep my lifestyle going. I try to have backup savings. I am realistic about money, but not necessarily prudent. I am not a big future planner with goals and lists. I tend to deal with long-term goals by breaking them down into shorter-term goals. I try to stay on some kind of work path so that it will lead somewhere. I consider where I might want to live. I think about my life circumstances and what would work best for me, and then think about where the money will come from. Abstract goals like retirement are more difficult for me to connect to. A tangible goal with an emotional draw motivates me more. I don't run numbers, but I know I need to be working towards something. I will consider what I can do to keep the wheels moving. I want my goals to motivate me but, even if they do for a while, it might not last long. I set goals, but often don't follow through on them. It's not just that I am undisciplined, but I stop caring about the goals when something else has got my attention. For example, getting out of debt has been the only thing that I have worked at consistently; but as soon as we get out of debt, I stop trying, and we go right back into debt.

As an "Outsider" SO 4, I am very sensitive to my image, and embarrassed when I fail. I can get mired in my emotional soup and forget that I had goals. I need structure to hold myself accountable, but I find it difficult to create structure for myself. Without structure, I sink into not-doing and can get self-critical. My system needs to be attuned to me. My goals need to be attuned to me. If they are, and I have structure, discipline, and accountability, I do much better. My goals tend to be modest, like having a roof over my head. I never specify a number because that would be restrictive and arbitrary. As a SX 4, I like to take on challenges and I can plan ahead professionally, though I am not apt to plan ahead financially. For example, I never think about retirement. I assume things will be okay and that my future will be fine. I have no anxiety around money except when I don't have any.

Domain 8 – Wealth Building

In longing, there is an acute awareness of what is missing and also an intense optimism that I will be able to get what I want. I sometimes long for money, but I tend to be more interested in making ends meet than building wealth. Savings seems impersonal and a bit abstract. I would rather use my money for something I can experience and connect to personally.

As a "Aesthete" SP 4, I want some savings for contingencies. Beyond this, I am not ambitious about amassing great wealth. Any wealth I do have tends to be in real estate, property, or other tangible assets that have personal resonance for me. I like investments I can see and touch. I've always felt that there is no such thing as security, so I would rather invest in something that is meaningful to me than stocks and bonds that could evaporate at any time. When I do invest in stocks, I am attracted to unique, exotic stocks like Brazilian stocks or biotech. I trust my intuition. As a "Dramatist" SX 4, I am less apt to save for contingencies, but investing in something personally meaningful that has great potential does appeal to me.

Domain 9 – Balance

Depending on my level of health, I can swing from great resignation to great optimism. When I feel scarcity, I feel special but alone, misunderstood, and undervalued because my creativity is not appreciated. I get by on what I have, but my feeling that something is missing creates jealousy and envy that keeps me in scarcity. The more I focus on my flaws and inadequacies, the more I feel blocked from love.

I must confront my fear of being ordinary, which causes me to ignore the normal rules and constraints of the real world. I must confront my fear of being undernourished, which causes me to use spending to soothe and compensate. And I must confront my feelings of being a nobody, which causes me to use money to build up my sense of identity. I can have the love I want, but I must work towards being in the flow of life and wealth.

When I feel abundant, I am connected to my creative energy, and feel that I can be or do anything. The world appreciates me and compensates me appropriately for who I am and what I create. I am special, but I know that everyone is special in their own way. I am grounded in my body, creative and productive. I feel capable and competent, and have a sense of my own agency, power, and self-reliance. I express my authentic nature. I don't have anything to prove, or any image to uphold. I am confident in who I am. I don't get preoccupied or anxious about money. Money is energy that moves in and out of my life effortlessly and supports my personhood. I believe that I am loved.

5. THE PARADOX

The fundamental paradox is that *Personalizing* never leads to knowing myself. It only leads to envy and a feeling that something is missing. Not only is the actual outcome the opposite of my original intent, but it can never be otherwise. What is identity? Is identity what I have when I separate myself from others? Is identity something that I can create? Or is identity something I am born with? *Personalizing* is supposed to help me be special. But when I overdo this strategy, I actually feel undistinguished and ordinary. The defenses I've employed bring about the very lack of identity that I fear.

The paradox is that *Personalizing* causes me to disconnect from the thing I care most about, which is finding out who I really am. I forget that my basic identity has nothing to do with external markers of who I am. There is a part of me that knows that I am not a nobody. But honoring this part of myself would create conflict with my ego structure, and that tension would be too much for me to bear.   So instead, I continue *Personalizing* in hopes that I can create an identity for myself. I sense that I am being blackmailed into *Personalizing* and that this entire structure is built on fear, but I do not know how to move past the fear. The more I fear being nobody, the more I try to be special. In continuing to search for identity, I can never actually find it.

The paradox is that in always always searching for ways that I am different, I forget that I am already special. In being attached to my emotions, I think I am my emotions. In always feeling flawed and inadequate, I do not leave room for how I am complete and perfect. In emphasizing the personal meaning of everything, I cut myself off from the universality of my experience. In resigning myself to what I cannot have, I cannot avoid envy.   My envy and jealousy cause me to be more ordinary and petty, which is the very thing I am trying to avoid. In learning to be ordinary and not setting myself apart, I can know the real me. In surrendering to my commonality, my identity radiates as a personal manifestation of the great identity. By going as deeply into myself as I can, I discover that our various personal paths lead to the same place.

6. BREAKING THE VICIOUS CYCLE

In order to break the vicious cycle of my personality, and move from Fear to Love, I must embrace and resolve the fundamental paradox of *Personalizing*. I have spent my whole life denying my flawlessness. This denial has cut me off from the true me. I have been crippled by needing to be unique and special. In keeping my perfect, dignified, intact self at bay, I have also held away love. As I throw off the shackles of my personality and orient to my true nature, I begin to own the whole me. I stay in contact with my own depth and see it in others. I remember what I care about and what makes life rich, meaningful, and worth living. I remember that my inner nature is a treasure trove. I recognize that everything I perceive is created anew each moment and that each moment is a creative gesture. I realize that what I am seeing is the painting, the production of reality, the world being produced anew, continually arising. The whole gesture of creativity and expression is part of our deeper identity. In surrendering to my core nature, I stop resisting the truth. I become embodied Love, with compassion in my heart, wisdom in my head, and well-being in my body.

My journey with money is a journey to equanimity, a journey to experiencing the calm blue skies behind the stormy clouds. By connecting my heart to my body and head, and nurturing a non-reactive heart that can accept love, I can relax knowing that I am a special somebody who does not need to craft a unique identity. Instead of trying to be different, I can relax knowing that I am a part of a vaster identity. I can be with both my flaws and my perfection. I can move away from self-absorption towards dignity and principled action. I begin to use everything that has happened to me for growth and renewal, of myself and others. I begin to entertain the possibility that there is nothing wrong with me, and that life is bountiful and abundant, and I am good. I acknowledge the universality of my particularity. In embracing these truths, I can move past my old beliefs and patterns and welcome abundance, prosperity, and love into my life. I can begin to feel more attuned and connected. But this is not comfortable or easy. I feel the pain as my ego resists losing its job. I feel remorseful about how I have lived my life and hurt myself and others. I am scared that I won't be able to survive on my own deeper knowing alone.

When I live abundantly, I feel utterly intact. I know that I am a manifestation of source and I don't need work at being special. I dance with the unspeakable depth of what is here now. When I feel loved and embraced, I can be fully me, and my identity is clearer and more defined. Dropping my story of failure and disappointment, I no longer deny my own capacities or refuse to step into my power. I let myself be who I really am. I let myself be supported and held, recognizing that who I am has nothing to do with how deep or turbulent my life is. My sense of a separate self is replaced by an interconnected personal self that is in communion with all souls. I am not an outsider. I do not have to distinguish myself because I am already special. I know I belong, that I am good and abundant, utterly intact and competent. I am supported in my search for depth, meaning, beauty, identity. I don't have to be starving or tortured around money and material comforts in order to be deep and special. I experience our common humanity and am humbled before it. It is our hallmark as humans for we are all part of this same mystery. We are all part of one vast intelligence that is the Beloved. We are all welcome. I am here, and I see what's real and relevant and what's not. From here, I am able to know directly the truth of things.

	Brief Description
"Aesthete" SP 4	I care about having a beautiful home that expresses who I am. I am aesthetically oriented, and want to be surrounded by sensory pleasures. I am resourceful, and will make ends meet however I need to. I tend to be more self-sufficient than a typical 4, and would rather have a margin than play things too close to the edge.
"Outsider" SO 4	I feel inadequate about managing money. I believe I deserve good things, and have difficulty being constrained by a budget. I fantasize about a life where I am an insider and nourished. I am generous to others, and feel that money is for others, not me.
"Dramatist" SX 4	The starving artist archetype fits me well. I must do work that I am passionate about, that allows me to express my deep well of emotions, but it feels impossible to be paid properly for my creativity. I spend to live intensely and have vibrant experiences.

Type 4	Summary
Gift	Going deeply into my emotions and expressing my unique identity.
Unconscious Belief	I am different. Something is missing.
Strategy	*Personalizing* – ascribing personal meaning to everything I have and do to express my unique identity.
Vicious Cycle	Because I must express my unique self in everything I have and do, I must stay away from the ordinary and mundane, and focus on being special and different. But because I am different, I feel that something is missing in me that makes me deficient, unable to connect to my true identity.
Defended Against	Being perfect and flawless
Operationally	• I must express my uniqueness. • I get roiled by my difficult emotions. • I focus only on the areas where I can be unique, special, creative, different.
Paradox	*Personalizing* does not generate authenticity.
Breaking the Vicious Cycle	I must recognize that my personal experience is universal, and that I am special and ordinary, flawed and perfect, all at once. Nothing is missing in me. I am an expression of love.
Direction of Growth	Being attuned to the love that exists here for me allows me to know what is true.

CHAPTER 11

MINIMIZING

Type 5

1. GIFT

    I can observe the world and make sense of things. I can see for myself what is true and what is not true. I am an independent and clear thinker, not easily pulled in by conventional ways of looking at things. I can see, for example, that money is just a means to an end. It is not an end in itself. It is just a thing and we shouldn't let it run our lives. I always try to have the proper perspective because, if we lose our perspective, then we lose our ability to orient ourselves to what is real. I can see how fragile and precious life is. We can be here one moment and gone the next. So it's difficult to get too wrapped up with material things. My ability to be detached brings me freedom from the disappointment and suffering that comes with being attached to things that you want but can't have. I prefer to meet each moment without an agenda, and allow the moment to provide what it will, without trying to control it in any way. If we can be here in the present moment, the moment will provide us exactly what we need. My ability to hold myself back and be detached, yet focused on the present moment, allows me to savor each moment just as it is. In this orientation, everything I could ever want is provided to me.

2. STRATEGY

My life and money strategy grow out of my sense of the critical importance of having some internal resources so that I can be okay. At the unconscious level, I register the world as unsafe and rejecting, though I repress this feeling at the conscious level. At the conscious level, my belief is simply that I must stay out of the strong tidal pull of life. *Minimizing* is about reducing my needs and desires, minimizing my financial encumbrances, and keeping my distance. It is obvious to me that needing people and things entrenches me in this world and sets me up to be hurt, so I instinctively hold myself back. Others might think that I am a strange recluse. What they miss is my desire to be safe and to have the wisdom that comes from observing life from a distance.

An aspect of *Minimizing* is my ability to pull myself back to be more objective. When we allow ourselves to get too comfortable, we can lose our perspective. When we get too focused on what we want, we can get caught up in things that are ultimately meaningless. The only way to make sense of this mysterious world is to stay detached so that we can figure things out. While being detached and observant is my gift, it can block my experience of being a part of life. *Minimizing* is a defense against going directly for what I want. My feeling that there is no point in trying to have what I can't have makes me somewhat nihilistic. I can get cynical about life. I don't want to make big commitments that would require putting too much of myself on the line. No point trying to play big if it's all pointless and going to end. I'm just going to live my small life and deal with what comes my way. I know what I don't want, but it's not so easy to know what I do want. I don't see the point of planning ahead for a life that is so unknowable, unpredictable and fragile. I don't have a sense of my ability to direct the flow of things or make meaning out of the meaningless. The difficulty with going for what I want is that I would have to be willing to be hurt. I'd have to be willing to enter the fray even if life might beat me up and toss me aside. I'd have to be willing to look death in the eyes and laugh.

Going after what I want is difficult because I would have to accept my own power to affect things. I would have to reach out without fear that I might be hurt or forsaken. Because I feel like an outsider. I fail to apprehend how life becomes meaningful through my direct participation. I fail to apprehend how much I miss when I observe life from a distance.

Having the proper perspective is not really about being detached and objective. Being objective assumes that there is some way to be separate from our collective life. At the deepest level, we are never outside, rejected, or forsaken, and there is no objective knowing, only direct subjective knowing. If I could accept this fact, I would not fear participating in life, even if it is fragile and our own mortal lives always end. It is only in participating directly that I will know what is real, true and meaningful about this life.

3. THE VICIOUS CYCLE

If I were to look at my life objectively, I would notice that I have essentially been trapped in a vicious cycle of fear and scarcity. Because of this, my relationship to love and prosperity is constrained. *Minimizing* is fundamentally about repressing my need for love. This orientation makes me feel dry and without resources. But my ego enthusiastically keeps this vicious cycle going so that it can keep its job. I get addicted to *Minimizing*. Even though I think I am moving along, I am merely moving in place.

When we are caught in a vicious cycle where our actions validate our beliefs, it can be very difficult to extricate ourselves. When we are stuck at a certain point along the scarcity-to-abundance spectrum, it is impossible to improve our position until we get out of the vicious cycle. If we are suddenly showered with new wealth, we will most likely dissipate it so that we can get back to our old set point. So in order to create new wealth, we must first become aware of the vicious cycle we are caught in. Once we become aware, we will be in a better position to consciously unblock what blocks us, and welcome new wealth into our lives.

My underlying assumption is that attachment brings pain. I will not accept help or be beholden to anyone. It is better that I keep my distance and stay detached. I don't want to have needs that require engaging with the world. I feel an overwhelming sense of the impermanent nature of things, and I get cynical. Am I just this physical body that will eventually wither and die? I will not allow myself to get angry though, because anger would mean I cared. I'll just stay cynical and not get too comfortable here.

It is hard to enjoy this life when I am not really part of it. The defenses I've employed to stay safe bring about the very alienation I fear. Somehow life does not feel real to me, but more like a game. We are all pieces in the game, but have no power to change the scope of the game –

which is that there is a beginning, middle and end. and there are winners and losers. The best way to survive is to play the game smartly, making logical, tactical moves. If you study the rules, you will play better. It's better to be a winner than a loser. But there is no point getting too invested in the outcome because, after all, it's just a game.

Life feels unknowable. I set myself apart and gaze outward at the world to try to understand it from a distance. I grasp for information and mastery as a way to make sense of this mysterious world. If I can stay detached, and not let my feelings get involved, I believe I will be able to figure things out. My feelings only impede my ability to understand. I keep my feelings and thoughts private, not letting other people know what I am thinking or feeling because that might subject me to shame or disappointment. Others may be allowed into my life, but only on my terms – otherwise I might get hurt. I am wary of attachments because they bring pain when they are pulled away.

I am intense. I focus on things that I am good at and know something about. I don't venture into areas I know nothing about or don't interest me. If money doesn't interest me, I may ignore it. If I lack confidence in some area, I can be indecisive. But by focusing my attention, I can go deep and control something in my life that otherwise seems random and uncontrollable. My focus could be on anything, constructive or destructive, from software coding to pornography, from string theory to poker.

People think I am greedy, but being greedy is overindulging in things you don't need. I am not greedy. In fact, I am repulsed by greed. The idea of taking more than I need is appalling to me, so I do the opposite. I try to take as little as possible. It's a lot easier to be self-sufficient when your needs are so minimal. I refuse to get caught up in the conventional social game of striving for income and wealth. I am a rebel by nature. I don't value what others value. In fact, I sort of feel superior that I don't need all the junk others seem to need. Having a lot of money feels uncomfortable, too. I consume what is readily available, but I do not allow myself to enjoy it too much. If I like something too much, I could get attached to it, and then I could get hurt.

Precisely because I do not go after what I want, I must hold onto the crumbs that I do have. My holding on is driven more by my stifled desire than a big appetite. I don't go after things because this would require wanting. But wanting something implies you might not get what you want and could be hurt. By holding on to what I do have, I can ensure that I will have something, even if just a little. This behavior might seem like hoarding to outsiders, but to me, it simply feels like a natural, logical thing to do. But by holding on too tightly, I prevent the natural flow of energy from moving in and out of my life to replenish and revitalize me. By not reaching for what I want and by holding on too tightly to what I have, I generate the very emptiness that I fear, leaving me feeling parched and dry.

I am not willing to go for something big or too far down the road. That would be too expansive. By stifling my desire, I don't have to make much money. By keeping my ambitions low, I don't need to interact with the world as much. I don't have to depend on people or owe people. This explains my deep reluctance to plan ahead, which implies wanting, even dreaming, which is scary. I don't want to put too much of myself on the line. I expect disappointment, so I protect my vulnerable heart by not allowing myself to be touched or hurt.

I am a one-man island. I am independent and can get by on my own. I am suspicious of help and kindness. I'll take care of myself because I am the only one I can count on. I don't want to get caught in any web that might suck me into the world of contact and enmesh me. I am naturally suspicious about money and believe there is something wrong with wanting so much that you become captive to it. I don't want to be owned by anyone. But being a one-man island ends up being more difficult and more of a fiction than I could have imagined. I want to be detached from the complexity and encumbrances of life, but by actively rejecting encumbrances, I often end up more encumbered by the very things I was actively avoiding. Things have to go very badly for me to be motivated to participate instead of withdraw. The dynamic of the ego structure keeps my ego employed and keeps me perpetually fixated on being self-sufficient and detached. I can never find safety and comfort, for then I would have no excuse for *Minimizing*. We are each caught in a vicious cycle of our personality and instincts until we decide to break free. This takes deliberate energy and momentum because the cycle is a compelling vortex. In order to create new wealth, we must see clearly the vicious cycle that blocks us from abundance. Then we must fight our way out of the vortex.

4. OPERATIONALLY

If my instincts are balanced, I will be able to attend to money in each of the Nine Money Domains in a healthy manner. If, however, my instincts are not in balance, then I will get stuck in my type fixation and I cannot be optimally effective. My motivation to minimize my needs and be self-reliant manifests in different ways depending on my dominant instinct. Instead of learning about and paying attention to areas I don't know about, I focus on the things that I do know about, am interested in, and have expertise in. As a SP 5, my *Minimizing* energy complements the frugality of the Self-Preservation energy, and I focus on being self-reliant about my physical needs and my money. As a SO 5, my *Minimizing* energy combines with my Social instinct to focus on ideas of social justice and fairness. Personal money matters tend not be a large focus of my attention. And as a SX 5, my *Minimizing* energy contradicts my sexual instinct and holds me back from my libidinal energy. How my instincts are imbalanced will impact how I relate to the Nine Money Domains – where I put my attention and energy and where I don't.

"ASCETIC" SP 5	"EXPERT" SO 5	"LOW ROLLER" SX 5

Domain 1 – Budgeting

The idea of budgeting seems simple – it's a matter of yes or no, can I afford it? It feels straightforward to know how much money comes in and goes out. But whether I do this in a methodical or loose way depends on my dominant and blindspot instincts.

As an "Ascetic" SP 5, I am generally frugal, attend to details, and am somewhat organized. I want to know where I am with the money. I try to have some organization, but I am not meticulous. I won't let a budget run my life. A budget is more of a flexible guideline. It makes me aware of the big picture and helps me understand what is going on. I might review my finances more frequently in tighter times. I try to keep things simple. I may not know exactly how much I spend, but I am pretty confident about the average because there is not a lot to keep track of. Typically, I pay my bills immediately after I get paid. Then I can relax and enjoy the money left over. The money I put away is not based on efforting or budgeting. It just happens naturally. I seldom bounce checks and I am reluctant to borrow. I try to pay my credit cards each month because debt makes me anxious. I don't like to owe anyone or be beholden. The tighter money is, the more likely I am to want to have a budget because I do not want to feel that I am living on the precipice. I am more averse to having no money than I am excited about getting more. I am not aggressive about bringing resources in, but once I have them, I don't want to squander them.

As an "Expert" SO 5, ideals and values are more important to me than money. I don't feel the need to do explicit budgeting or be super organized. I can keep track of things in my head and I trust that money will be available when I need it. If money gets tight, I might pay a bit more attention. But I just don't worry much about it. If I am a SO 5 with a Self-Preservation blindspot, I most likely ignore budgeting altogether. I fear that if I were on a budget, I would be denied. I have this irrational fear of becoming a bag lady, but at the same time, I don't want to be denied things in the present. For example, I want to look decent and I don't want to eat leftovers. It might seem paradoxical that I would ignore things that scare me, but I don't want to think about things that make me feel ignorant and powerless. I just hope that money will take care of itself.

As a "Low Roller" SX 5, my Sexual instinct contradicts my *Minimizing* energy. I am more spontaneous and casual about money than a typical 5, and can spend easily as I pursue what interests me. I use spontaneous spending to give myself small charges. I will get anxious when I am close to my limit, and know how to put the brakes on when money is tight, for fear of being destitute and beholden to others. I can do budgeting when I have to, but it's not my favorite thing to do. If Self-Preservation is my blindspot though, budgeting feels less important and more boring. I have always found ways to get by. I'm not interested in maximizing my wealth. I just want enough money to be self-reliant, free, and spontaneous. I am not great at tracking and organizing around money. It helps if I have a desk, a filing system, and some built-in structure. But it is not where my strength lies. I may clamp down and follow a budget for a few weeks, be frugal, pay my bills on time. But then I get distracted and can't stay on track because it gets boring. It tends to be all or nothing for me. My bills pile up and then I pay them all at once. Money is only interesting insofar as it allows me to do things like travel and have experiences. Having a huge bank balance does not give me a charge. It feels like there are a lot more interesting things to pay attention to.

Domain 2 – Spending

I am both skeptical and respectful of money. I've always tried to live minimally. I don't want to get attached to money. At the same time, I respect money because money enables me to be self-sufficient. I have a much easier time dribbling money away on small things than spending just as much on one or two big items. Learning to be okay using money for comforts and my well-being is a growth edge for me. My *Minimizing* strategy cause me to exhibit greater distortions in my spending relative to my needs at lower levels of income and wealth. I am a lot more frugal and self-denying when things are tight than when things are flush. When I fear having nothing, I try to hold on to what little I have. When things are relatively flush and there is a larger cushion, my spending can be looser. In general, though, I am naturally cautious about big purchases, and tend to avoid debt. It can be difficult for mc to spend money on things that I might enjoy. In lacking a strong desire for things, I can feel cut off from life. My *Minimizing* strategy is to avoid being hurt. But, at the same time, this strategy hurts me because I can't feel what I want. How are you supposed to go after a relationship, or have sufficient motivation to do things if you aren't in touch with your desires?

> I hoard myself. I feel an inner desert in my heart that is praying for rain.

As an "Ascetic" SP 5, I can be frugal. It is clear to me that the less money I spend , the more money I save and the more self-sufficient I can be. I am practical. A nice but modest home is fine for me. I like utility, functionality, workmanship, and value. I don't really care what others think about my image. I pride myself on not desiring the material things that others seem to be driven by. I might buy used and recycled stuff, and find things others have discarded. I am not necessarily self-denying. I just want to get good value for my money. I can splurge on books, travel, personal development, etc. I am willing to negotiate to get a good value and could care less about the image it projects to others. I can be very picky about how I spend my money. It might take me three hours of research to buy a $200 item. I am, however, willing to spend a lot of money in the right context. For example, it might make more sense to spend $50 on a good meal than $5 on a McDonald's meal. I am more apt to be generous about money than time. Time feels more precious to me than money – I can always make more money, but I cannot get back my time. I am willing to give discounts and charge less. It is more difficult, however, to give away money that is already in my pocket. If my Self-Preservation instinct is severely imbalanced relative to my other instincts, then I might go to such an extreme in minimizing my needs that I become eccentric and unkempt, neglecting hygiene, dental care, etc. I may deny myself all physical comforts and live austerely. I may wash my clothes only once a month and walk everywhere. I may become paranoid about losing the few possessions I own. I might not be able to get a job because I seem so strange, even if I am brilliant in my field.

As an "Expert" SO 5, my Social instinct is to be generous. I spend money as an expression of my ideals and values. For example, *not* spending a lot of money on clothing makes me happy, but I am willing to pay what something is worth. I would rather not worry about the cost of something and enjoy the experience than do hard bargaining. If I drive a hard bargain, I feel like I'm cheating. I like to tip extravagantly. I like being generous to other people. I'd rather spend on people than things. I'd rather save $20 on a shirt and be able to tip someone extra.

As a "Low Roller" SX 5, my Sexual instinct helps me to be more in touch with what my heart desires. When I see something I want, I know it. I like to spend on things that interest me. It is a lot easier to spend on workshops, relationships, and travel than on a leaky roof. I like to buy things that make me look good like jewelry, shoes, and clothes. I like to spend on experiences. I want to be able to do what I want. I have a very simple relationship to money that way. It is more important to me that I get what I want than save money. And I don't want to waste my time. When I shop, I like to go in, get it, and go. I won't necessarily buy the cheapest thing. I don't need my things to be cutting edge, but they need to be functional and reliable. Since I am the only one I can rely on to take care of myself, I can be rather self-centered and hedonistic. When I don't have the emotional reserves to watch my budget, my spending is not very restrained. Sometimes I pamper myself because I am so stressed from working. I don't necessarily completely figure out if I can afford something before I buy it. I just base it on my gut sense. I like being spontaneous in enjoying the here and now. I have an easy-come, easy-go attitude about money. I have been known to spend tens of thousands of dollars on my book or music collections. I won't spend this money all at once but, over a period of several years, it can add up. Money escapes me in small dribbles. Small purchases feel emotionally more acceptable than large ones. For big purchases, I tend to think about it a lot and do a lot of research. For example, the benefits of owning a house as an investment might be overshadowed by the emotional difficulty of spending such a large amount of money on one item and the burden of taking on so much debt. This reluctance to spend on big ticket items stems in part from my sense that it is not okay to have needs and not okay to be comfortable. It feels scary to exchange resources that provide self-sufficiency to buy comfort and fulfill needs. Spending or investing on big ticket items induces a large emotional charge and can trigger fear and anxiety in me.

Domain 3 – Earning

Work, money, and life feel like a game, a bit like Monopoly. Maybe I will amass enough money to put hotels all over the board. Or perhaps I will just buy some rentals. Or perhaps I will opt to not own at all. Regardless of what I choice I make, I never lose sight of the fact that money matters on the game board. I recognize the value of money, but I'm also cognizant of the compromises we must make to exchange our time, energy and knowledge for paper money. I intuitively try to minimize the world's hold on me. I don't want to be owned by anyone.

Money has never been a big motivator for me, but it feels good to be paid for my expertise, and I like to make money so that I can be self-sufficient. I tend to choose my profession based on what I am interested in, good at, and enjoy, not what pays the most. Being an expert has always been important to me. I intuitively realize that if I have an expertise, no one can take that away from me, and I can always be valuable. However, I am not willing to sacrifice my precious time to make money in a way that is not worthwhile for me. I'm fairly confident in my ability to make money and earn a living, because I have skills and knowledge that are useful to others. But I've never had a huge ambition to make a load of money. It's always been about what I was interested in doing. I don't aspire to be successful in the conventional sense. I intuitively recognize the potentially entangling web of compromises that one has to make to work for big name companies like IBM and Goldman. More likely than not, I won't be interested in making these Faustian bargains. I am sensitive to the encumbrances of rules and authority. I value my autonomy and like to set my own hours and work in my own way.

I don't have a massive need for status or symbols to show people what I'm worth. I don't have an inflated sense of how great I am, but people have mostly been happy to pay for what I offer and opportunities always seem to open for me. I'm not comfortable selling myself, but word of mouth has usually worked well. I have always focused on doing what I enjoy doing, and have never been hard-nosed about how much I'm paid. I know I am valuable to others and I expect to be compensated fairly for the work that I do. But I won't necessarily be aggressive in arguing for a higher salary. As long as I don't feel like I'm being exploited, I can be fairly quiet. But if I think someone is taking advantage of me, I could blow up and leave. It is true that I may go a few years not standing up for myself because I really want to keep working, and don't want to look for new work. Sometimes, I don't even pay attention to how much I am being paid. Mainly, I want to make sure there is enough to pay my bills and buy what I want, when I want it. If I tried to make more money, I would probably have to compromise something else in my life – I'd have to pay more taxes and would have less time for myself. So I am always careful in weighing the tradeoffs before changing jobs.

As an entrepreneur, I can be stymied in going after big accounts. I don't like to do a lot of posturing, pitching, and angling. When I set my fees, I try to be fair. I don't want to be too greedy. Part of this is out of fear that I will price myself out of the market, but part of this is also driven by my repulsion of greed. I want to leave something on the table for the other side. My *Minimizing* strategy causes me to not want something so much that I would risk rejection. Rather than go after things, I tend to wait for things to draw me in. I don't set career goals and I don't try to control how life unfolds. Life seems to unfold apart from me.

Domain 4 – Beliefs

My beliefs stem from my ideals and principles. First of all, money is a means to an end, not an end in itself. Work, books, arts, real things, etc. are more interesting than money, which is man-made, artificial, and simply a medium of exchange. I certainly wouldn't want to live without money because money does give you freedom and options. So I engage money out of necessity. Second, greed is bad, and having money is embarrassing. Going after money signifies an attachment to and dependence on it. Third, caring too much about money can cause you to miss what is here now. Angling for money and one's own self-interests is dangerous. There is something wrong with wanting something so much that you become captive to it. When you always have an agenda, you lose perspective and focus on the wrong thing. We should never compromise ourselves or our work for the sake of money. As much as money can give us freedom and options, it can also weigh us down. The more you are enmeshed and encumbered by financial obligations, the less freedom and flexibility you have.

> Money can cause us to run away from the important things and from ourselves and love, and get preoccupied with material concerns. And on our deathbed, we think about our relationship with ourselves, others, and God and we wonder why we spent so much time on material issues.

As an "Expert" SO 5, I am moved by my ideals and principles. I believe that if I'm generous to the world, then the world will support me back. If I'm generous and responsible and affirm my principles of abundance, this will be reflected back to me. Being generous demonstrates that I'm plugged in, acting in correct ways, and am an effective player in the movement of money in this system. When money flows from me, I am creating room for more money to flow in. Money flowing from me is an expression that it came to me. If I spend too much time looking at it and analyzing it, I'd be dishonoring the system.

Domain 5 – Understanding

Yes, money is a necessity in my life but, emotionally, money does not feel real. If I do understand money, it is in the context of a game. Life feels like a game where I am an outsider. To the extent that money is part of a game, I may be motivated to learn the rules and play the game well. To the extent that it is a game, I can be quite logical and analytical and unemotional about the stakes of the game. I will find out what experts say, what rate of return I need to earn, how to budget and plan ahead. I understand that when I play a game, I could win or I could lose, so I have to be okay with losing if I take the risk of playing. Stock investing is essentially gambling, but that's the fun of it. I might decide to be aggressive about playing the game. But if the stock market tanks, I don't get destroyed by it because I recognized the possibility of loss even before

I began. I try to learn from my experience. I have a sense of prevailing optimism that, in the end, I'm going to win the game.

> Money is only interesting in the context of a game. Else there is not much inherently interesting about it.

Of course, money is not really just a game. Money can be very polarizing because so much is at stake. It's difficult to sort through all the conflicting advice of brokers and salesmen with their own agendas. I always wonder if they are trustworthy, knowledgeable, competent. It's hard to know what is really true. Because money can be so opaque, I might be averse to learning about it. And if I do not feel competent, I may also reject learning about it. When I don't understand something, though, I get a hopeless feeling that I can't do it on my own. Getting help and learning a little about money would vastly improve my relationship to money, but it is difficult for me to reach out for assistance.

Domain 6 – Risk Management

In general, I don't get too wrapped up in what could go wrong. All of life is fragile and I accept death as a part of life. I don't fear it. I don't try to have insurance policies against reality. What I fear is being without resources to deal with life while I'm here. Risk is about what might happen down the road. For me, the here and now has my attention. I don't purposely court danger, but I don't go out of my way to avoid what is inevitable. I regard my expertise and competency as a reliable form of insurance. In any case, a disaster could become a blessing in disguise. It all depends on your perspective.

As an "Ascetic" SP 5, I try to have a savings cushion in case of emergency. But once I have the savings, I am reluctant to spend it. I want to be self-sufficient and not depend on others. I try to hedge my bets and I don't have a problem buying insurance for things that I can't replace, as long as the insurance rate is reasonable and I'm not getting gouged. As an "Expert" SO 5, I have always been involved in social movements and I am called to make the world a better place. By being a facilitator, servant, catalyst, I want to be able to look outside myself and see that what I am doing is working and I've done my job well. I don't depend on others to take care of me. I don't have a lot of concern about risk management, but I do need to be reasonable. I take reasonable precautions and have medical insurance and long-term disability insurance, even though I don't know how much it pays out. I rely on my personal resources not money. My education and relationships would enable me to get another job quickly if I had to. When Self-Preservation is my blindspot, planning for contingencies and emergencies is even less natural. I may find myself trying to play catch up. I don't tend to cultivate savings as a form of risk management.

Domain 7 – Planning

My *Minimizing* strategy keeps me in the now. I don't have big dreams or visions about the future. In fact, I'm hardly curious about the future. The present is where life is, and I enjoy my life here. The future seems like a fantasy. Whatever happens will be cool. I let it take care of itself. My satisfaction is not based on external circumstances much. I'd be just as happy playing with a cardboard box as a fancy car. My anti-libidinal nature goes against planning, which requires having an idea how life could be better, believing that you can get what you want, and then planning how to get from here to there. It requires a sense of control over your own destiny.

To me, it feels absurd to try to control the future. I don't even know how long I'll be around. If I think about the future, it's as a pure thought, absent any inclination to go in that direction. I don't conjure images of myself living a particular future. I know there is a value in tactical planning, for example – for a vacation. But further into the future, I just see a fog. I never assume that tomorrow will look like today. So much is unpredictable.

> I am too aware of the wild card factor of life – both individually and collectively.

Logically, I would like to have the resources to deal with the vicissitudes of life and have a cushion to deal with what arises. I like for my affairs to be squared up and I don't want to be a burden to others. But emotionally, it is not easy to think ahead and prepare for a vague future. Long-range planning feels absurd. It feels presumptuous to think I can know what the right long-run plan ought to be. If I earmark money for some future goal, I will probably be disappointed, because who knows what contingency may arise to divert the funds. It seems emotionally futile and senseless to plan ahead. It's more sensible to withhold desire and just enjoy the small joys in the present. I want self-sufficiency, but I'd rather ensure my self-sufficiency through minimizing my needs than wanting more either now or later.

Domain 8 – Wealth Building

The wealth that I naturally build up is my own competency. I enjoy the time I invest to build up my skills. Comparable to a financial asset, I recognize that when I cultivate my knowledge, my competency becomes more valuable over time. Building financial or physical assets, in contrast, requires committing myself to a path of action and feeding a desire to have more. I am reluctant to work towards greater wealth. I worry about losing myself to the world like that. Too much stuff can feel like a burden. More stuff means more to take care of, more responsibility, more embeddedness. Perhaps there is a slight sense of superiority that I don't need all this.

As an "Ascetic" SP 5, I am more comfortable amassing resources passively. As long as I get paid more than I spend, I will have savings to buffer me against unexpected contingencies. I am willing to play the "investing" game and take my chances if I can afford to. I understand that it takes big risk to earn big returns. I don't get too emotionally caught up in market gyrations. As long as I don't need to win, I am willing to take smart gambles that I might lose. I have qualities that make me an excellent investor. I am naturally logical, inquisitive, and analytical. I can be very objective and detached, and pay attention to details. I pride myself on my intellectual savvy and my ability to make good assessments about firms and market situations. I might suffer from over-confidence and over-trading, but that does not deter me, especially if I win some big pots once in a while. I wouldn't invest the money if that money really mattered to me.

As an "Expert" SO 5, I don't believe in hoarding money. Money should be moving and active. Whether I'm rich or poor, I sense that I'm going to be fine. I don't need material things, so why bother spending energy on material things. But I do like the idea of wealth being a measure of how smart I am. If I had to choose, I'd rather be smart than rich. There is nothing out there I need to have. Being rich is okay because then I can be more generous. The sin of greed is the sin of attention more than the sin of having wealth. I don't want to put attention on anything material. Ideas like kindness, compassion, justice, are eternal, dependable, and can't betray you the way people and material things can.

As a "Low Roller" SX 5, I like challenges and I prefer to invest and build sweat equity rather than save in a bank. Where's the juice in squirreling away money to earn 1%? My Sexual instinct is interested in being bold and creating something from nothing. I am more cavalier about risk taking and I don't care as much about creature comforts. I'm more interested in having my autonomy and creating something new. I like the challenge of building something where I can invest in my knowledge base and become an expert in a new field. However, my *Minimizing* energy can act as a drag on my building efforts because I am reluctant to ask aggressively for what I want. I tend to sit back and think, rather than just go out and do things. It's difficult for me to see the bigger picture, live into the bigger vision, harness my strong desire and pursue what I want. I struggle with thinking big, giving direction and managing others. My power lies more in my expertise than my leadership skills.

Domain 9 – Balance

Objectively, I sense that there is plenty. I understand how great wealth starts from an idea. And how powerful knowledge can be. What blocks me from abundance is my fear of being without resources and knowledge, and my sense that I must hold on tightly to what I do have. It also comes from a sense that it is not okay to be comfortable, and that I cannot have what I want. This keeps me out of the flow and keeps me from experiencing prosperity. I have always sensed the finiteness of resources and human life. This fear of being without resources can grab me with such intensity that all I want to do is hold on to what I have. I hold onto knowledge and information to help me feel more filled up. I am afraid to want because wanting makes me vulnerable to being hurt and there is no end to wanting. Material things don't make us happy. They may delight and satisfy for a time, but then the mind will ask, What's next? Because I am so scared of being hurt, I try to stay detached. I must remember the adage from Tennyson's poem "'Tis better to have loved and lost Than never to have loved at all." I must confront my reluctance to go for what I want. I must recognize that my perspective can be improved when I am in the flow of life rather than outside of life. Just because the future is unknowable, doesn't mean I can't be part of that unfolding. And I must examine my belief about being detached as a valid way to understand the nature of reality. I can have the love I want, but I must work at being in the flow of life without blocking love out.

5. THE PARADOX

The fundamental paradox is that *Minimizing* never leads to objectivity and direct knowing. It can only lead to a false sense of what is true. Not only is the actual outcome the opposite of my original intent, but it can never be otherwise. What is the proper perspective? Is objectivity something that I can have when I have fully separated myself from others? Can I really distance myself from life itself? Or is proper perspective only possible when I actually stay connected to life? *Minimizing* is supposed to help me get proper perspective. But when I overdo this strategy, I actually have a poorer understanding of what is true. In defending against my intrinsic desire to be lusty and alive, I withhold myself because I do not believe that I can have what I want. The defenses I've employed bring about the very lack of resources that I fear.

The paradox is that *Minimizing* causes me to disconnect from the thing I care most about, which is knowing directly what is true and seeing the world as it really is. I forget that I am a part of the natural laws of life and death, and that my desire is a natural part of life itself. What I do not perceive is how I still feel without resources with all the *Minimizing* and holding on that I do. I forget that having proper perspective does not come from withdrawing but staying in the flow of life. There is a part of me that knows that I am not rejected and without resources. But honoring this part of myself would create conflict with my ego structure, and that tension would be too much for me to bear. So instead, I continue withholding and pulling back. I sense that I am being blackmailed into *Minimizing* and that this entire structure is built on fear, but I do not know how to move past the fear. The more I fear being forsaken, the more I withdraw and separate myself.

The paradox is that in resisting what might cause me pain and hurt, I cannot avoid fear. In holding myself back, I cut off the flow and the joy. My resistance to desire and wanting causes me to be more hurt and empty. In learning to embrace desire, I can have what I want. In joining the fray, I become not more rejected, but more embraced. When I can honor my own power and strength to be here with it all, I experience greater wisdom. This wisdom brings joy and fulfillment to my life.

6. BREAKING THE VICIOUS CYCLE

In order to break the vicious cycle of my personality, and move from Fear to Love, I must embrace and resolve the fundamental paradox of *Minimizing*. I have spent my whole life being afraid to make contact. This has cut off from my own vitality and strength. I have been crippled by this separation. What incredible possibilities could exist if I didn't resist contact? In keeping the fear of hurt and disappointment at bay, I have also kept away the love. As I throw off the shackles of my personality and orient to my true nature, I begin to own the whole me. I move past my story of being rejected, forsaken and without resources. In surrendering to my core nature, I stop resisting the truth. I become embodied Love, with compassion in my heart, wisdom in my head, and well-being in my body.

My journey with money is a journey to interdependency and true knowing. Participating in the knowing requires me to connect my head to my heart and body. By nurturing a vital physical self that can be present with my true needs, I can participate in life, knowing that it isn't an impediment to knowing but in fact a conduit to my direct knowing. I no longer feel scarcity driven by my need to withhold and be safe. I can be fully naked experiencing things in all their intensity and unbidden forms. This nakedness illuminates my consciousness. I can laugh with joy and enchantment as I recognize what is true. I experience my vaster identity and participation, and feel the love that is here for me. In embracing these truths, I can move past my old beliefs and patterns and welcome abundance, prosperity, and love into my life. I can begin to feel more powerful, vital, and alive. But this is not comfortable or easy. I feel the pain as my ego resists losing its job. I feel remorseful about how I have lived my life and hurt myself and others. I am scared that I won't be able to survive on my own deeper knowing.

When I live abundantly, I fully participate in life unfolding. I do not have to deny my desire. I recognize that I am meant to be fully human and live as I am. This enables me to be engaged in the flow of life. I can be with all the potential hurt, mortality, failure, and deprivation, without resisting it. I don't have to withdraw myself to be safe. I do not have to resist my own humanity, because it is only through my humanity that I can know what is true. By participating in life, my real wisdom develops. From here, I am able to have faith in a supportive universe, and allow myself to support and be supported.

	Brief Description
"Ascetic" SP 5	I am generally frugal and tend to save naturally because I spend less than I make. I am more comfortable amassing resources passively than effortfully. I need to be self-sufficient about money. I am practical and utility oriented. I don't care what others think about my image. I want to get good value for my money.
"Expert" SO 5	Ideals and values are more important to me than money. I keep track of things in my head. I am generous and believe that my generosity will be returned in kind. Money flowing from me is an expression of the money that came to me. Money should move and be actively circulating. The sin of greed is the sin of attention more than the sin of having wealth.
"Low Roller" SX 5	My Sexual instinct contradicts my *Minimizing* energy, which makes me more spontaneous and casual about money than a typical 5. I spend easily in pursuit of what interests me, but small spending for small charge is easier than large expenditures for big charge. I prefer to invest for higher returns than save passively.

Type 5	Summary
Gift	Being observant and making sense of things.
Unconscious Belief	The world is unsafe and rejecting.
Strategy	*Minimizing* – pulling back my needs and desires so that I can be self-sufficient and safe.
Vicious Cycle	Because I pull myself back, I can have perspective on the world and know things from a distance. But because I cannot join the fray, I feel even more rejected. And I cannot know things from direct experience.
Defended Against	Desire, wanting, lust.
Operationally	• I must hold back my desire. • I must stay out of the strong tidal pull of life. • I focus only on the areas that I can know well and be expert in.
Paradox	*Minimizing* does not generate safety or proper perspective.
Breaking the Vicious Cycle	I must recognize that the universe is friendly and loving. In order for me to know what is true, I must participate in the flow of life and be the eyes and ears of knowing from the inside out.
Direction of Growth	Participating fully in my life allows me to feel supported and be committed.

CHAPTER 12

SECURING

Type 6

1. GIFT

I have an innate sense of the importance of allegiance and faith. My faith upholds, maintains, and strengthens the structures that in turn support us. In giving support, we are also supported. My fealty and loyalty is my gift. I feel the honor and duty that this allegiance brings. By believing in structures, working dutifully for these structures, and giving our loyalty and support, we enable institutions like the Red Cross, the Federal Reserve System, and the World Bank, to exist and serve us. If we collectively withdrew our faith, these institutions would crumble.

By upholding and maintaining these structures, we can stay grounded, oriented, and secure. Together, we can move mountains. The world needs me to believe in it, support it, and uphold it. The world needs my faith. It needs me to not be cynical. My allegiance gives life to the structures that matter to us. Without my gift, the world could not harness the power of institutions and structures to organize our lives, protect us, and give us purpose. The devotion inside me fuels my energy of loyalty and allegiance. Being dutiful, faithful, and trusting feeds my soul.

2. STRATEGY

My life and money strategy grow out of my sense of the critical importance of being supported. At the unconscious and conscious levels, I register the world as a scary place. *Securing* is about attaching myself to structures that can support me. Others might think I am a bit fanatical in my devotion to structures, but what they miss is my desire to live from a place of faith and trust, aligned to my own devotional energy. For me, *Securing* is about allying myself with and upholding that which supports us. One aspect of upholding structures is the responsibility to guard against worst-case scenarios, and working to make sure that there are always escape routes that can bring us back to safety. This is my gift and my service to the world, but it can block my experience of trusting that things are as they should be.

Securing is a defense against being okay and differs radically from the *Settling* strategy. In *Securing,* I focus on what could go wrong as opposed to what is okay. I want to be proactive about what might go wrong and prepare in advance so that these things don't catch us off guard. *Securing* is not about trying to be peaceful and rested. It is about being vigilant so that we can be secure. I am always in the process of checking in with my inner radar and discerning what is safe and trustworthy and what is not.

I enjoy the challenge of exploring worst-case scenarios and putting safeguards in place. I would rather prepare in advance for what could go wrong than be caught off guard. I assume that the world requires *Securing* because it is inherently rudderless. I do not trust that there is an inherent support system in place that keeps me or the universe from being set adrift. Security is not just local, but global as well, and requires more than just preparing for worst-case scenarios. At some deeper level, security is about not letting our fear of what could go wrong keep us small. It is about being secure enough to explore the big world. If we are really secure, then we do have to live anxiously. We intrinsically cannot prepare for that which we do not know or cannot anticipate. But if we let fear stop us in our track, we are not secure at all. We are only truly secure when we can trust that we have the capacity to meet whatever comes our way. An orientation to letting go and living fully requires being okay with the possibility that life is not always going to be safe, predictable, knowable. But I am not so comfortable with this reasoning. I prefer the known over the unknown. I prefer to stay close to what I know as home base.

For me, having security is about having the support that will keep me oriented and safe. I don't associate it with having confidence in myself or the universe. Stepping forth into my full potential would require that I move into the unknown where I couldn't even begin to anticipate the ways in which things could go wrong. But how am I to navigate this enormous world if I can only go places that I know? Without being able to travel to places that are unknown, unpredictable, and possibly exhilarating, life remains dreary and small. I just don't know if I am ready to bear the cost of moving beyond my strategy of *Securing* and venture into the realm of the unknown.

3. THE VICIOUS CYCLE

If I were to look at my life objectively, I would notice that I have essentially been trapped in a vicious cycle of fear and scarcity. Because of this, my relationship to love and prosperity is constrained. *Securing* is fundamentally about holding back danger. But in seeing the world this way, I continually reinforce the fact that danger and the abyss are out there to be feared. This orientation makes me anxious and scared. But my ego enthusiastically keeps this vicious cycle going. I get addicted to *Securing*. Even though I think I am moving along, I am merely moving in place.

When we are caught in a vicious cycle where our actions validate our beliefs, it can be very difficult to extricate ourselves. When we are stuck at a certain point along the scarcity-to-abundance spectrum, it is impossible to improve our position until we get out of the vicious cycle. If we are suddenly showered with new wealth, we will most likely dissipate it so that we can get back to our old set point. So in order to create new wealth, we must first become aware of the vicious cycle we are caught in. Once we become aware, we will be in a better position to consciously unblock what blocks us, and welcome new wealth into our lives.

My underlying assumption is that life is scary and I could fall forever without support. Thus, I must work hard to find security so that I don't fall into an abyss. I cannot let my guard down and relax. I cannot trust that things will be okay and that I am supported. I cannot trust that the universe is friendly, and that I am guided. I must be constantly vigilant. I must figure out who I can trust and who I can't trust. I must figure out where my security lies. I must be prepared for whatever might happen so that I will be safe. Structures either support me or they don't. I prefer black-and-white thinking to fuzzy thinking. In the gray, there might be no such thing as security, and I don't want that to be true.

Danger and insecurity exist in the realm of the unknown, so I try to stay close to what I know. To me, big dreams and visions have nothing to do with making the world a safer place. I choose to focus my attention on the things around me that I can control. I do not interest myself with things beyond my duty and responsibility. I am a realist about the dangers that might meet us at every turn. To me, things are either safe or not safe. I find it a challenge to go beyond this type of black-and-white thinking.

The problem is that when I don't know which way to go, it is difficult to trust that I oriented correctly. I constantly scan the landscape to determine whether I have made the right choices or not. I want to validate my choices, commitments, and allegiances. I want to know that the choices I have made are correct. I want to relax, but I also feel I must be vigilant and on guard. Out of sheer exhaustion and the feeling that I can never be secure enough, I can get quite reactive. Sometimes I redouble my efforts for security. Other times I give up and go looking for security elsewhere.

I look outside myself for guidance. The more lost I feel, the more I try to attach myself to structures, even though I am not sure they will help. I feel the fear first, and then I try to find something that might alleviate this fear, even if it can only bring temporary relief. My general anxiety stems from an existential problem of being in a world without any intrinsic support or direction. I must recognize this fear for what it really is. It's like I went out to sea, hit a terrible storm, and everything got knocked out. I awoke, but found myself lost without any navigational devices or landmarks in sight. Imagine my horror and fear. In which direction should I go? Will I be lost forever? Am I going to make it? All I want to know is what I should do. I had better stay awake in case anything else bad happens. I don't want to get knocked out again. I will do what it takes to be prepared this time. I am going to find something to orient towards and go for it. Better to have some direction than none at all. I have always been seeking safe harbor. But it has been difficult to trust the places that I have chosen. Even when I land somewhere, I am not sure that this is where I am supposed to be. Do I stay or do I keep going? Who can I trust? When can I rest?

On the one hand, I crave authority and structures that give me orientation and direction in my life. I look for authority, and look for bosses who I can respect. I want my boss to know that I am a good worker. I like to be right under the boss, because then I have someone to bounce ideas off of, and someone to confide in. I like to be able to speak to someone I trust because I don't want to make decisions on my own. On the other hand, I can distrust and resent authority. This ambivalence can result in very puzzling behavior. I look outside for advice and confirmation about my own thinking. I am sorely tempted to depend on others. But then, I get angry at myself for this dependency. It is easy for me to look to an authority figure, but I know I can't just depend on someone else. I know I need to look inside for this wisdom. I want to be self-directing, self-trusting, self-confident. Yet, it can feel so difficult to be this way. I can spend a lot of time thinking things through, rehashing scenarios, figuring things out, which often causes me to procrastinate.

Money, like authority, seems like the answer to all my problems. It represents security, safety, and direction, and I don't have to think too hard. It seems, for a while, that I can be okay if I just dedicate myself to working for money and placing my power at money's feet, and trusting that I will be guided properly. But like with authority, I get resentful about how money ends up leading me around by the nose. I resent having to worry about money and having to do things for money. So I oscillate between extremes – being frugal sometimes, and then spending lavishly at others. It is difficult to walk the middle road. Either I give my power to money, or I try to take my power from money and reject its authority.

I give my power away to the structures and authority figures that provide me with security and guidance. For if I am not loyal and committed to these structures, I believe that my needs will not be met and I will be lost forever. I believe I must stay attached to the structures that are working for me. I check-in constantly and am a good team player – diligent, cooperative, collaborative, and responsible. I hope that these structures, in turn, will support me. But I can be torn between my commitments to different alliances, and I can also be torn about how best to honor my commitments. Is it better to speak up for what I believe or is it better to not rock the boat? Sometimes I am hurt by being too trusting. By unquestioningly following the lead of the group or person to which I am allied, I might put myself or others in danger, or betray myself. I struggle with these tensions.

I don't know where to turn, I can't let my guard down, I am tired, pulled in so many different directions, and nothing seems to help. This global anxiety seems to have no cause and seems to be impossible to manage. It is difficult to be courageous and relaxed when my head feels so cut off from my internal compass which is my body and heart working together in unison. I lack faith in myself and in my direction. I fear being the shiny lonely star without support. Fear keeps me small. I fear my own success. I fear being untethered. I often sabotage myself so I don't shine too brightly.

Because I am constantly worried about who or what can be trusted, I find myself testing people and alliances. I can be at turns docile, compliant, and trusting, and then doubtful, reactive and argumentative. My early warning system is on high alert. If something or someone does not prove trustworthy, I need to cut my losses. My pattern is to trust for a while, and then turn skeptical and cynical. Either I trust someone, or I doubt them. This testing and skepticism can devolve into self-defeating behavior as I damage good relationships. It can also be difficult for me to trust that money supports me and that there is abundance in my life.

The problem is I simply don't know which way to go, who to believe, what to do. Lacking confidence in myself and in others, I worry. I worry about things that might threaten my security. I worry about who to be loyal to and who has my back. I worry about doing the right thing. I worry about what might befall me in the future. I try to anticipate what might go wrong and prepare for the worst. Bracing for future collisions, I live in contraction and fear. My efforts to keep myself and everyone around me safe is fundamentally based on my fear of life itself. My anxiety keeps me from coping in a calm and collected way. I become reactive to my environment, and get set off in reaction to things that happen around me. Rather than setting my own direction, I get triggered by things that don't go well. It is easy to get upset, feel criticized and attacked by things that happen outside of me. I find myself being reactive because I do not trust myself enough, do not have my own sense of what I need, and worry that I am not doing things correctly. I feel besieged by criticisms from outside and from inside, and I lash out in defense.

Sometimes I want to just forget everything and indulge. This extreme behavior does not serve me well. Either I totally trust someone or I reject them. Either I am frugal or I binge spend. Either I am careful or I am impulsive. It is hard for me to walk the road of moderation without feeling torn in two different directions. The defenses I've employed bring about the very insecurity I fear. *Securing* actually generates more anxiety than it relieves. In being afraid of living, I cannot connect to my inner guidance and courage.

This is the very paradox of my ego strategy – the strategy of *Securing* causes me to disconnect from the thing I care most about, which is finding my own inner guidance. If I were to embrace the fact that I can manage, no matter what curves life throws at me, then I would have to give up my belief that I am not secure. Honoring myself would create conflict with my attachment to structures, and that tension would be too much for me to bear. So instead, I continue searching for safety and guidance. But the more I fear being lost, the more worried, anxious, and suspicious I become. In continuing to search for security and safety, I can never actually relax. Things have to go very badly for me to give up on trying to find security. The dynamic of the ego structure keeps my ego employed and keeps me perpetually fixated on the question of what can I trust. I can never find security for then I would have no excuse for *Securing*. We are each caught in a vicious cycle of our personality and instincts until we decide to break free. This takes deliberate energy and momentum because the cycle is a compelling vortex. In order to create new wealth, we must see clearly the vicious cycle that blocks us from abundance. Then we must fight our way out of the vortex.

4. OPERATIONALLY

If my instincts are balanced, I will be able to attend to money in each of the Nine Money Domains in a healthy manner. I am both prepared for what could happen and confident that I can handle what I comes up. If, however, my instincts are not in balance, then I get stuck in my type fixation and I cannot be optimally effective. My motivation to be secure manifests in different ways depending on my dominant instinct. I tend to focus on the areas which I deem most important for my security and ignore the areas I deem unimportant. As a SP 6, I focus on being secure in terms of having safe water to drink, safe food to eat, a safe place to live, a safe car to drive, and so on. I also focus on having enough money so that I will not be in danger. As a SO 6, I focus on allying myself to social groups and institutions. As a SX 6, my *Securing* energy reinforces my Sexual instinct, and I continually test the trustworthiness of my connections. How my instincts are imbalanced will therefore impact how I relate to the Nine Money Domains – where I put my attention and energy and where I don't.

"GUARD" SP 6	"ALLY" SO 6	"PARTNER" SX 6

Domain 1 – Budgeting

Which areas I define to be important for my security depend on my dominant instinct. In those areas, I try to be responsible. Other areas I just ignore so that I will not be overwhelmed by worrying. I tend to have trouble enlisting the satisfactory cooperation of my partner around finances and feel frustrated that my partner doesn't give me the support I need to create the security I crave.

As a "Guard" SP 6, I try to find the structures in my life that will give me physical and financial security. I believe that money can provide me with security. Therefore, I tend to focus a lot of my attention on money and worry about it a lot. I have a sense that budgeting is something I should do, but I may or may not stick to a budget. A budget helps me feel more structured and secure but the budgeting process itself often creates more stress than security for me. So my discipline runs hot and cold in this area. I want to track my spending to get relief from my anxiety, but the anxiety doesn't really ever go away.

As an "Ally" SO 6, I tend to be less anxious about money and more anxious about social alliances. But I do pay some attention to money. I may be organized and keep meticulous records, but resent having to do so. I don't like to be constrained by a budget. My budgeting process feels somewhat forced, like it is being imposed from outside of me. I feel obliged to track my spending, but do not use the information that it generates. I feel reactive about the budgeting process. I will do it, but cannot embrace it.

As a "Partner" SX 6, I tend to swing to extremes even more. My Sexual instinct causes me to be daring, bold, and impulsive. Coupled with my reactive type energy, I swing to extremes. I might consider budgeting and tracking to be completely boring and either ignore it completely or have someone else deal with it, or I might be very determined to control and tame it. I will want to know where things are at, be organized, and try to be frugal. But then something will come along and completely derail my good efforts.

Domain 2 – Spending

I like to think of myself as frugal. I like the idea of being frugal and love bargains, but in truth, I am not really frugal. My spending tends to go back and forth between being frugal and splurging. Sometimes I pay careful attention to my spending. Other times, I zone out and do not pay any attention at all. When I splurge, there is a feeling of release, like I can't hold the tension and anxiety anymore. I notice this desire to let go but, at the same, I feel it is important to be responsible, proactive, and in control. So I vacillate between being anxious, worried, and burdened by money decisions, and wanting to be on auto pilot, not thinking about it.

I like to spend on known quantities that are reputable. Spending, otherwise, can be fraught with indecision. For example, when I have to choose from dozens of LCD HDTVs, the details overwhelm me. I don't want to make the wrong choice. But it can be difficult to think clearly about everything. To diffuse the anxiety and get the process over with, I might make an impulsive decision without having a good reason.

I want to stay on track and do what will enable me to be secure. But when I get disappointed because I don't feel secure, and I feel let down by the structures that I have put my faith in, I get reactive. My reactivity makes me go the other way to blow off steam. This is why my spending can be so back and forth. It's difficult to hold the line and aim straight when I feel this kind of anxiety inside me.

As a "Guard" SP 6, I want security around food, money, shelter, and safety. I like to spend on safe cars, reliable clothing and furniture, good housing, and live in safe neighborhoods. I want to have savings in case of an emergency. I am torn between spending on the things that keep me secure now and saving for a rainy day - this makes me anxious about spending. Because of this, I tend to be more generous with my time than money. You would think that because I worry so much about having savings, I would be a good saver. But because spending is fraught with anxiety, I tend to blow off steam by spending that undermines my savings. For example, when I am with the kids at Disneyland, I may know that I don't really have the money to spend, but because I want so badly to relax on vacation, I just charge everything to my credit card and deal with the consequences later. At the other extreme, I might be incredibly frugal, afraid that if I open the spigot, I won't be able to stop myself. In addition, I often feel frustrated by my inability to control my spouse's spending because this might generate too much conflict and insecurity.

As an "Ally" SO 6, I want to know the rules and adhere to the implicit social mores. I am less concerned about having savings and material security than I am in having social connection and alliances. I want to be in the right place with the right people. I want to look appropriate, dress appropriately. I want to support my family and my community. I want to belong. Security in the form of social bonds is much more important to me than money in a bank account or the stock market. I may seem "easy-going" about money on the surface, but inside, I can be nervous and indecisive. Sometimes I just want to stay away from money because it's too complex and overwhelming, and I am afraid of making the wrong decision.

As a "Partner" SX 6, I spend money on my passions, to look good, and to have intense experiences. My desire to find the juice can outweigh my anxiety about spending. My Sexual instinct makes me impulsive and makes me want to go after what I want in an aggressive and assertive way. Sometimes I throw caution to the wind and buy what I want, even if I know I'll have to deal with the consequences later. I feel rebellious against my own rules. I can only be disciplined about money for so long. Then I can't handle the routine any more. In relationship, I can be reluctant to say no to my spouse's or partner's spending whims because it feels riskier to disrupt the relationship than to take a stand for money security.

Domain 3 – Earning

When it comes to making money, I tend to be very responsible and hard working. As a "Guard" SP 6, I want to have a decent lifestyle and I am paid well since money promises security. I like having a stable income and I am not comfortable when the atmosphere is ultra-competitive. I like the stability of a government or academic job. I am a responsible, diligent worker who will do what is required. I am fairly ambitious, but I am not a big risk taker who would bust out in a completely innovative direction. I can be very loyal to my company and I want a boss who knows that I am a good worker.

As an "Ally" SO 6, I am more concerned about fitting in and collaborating with others than about my lifestyle or money. I want a secure job that I can count on but don't have to think about too much, since I already spend so much time checking in on my support structures. It is nice to be a part of something, and be able to work collaboratively and cooperatively. I enjoy working with a group or team. Because I tend to lack confidence in myself and don't want to draw too much attention, I tend to hold myself back from the best jobs and leadership positions. I don't want to create unsafe structures by setting expectations high. I have even done some self-sabotage in my life. I might know the next step and yet not do it, create a situation that doesn't work, or stop short of my potential and then change directions.

As a "Partner" SX 6, my Sexual instinct makes me more confident and competitive than a typical 6. I feel sure of myself in a way that does not feel grounded in facts. My Sexual instinct desires freedom and autonomy to do my own thing. I want to be the master of my own destiny, and am willing to endure difficult hours and more stress and anxiety than most. My lifestyle is not as important to me as doing what I have a passion for. I might be attracted to being an entrepreneur who has more control, even if it comes with more headaches and risk. I am committed to the impact of my work and figure things will work out somehow.

Domain 4 – Beliefs

On the surface, money represents security, safety, a way to contribute, and a way to pursue my dreams. I am very apt to get pulled into the temple of money and worship money as a god that can bring security and direction to my life. I want to believe that it will bring me security if I devote myself to it. In a black-and-white world, money tends to be one of the good guys in my book. I am apt to trust in money completely, until I get to a point of recognizing that it is my overconfidence in money as a structure of security and support that does me in. There is another part of me, however, that knows that no external structure, including money, can ever really bring me the kind of security I crave. Real security comes from trusting myself, having confidence and faith in myself. When I get disappointed in the power of money to bring me security, I tend to react in the opposite direction and give up on money.

As a "Guard" SP 6, I am almost always anxious about money. Money represents stability and security for me and I want to be so well off that I don't have to worry about money. I wish I could be more generous with my money, but all my neuroses go into the future. I would be willing to completely sacrifice today for tomorrow but there are bills to be paid now which makes it difficult to feel secure. As an "Ally" SO 6, money is about having a place in the group. A lack of money signifies a lack of status, value, and contribution. Money enables me to maintain my relationships and belong to a community. As a "Partner" SX 6, a lack of money signifies a lack of opportunities and experiences. The complexity and potential worry associated with managing large sums of money can deter me from that.

Domain 5 – Understanding

Money is an object of security for me. I am attached to it but I am also anxious about it. I don't tend to think about money from lots of different angles. As a "Guard" SP 6, I am a bit more motivated to learn about money because I want to be self-reliant and in control. When Self-Preservation is my blindspot, though, I tend do very little thinking or learning about money, until I worry about hurting myself. I can feel overwhelmed just talking about it. The future feels too big to think about. I can only sustain interest in money for a short time before it slips out of my focus. I have a lot of anxiety about understanding money and getting it right. I can get so afraid of my incompetence that I endlessly defer money tasks. My anxiety, fear, and sense of incompetence can be a deterrent to learning. At the same time, I can use my counterphobic energy to force myself to gain some competency and break through the fear. Otherwise, the fear of not being able to figure things out as I go along can stop me in my tracks. It feels difficult to think clearly about money, what it means to me, what role it plays in my life, and how it works. I would rather hire someone else to figure it all out for me – someone that I "trust" to act on my behalf. Often, though I get burned from over-trusting because I farm it out to someone else before doing enough due diligence about their motives.

Domain 6 – Risk Management

My mind naturally goes to what could go wrong. Whatever I can do to keep the floor from falling out from under me would be great. I instinctively think about worst-case scenarios so risk management comes naturally. But it can be a burden to have such a heightened awareness of what could go wrong. Mostly I only see the downside.

As a "Guard" SP 6, I am motivated to manage potential risks. I want to make sure that I have what I need and am very motivated to build up a rainy-day fund. My motivation for saving has surprisingly little to do with building wealth for bigger possibilities. Savings is almost entirely to guard against potential future pitfalls. Saving for anything beyond contingencies is difficult for me to consider because it feels so abstract. Contingency planning feels more compelling because it feels like I can control it. In contrast, the distant future where anything might happen feels too abstract for me to think about. For me, the best way to deal with the abstract future that I can't get my head around is to put money into a "black hole" and not touch it. Like a Type 1, money that is abstract and for the future is difficult for me to pay attention to and connect to now.

> I think liquidity is more important than retirement savings. I have $30,000 in a savings account that is earning barely anything, but I like the base it gives me, even if it doesn't earn a big return. Intellectually, I understand that the stock market will return more, but it makes me feel good knowing that the base is there earning 3%.

As an "Ally" SO 6, the focus of my contingency planning is centered more around cultivating my social network which is something I can count on in case of emergency, perhaps more so than money. My social relationships are resources to me. Perhaps I should worry about money more, but I just trust that the money stuff will be okay.

As a "Partner" SX 6, the focus of my contingency planning is centered around cultivating my passion, my health, and my partnerships, rather than money per se. My sense is that if trouble hits, I can always rely on my own wits, capabilities, and relationships to bounce back.

Domain 7 – Planning

There is a part of me that loves the idea of planning. But the kind of planning that I do, if I do it at all, is more tactical than strategic. I like to know where I am going to be staying, what I'm going to be doing, what time I am going to be leaving, etc. This type of planning makes me feel more secure. I'm very good at the kind of planning that requires thinking about the logistics, scheduling, and details. The kind of planning where I need to think through what-if scenarios. What's the weather going to be? What time do the trains leave? What if we miss the first train? I can be very skillful at planning for future things that are relatively parameterized. I'm averse, though, to projecting out to where things get fuzzier and more gray and blurry. Planning at this distance requires clarity of vision and a big picture perspective that my mental chatter doesn't allow me to have. This kind of planning feels overwhelming. I am more oriented to having a strong foundation that supports me than optimizing or maximizing for a bigger stockpile that would just create more worry and anxiety.

I resist big, long-term goals, financial or otherwise. I don't want to have to "worry" about things. The problem is that the planning itself can generate so much anxiety that sometime I just want to close my eyes. A part of me is also afraid that if I set goals and don't meet them, I will be disappointed. I don't want the insecurity of failing. This resistance to planning and thinking ahead only perpetuates the vagueness, insecurity, and dread. Whenever I resist something, it is usually a reaction to feeling disappointed. The anxiety that keeps me away from being able to plan long-term generates more insecurity in my life.

As a "Guard" SP 6, I am more likely to have financial goals, but I am more methodical than visionary in my approach. If I put money away in a retirement account, I generally use the "black hole" strategy where I put the money away and am not allowed to touch it because I don't trust myself to not mess it up. I don't want to give myself the flexibility or opportunity to optimize my financial situation. I prefer a cut-and-dry system to anything gray and complex.

As an "Ally" SO 6, I am not as oriented to having financial goals. Saving feels abstract and difficult because that would require that I have an idea and plan for what to do with the money. I know I don't like to waste or hoard. I don't want too little or too much. I don't want to be greedy or stingy but concrete planning is very hard for me. I don't seem to take the steps I need to take. I find myself spending more energy worrying about what could go wrong than actually saving the way I could, given what I make. I know I am playing roulette and that it is a self-sabotaging behavior, but there is something in me that resists goal-setting pretty strongly.

As a "Partner" SX 6, my Sexual instinct prefers to be more in the moment, impulsive and opportunistic than planful. I tend to jump in and out of the moment, and worry less about the future and more about today. I want to trust someone else to plan for me, but I don't know if I can.

Domain 8 – Wealth Building

Security is more important to me than wealth building. I prefer to earn stable, decent returns. Wealth building for me is more about having a secure foundation than wanting money to open up new possibilities. My responsibility is to do what there is to do and no more. For things I don't understand so well, I either avoid them or try to be moderate, and not take too much risk. I can be very disciplined about savings if I don't get deterred by my anxiety and reactivity. My weakness is that I lack a vision of what to do with the money. Either I will be a lazy investor, and pay little attention, or my insecurity, coupled with my desire to get ahead, will make me reactive and jump around looking for better results. By making constant changes to alleviate my emotional distress, I tend to worry even more. I want to trust that I have made the right decision, but any small thing can trigger me to be skeptical, distrustful, and want to switch course. When the market goes down, it can be very difficult for me. I don't want to get upset, but I do. I can be very reactive and bounce from investment to investment in an attempt to avoid more losses. Thus, long-term investing and wealth building, buying and holding can be difficult for me. There is something at once appealing and yet deeply worrisome about being fully invested in something and actually staying put for the long haul. Part of the problem is that I don't like to do the research about the details of potential investment options myself. Too many possibilities and options make my brain go haywire, and I just don't want to be responsible for this kind of big decision. I would rather someone tell me what to do.

> I look for people I can trust. If I have a deep affiliation to them, I would give my money to them to manage because I feel they have my interests at heart.

I don't stop to think that the incentives, compensation structure, and motives of financial advisors can create a conflict of interest. For example, I don't stop to think about how they get bigger fees if they churn my portfolio a lot, or invest my money in mutual funds with load fees. Because I go in with this hope and desire to off-load my own worries, I can get burned by being over-trusting with financial advisors. I have to learn this lesson the hard way before I recognize what it is in me that causes this dynamic to happen repeatedly in my life.

As a "Guard" SP 6, I try to be proactive in building wealth because I want to be self-reliant. I tend to avoid junk bonds, penny stocks, and other exotic and risky investments. I try to do my due diligence and ask questions and do my own research and then go to the experts to help me. I like to have someone watching over my retirement assets. I only know enough to figure out if they know enough. I tend to be moderately conservative. I understand the benefit of stocks for the long-term horizon, but I also like to have a decent amount of liquidity for emergencies. Low-cost index funds make sense to me. I am willing to take moderate risk because I know that if I don't earn a decent return, I could outlive my money, and that's a big fear for me as well. I try to do things myself, but if I am not able to manage on my own, I will ask for help.

> I put away $16K/year into my 401K religiously. I don't like to know or check on my money every day. Then I'd have to deal with all the emotions, and I'd get upset with market falling and there's nothing I can do about it, so I just don't look so often. As investor, my notion is that I won't look at the account balance till I am 70.5. I have not rebalanced and I won't go look at it, because I don't want to know and get upset. I rely on my broker, who has custodianship of my money. I trust him to take care of things.

As an "Ally" SO 6, I tend to be less proactive about building wealth for security. I don't want to be selfish, and I don't want to set the bar too high. I don't even know if I deserve to have a lot of wealth. I feel a bit guilty about wanting more. Also, managing a large pot of wealth myself is a huge responsibility and I don't know if I am up to that. I'd have to find someone to help me. As a "Partner" SX 6, I want to invest in areas that I have passion for. Building wealth through sweat equity is more appealing to me than money in a bank. I find that I gravitate to ventures that are challenging and slightly risky and daring. I'm not in it for the money so much as I am in it to prove to myself and the world that I can do it and succeed. It scares me, but is exhilarating at the same time.

Domain 9 – Balance

I forget my successes. It's difficult to feel abundant when I feel so much fear and insecurity and habitually see the downside but not the upside of things. This perspective keeps me anxious, reactive, and lacking in confidence. Balance for me is about remembering my successes, recognizing the support that has existed in my life, and being grateful for the way life has worked out. It means reminding myself that I am supported even when I don't see it. Balance requires trusting myself and the universe in the darkest of times, when I am most anxious and worried that I will fall forever. Rather than looking for evidence in the external world that would allow me to trust, I must look within. Haven't I held up even in the worst of times? Hasn't some internal guidance system always clicked on when I needed it? Wasn't I the one who knew what to do when there was an emergency? If I can make it through the worst of times, why wouldn't I be able to make it through the easy times? There is nothing to stop me but me. I must recognize how supported I have been and integrate this into my experience of money. I must confront my unwillingness to step forth boldly and be heroic. I can have the love I want, but I must work towards being in the flow of life and wealth without blocking love out.

5. THE PARADOX

The fundamental paradox is that *Securing* never leads to the security I want. It only leads to doubt and anxiety. Not only is the actual outcome the opposite of my original intent, but it can never be otherwise. What is security? Can security come from some object or structure outside of me? Or is security something intrinsic to my own nature? *Securing* is supposed to bring more security to my life. But when I overdo this strategy, I actually feel less secure. In defending against my essential nature, I cannot shine brightly. The defenses I've employed bring about the very insecurity and doubt I fear.

The paradox is that *Securing* causes me to disconnect from the thing I care most about, which is finding support and guidance. I forget that the support I want cannot come from outside; the support I crave can only come from within. Until I recognize this fundamental truth, I will always be disappointed and reactive. Hiding out at home base, afraid to strike out boldly, and lashing out in disappointment, will not give me the security I am looking for. There is a part of me that knows that I am not unsupported. But honoring this part of myself would create conflict with my ego structure, and that tension would be too much for me to bear. I sense that I am being blackmailed into *Securing* and that this entire structure is built on fear, but I do not know how to move past the fear. In continuing to search for security, I can never actually feel it.

The paradox is that in always paying attention to how things are not secure, I become part of the insecurity. In always trying to make things safer,

I can only see what's risky. In always needing to be safe, I feel more threatened. In always needing to control, I can never eliminate danger. In learning to take a leap of faith, I can learn to trust and have confidence in myself. In surrendering to the fall, the fear of falling no longer has power over me. What I resist makes me more anxious and insecure, while what I embrace enables me to relax and brings real security to my life.

6. BREAKING THE VICIOUS CYCLE

In order to break the vicious cycle of my personality, and move from Fear to Love, I must embrace and resolve the fundamental paradox of *Securing*. I have spent my whole life being scared, cut off from my own courage. I have been crippled by this fear. How can I relax and be here with what is? What incredible possibilities could exist if I didn't have to be scared? If I could take a leap of faith and be strong, I could honor myself. In keeping the fear at bay, I have also held away the love. As I throw off the shackles of my personality and orient to my true nature, I begin to own the whole me. When I do this, I move past my story of being unsupported. I move past my anxiety. In surrendering to my core nature, I stop resisting the truth. I become embodied Love, with compassion in my heart, wisdom in my head, and well-being in my body. I experience my vaster identity, and feel confident. I step into the light, knowing that I am meant to take my place and shine.

My journey with money is a journey to real security. My journey to real support requires me to be open, clear, awake, knowing what to do and how to be without referencing external structures for direction. When I take this journey to real security, I can relax knowing that I am meant to be here, courageous and brave. I can be confident that I will know what to do and how to be when the new moment arises. I trust that the universe supports me and I can show up fully. In embracing these truths, I can move past my old beliefs and patterns and welcome abundance, prosperity, and love into my life. I can feel confident and secure. But this is not comfortable. I feel the pain as my ego resists losing its job. I feel remorseful about how I have lived my life and hurt myself and others. I am scared that I won't be able to survive on my own deeper knowing alone.

When I live abundantly, I have confidence, trust, and faith in myself and the universe. I no longer feel scarcity driven by my need to have more security. I no longer need to sort things into safe or dangerous, with me or against me. I no longer believe that money is about security or insecurity. I can be with what is here right now, sensing the support that upholds everything. In this space, I can be with all the scary things without being afraid and needing to hide. From this place, I can see the larger vista ahead. I can take my place confidently in the world. I can relax. When I can shine and live to my fullest potential, I can see how I am supposed to participate in the unfolding, just being fully who I am.

	Brief Description
"Guard" SP 6	I believe that money can provide me with security, so I focus on and worry about money a lot. I am almost always anxious about money. I want to have a rainy-day savings account to guard against potential future emergencies. My discipline, however, runs hot and cold. When I feel unsupported, I get reactive and my spending becomes undisciplined as I discharge my anxiety.
"Ally" SO 6	My anxiety centers less around money and more around social bonds. I want to know what the rules are and adhere to implicit social mores. I want to look appropriate, support my community, and belong. I like to have a secure job and be collaborative. Financial goals feel abstract and difficult to orient towards.
"Partner" SX 6	My anxiety centers around my relationships more than around money or groups. I want to look good and I want to be where the action is. I will often throw caution to the wind and buy what I want, even if I have to deal with the consequences later.

Type 6	Summary
Gift	Being loyal and responsible.
Unconscious Belief	I don't know what to trust or how to orient myself
Strategy	*Securing* – trying to determine who and what I can trust and attaching myself to trustworthy structures to be secure.
Vicious Cycle	Because I need to find security, I must be loyal and responsible, focus on cultivating my inner circle and repelling untrustworthy outsiders. But because I can never be sure who or what to trust, I must be hyper-vigilant, which causes me to feel insecure.
Defended Against	My wholeness and connectedness.
Operationally	• I must figure out who and what is trustworthy. • I need to be supported to feel secure. • I focus only on the areas where I can be responsible and secure.
Paradox	*Securing* does not generate security.
Breaking the Vicious Cycle	I must recognize that the universe supports me, and I will not fall forever without support and security. My job is to trust myself and the universe and be courageous in the face of the unknown.
Direction of Growth	Performing to my fullest potential allows me to have a wider vision of what is possible.

CHAPTER 13

OPTIMIZING

Type 7

1. GIFT

My spontaneous enthusiasm contributes to the joyfulness in the universe. My energy lights others up. My openness to new ideas fills the world with possibilities. I am an expression of our expansive spaciousness. I have a childlike enthusiasm for life. I understand that life is supposed to be stimulating, interesting, and wonderful. I am effusive and unbounded. I have a large appetite for the good things in life and I share that enthusiasm with the world. I can see quickly what is not working well and what could be improved. When I combine discipline with spontaneity, I become incredibly productive and creative. I can see all kinds of possibilities and I can harness my creativity in service of the world. I am gifted at managing complexity and getting the most for the least. When I surrender my own plans to the universe, and simply respond to each moment as it unfolds, I bring my best to the world. I savor the qualities of each moment, enjoy the pleasures of all the senses, and take in impressions fully. I see and experience heaven on earth and share that with others.

2. STRATEGY

My life and money strategy grow out of my sense of the critical importance of freedom and joy. For me, freedom is about being free of inhibitions, rules, and constraints. At the unconscious level, the world is a box that constrains and potentially deprives me, though I deny this at the conscious level. At the conscious level, I believe I can generate spontaneity, freedom, and happiness. *Optimizing* is about making the world better than it currently is. Others might think I am frenetic in my acquisitiveness and consumption of material things and experiences. What they miss is my desire to live from a place of satisfaction, freedom, and joy.

An aspect of *Optimizing* is the ability to visualize how things could be better so that they would suit me more. I feel compelled to continually make things better and more fun. I cannot be satisfied with the way things are. It's not that they are wrong, but just that they could be made more satisfying. I feel that I am at the center of the universe and can guide the unfolding of things. *Optimizing* is a defense against being without resources and deprived, and is the opposite of *Minimizing*. In *Optimizing,* I deny my ability to be satisfied with little or nothing. I refuse to be denied material pleasures and experiences. I assume that it is up to me to get satisfaction. The world will not naturally bring it to me. I must go out and get satisfaction for myself. I deeply fear a life that is not pleasurable and free.

But being free and satisfied is not really about being unconstrained. Being free is about being able to embrace our life in our bodies and still experience the freedom of our consciousness. If we have to push away constraints to be free, we are not in fact free. To live freely is to be able to be spontaneous within whatever restrictions exist in our physical lives. It is about participating in life just as it is. It is about trusting that the universe is unfolding in the way it is meant to unfold. If I cannot trust that I have what I need, it is difficult to live in the present instead of anticipating a better future. It is about not letting my fear of being deprived keep me from being fulfilled now. We are only free when we can be with deprivation and plenitude, constraints and freedom, with equal ease. But I am not so comfortable with this. I am used to spending my energy breaking free, not experiencing the freedom that I do have.

3. THE VICIOUS CYCLE

If I were to look at my life objectively, I would notice that I have essentially been trapped in a vicious cycle of fear and scarcity. Because of this, my relationship to love and prosperity is constrained. *Optimizing* is fundamentally about trying to make things better because I can never be satisfied with the way things are. I am frustrated that I have to work so hard to improve things, but my ego enthusiastically keeps this vicious cycle going so that it can keep its job. I get addicted to *Optimizing*. Even though I think I am moving along, I am merely moving in place.

When we are caught in a vicious cycle where our actions validate our beliefs, it can be very difficult to extricate ourselves. When we are stuck at a certain point along the scarcity-to-abundance spectrum, it is impossible to improve our position until we get out of the vicious cycle. If we are suddenly showered with new wealth, we will most likely dissipate it so that we can get back to our old set point. So in order to create new wealth, we must first become aware of the vicious cycle we are caught in. Once we become aware, we will be in a better position to consciously unblock what blocks us, and welcome new wealth into our lives.

My underlying assumption is that I must do what it takes to avoid deprivation. I assume that things are not good enough the way they are and could be made better. This leads me down the slippery slope of living as if today is not good enough and tomorrow will be better. I employ a strategy of *Optimizing*, always going for something better, so that I will not be boxed in and deprived. I reach for what I believe will satisfy me and make me happy. And then I go on to the next thing. Keeping commitments is difficult for me because if something better comes along, I want to be free to pursue it. Why shouldn't I be able to have what I want? I hate being deprived. It can be difficult to master anything. I tend to be on to the next thing before I have mastered the last thing.

Going where the grass is greener is my way of dealing with this constant feeling of being constrained and boxed in. The problem is that in continually looking for something better, I never enjoy what I already have. This causes me to stay hungry and continually unsatisfied with what is in front of me, leading me to look for something better. I optimistically believe that I will eventually find what will alleviate my hunger, not recognizing that this behavior only perpetuates my hunger. My relationship to goals is interesting. On the one hand, I like to anticipate and plan ahead. On the other hand, I do not like to be constrained. Therefore, I may be goal-oriented, or I may not be, depending on whether I perceive a goal as a constraint or an escape route. I enjoy having a vision to move towards, but I also enjoy making things up as I go along. It is true that decisions cut off options, but new options and possibilities continuously open up as life unfolds.

I want to have maximum flexibility with my job, schedule, spending, investing, living options. I do not like to be limited by anything. I am an energetic person with lots of ideas. I am creative and can see all kinds of possibilities for the future. I like to control things, so that other people's visions aren't imposed on me and so that I can maintain maximum freedom for my own life. I am playful, inventive, optimistic. I don't want to have to say no to better things that come along in my life. I am, in fact, always scanning the landscape for "better" – a better job, a better house, a better lover, a better education, a better car. I want to figure out what I can do with myself that would enable me to make money, but also allow me freedom and mobility, control over my own life, amusement, challenge, and enjoyment.

I can't understand "no" very well. I feel like a caged animal that needs to break free. It may seem that I am rebellious, but what I am really trying to do is to be free. I am almost always in motion as my large appetite for more propels me forward. I equate freedom with lack of constraints. Anything that stands in my path to satisfaction is an obstacle to overcome. I can be aggressive about getting what I want. But if something takes too much effort or gets too difficult, I might go for something else. Changing directions is not an issue for me. What is difficult is staying on track if it requires saying no to other interesting options. I am eager to take advantage of opportunities as they come my way. When staying the course requires an ability to live within boundaries, and persevere through difficulties, I often fall short. It can be difficult to finish what I start.

Sometimes my spontaneity can be taken to an extreme, and my impulsiveness can lead to poor decisions because I don't think through the consequences. I can be a compulsive and impulsive shopper. Delayed gratification feels frustrating and punishing. The problem is that I am never satisfied. I have difficulty focusing and staying with what is, because I am always imagining that there is something better out there. Every choice I make feels like it cuts me off my freedom to embrace other options. The insatiable quality of my gluttony comes from a place of feeling internally bankrupt, disconnected from myself and what is real right here. I never feel like I can get enough. The truth is that I cannot get enough satisfaction, fulfillment, and contentment because I do not savor my experiences deeply. I am like a hungry ghost that never rests because I am always seeking what I believe will satisfy me. There is never enough money, never enough experiences, people, things to keep me entertained for long. Even if I overdose on these things, I still feel hungry.

Ironically, if I were totally free and unconstrained, I would get lost. My energy would get so dispersed that I wouldn't know which way to move. I am actually more effective when I operate within constraints. I can be grounded, sensible, organized, creative, resourceful and decisive. I can accomplish tasks, meet goals, and enjoy myself. Yet I don't recognize that I do much better within constraints than I do without constraints. My assumptions lead to thoughts, actions, and consequences that validate my assumptions. In this case, the more I try to break free, the more hungry I become. This dynamic keeps my ego employed and keeps me perpetually fixated on being free and satisfied. I can never find satisfaction for then I would have no excuse for *Optimizing*. We are each caught in a vicious cycle of our personality and instincts until we decide to break free. This takes deliberate energy and momentum because the cycle is a compelling vortex. In order to create new wealth, we must see clearly the vicious cycle that blocks us from abundance. Then we must fight our way out of the vortex.

4. OPERATIONALLY

If my instincts are balanced, I will be able to attend to money in each of the Nine Money Domains in a healthy manner. My big appetite motivates me to make the world a better place to live. I understand that it is important to be of service to the world, and not just selfish about my own needs. I am balanced between taking in and giving back. If, however, my instincts are not in balance, then I will get stuck in my type fixation and act selfishly. My motivation to be spontaneous and free manifests in different ways depending on my dominant instinct. Instead of focusing on areas that could satisfy me, I instead focus on possibilities that could be even more satisfying. As a SP 7, my *Optimizing* energy is focused on having what I need and keeping my options open in the self-preservation realm. As a SO 7, my *Optimizing* energy is focused on being comfortable and keeping my options open in the social realm. As a SX 7, my *Optimizing* energy is focused on finding the charge and being opportunistic about where I put my energy. How my instincts are imbalanced will therefore impact how I relate to the Nine Money Domains – where I put my attention and energy and where I don't.

"OPTIONEE" SP 7	"PLAYBOY" SO 7	"JUGGLER" SX 7

Domain 1 – Budgeting

The way I relate to budgeting reflects my *Optimizing* strategy. I want to figure out how to make the best of my situation. If I can understand a budget as something that helps me to optimize my choices and make better decisions, and feeds my needs and wants, then I could get interested in it. Learning to live within a budget is about learning to savor what I have and finding freedom and satisfaction within constraints. When I actually abide by a budget, I can experience a great relief at the simplicity and relaxation that it provides. The containment forces me not only to enjoy what is in front of me, but also to be more disciplined, focused, and productive.

As an "Optionee" SP 7, I like to get the most bang for the buck, the best value, and the most out of each experience. If I am able to optimize within constraints, and view budgeting as a means for having greater options, freedom, and autonomy, then I can embrace budgeting and be motivated to be frugal and save. I can see that having a budget and having savings is a way to keep my options open. If, however, as an "Optionee" SP 7, I see budgeting as a barrier to my freedom, then I will want nothing to do with it. When I have this perspective, budgeting feels suffocating and intolerable because it gets in the way of my living a spontaneous life. I like to put my attention on positive options and make light of scary situations. Budgeting can be scary. I don't want to face up to the reality of how little money might be available for me. I don't want to be deprived, so I act like there are no limits. Expecting the worst, I avoid looking at the numbers. Underneath, there is anxiety, but I try to gloss over it. Staying within a budget can be challenging because there are so many things that I want to do. I tend to have a multitude of friends, activities, and projects that I am doing at any one time, and they all require money. I don't want to deny myself just because of money. When I get stressed out and anxious, though, I can swing to the other extreme, and become quite exacting about budgeting. I might spend a whole weekend recording my expenses in a spreadsheet. I might put myself on a budget to relieve the anxiety and reign in my impulses. But this discipline generally only lasts a while, until my anxiety subsides and my interest fades. Then I rebel against it.

As a "Playboy" SO 7, my life is so busy that budgeting can be difficult. I am not naturally organized, detail-focused, or inclined to be limited. When bills come in, I stack them in a corner and, later, pay them and file them in a haphazard manner. I don't tend to balance my checkbook or follow any budget. I spend like there is no limit. There is a lot of clutter in my life – in my house, in my office, in my garage. Various activities claim my attention and I don't take the time to tidy up and get organized. Life feels like a whirlwind to me. I have a lot of enthusiasm for different activities. But I don't take the time to get caught up with budgeting and money management. I am not a long-term budgeter because it feels too limiting to me. When money is plentiful, I tend to relax and enjoy. But when money is tight, my anxiety kicks in and I try to be more careful. I do have a perfectionistic streak that can interrupt my ability to be effective. With all the clutter in my life, I can get obsessed about cleaning, labeling, and making things perfect.

As a "Juggler" SX 7, budgeting is boring. Things pile up and get lost. I don't really have a good system. I try, but the truth is that my life is moving so fast that everything gets messy. I'm no good at bookkeeping or tracking. My attention is on what's next. When it comes to accounting for where all the money went, it's a mess. Even if I write it down, it's a mess. I am not detail-oriented. I am clever-oriented! I'm clever at getting out of jams. I wouldn't mind trying to take on budgeting as a challenge or game, but it would be difficult to stick to a budget for long. I don't have a strong orientation towards saving because I want to enjoy life right now. I certainly don't want to deal with the negative stuff around money. For example, if my spouse gives me a budget, I might not even look at it. I just couldn't be bothered. I don't want to be so careful because being careful would slow me down. I don't want to see all the details, because if I make a mistake, I don't want to know. I want to believe everything will be okay. I have fear, but I block it out, hoping that I will figure out a way to deal with things down the road. If I want something, I just go for it, whether I have money for it or not. I feel that budgeting would distract me from bringing money in and from the more "important" things of life. I fear that if I hear the bad news, it will ruin my day and I won't be able to stay in action.

Domain 2 – Spending

Material things amuse me and make me happy. *Optimizing* is about continually searching for things that satisfy me. Shopping is fun. It's entertaining, stimulating, and enjoyable. If there is a sale in front of me, it can be difficult to resist. I can easily rationalize a purchase, so it is easy to spend beyond my means, and be in debt. Spending spontaneously to feed my large appetite, I can easily overspend and fill my home with clutter. With all my interests and hobbies, there is always more to buy. The volatility in my spending is due to my own volatile nature. I change jobs often, move homes often, and change hobbies and interests often. I try to avoid being "trapped" by money. I equate spending spontaneously with being free. But I may also equate saving and having money with being free. It's not the spending behavior that defines a Type 7 so much as it is the large appetite for material things and the desire to be free. I may be a spendthrift 7 who indulges my appetite or I may be a frugal 7 who represses my appetite (in reaction to a sense that there might not be an end to the spending if I let go). Either way, what is true is that I revel in material experiences. I get pleasure from material objects and look to the material world to satisfy my hunger. Part of my growth is to recognize my pattern of always looking for something better – a new house, a new kitchen, a new car – and to recognize that perhaps my real satisfaction will come not from more material things on the outside but from satisfaction on the inside.

As an "Optionee" SP 7, being comfortable is about keeping my physical options open at all times. I want the option to eat well, live well, live in a nice home, be secure and be self-reliant. As long as I am free to exercise my option to be comfortable and secure and live well, I feel okay. If I feel that I don't have options, though, I get very frustrated with my situation.   Being free to chase down what I want pleases me. I may find myself driving all over town to get the best price. I love bargains, deals, and loopholes. I may spend ridiculous amounts of time online to get a good deal. I am always looking for the easy way or the best way. I like to buy whimsical, funny, silly things. I like new gadgets, useful things, beautiful things, designer things. I think of myself as a clever shopper who always gets good deals. I love buying gifts for people. I like to express my love through things and to feel connected to others through pleasure. I also like the enjoyment and stimulation of traveling. I might be reluctant to buy property that could tie me down physically and financially. But I may also choose to buy a house if I know that I can exercise my option to move if I am not happy with it. I do like to have options in case of an emergency. I may count on insurance products to bail me out, or I may count on my own reserve of savings.

> I buy clothes all the time. It's spontaneous and not meaningful. Then I feel guilt and shame – like what was I thinking? I don't think about what else I could have bought with the money. I constantly spend money fixing up where I live. A lot of it is eclectic, cheap and disposable. I buy things because I want it to be done right now. What fills me up? When will I be satisfied? I don't know. When will it be enough? For me, it's hard to know until I get nauseous. Acquiring experiences and having fun is very important to me. I spend money in a constant search for what is fulfilling. I've done so many activities.

As a "Playboy" SO 7, I want to have fun and be a part of things. I am more focused on sharing experiences with others and fitting in than I am on security per se. My Social instinct makes me prone to feeling guilty about buying for myself, so I am generous to others when I indulge my own appetite. My optimism dials me into the possibilities rather than the limitations of life. I love the excitement of going to new places. I love different cultures and the excitement of new languages, new ideas, and new people. If I go out to dinner, I want to enjoy myself. If I have to put it on my credit card, and pay it off later, I will. I want what is trendy and popular and what my friends have. I may buy clothes a few times a month. I buy things we need for the house. I travel all over the world. Why shouldn't I? There's no reason not to.

> To spend $20 on a dress for myself was very difficult for me, even though I'd spend a ton of money on others. I wanted to do social work but I also wanted to have nice things.

> The expensive furniture we bought when we moved to this house was mainly bought because it was trendy and the store we bought it from was very popular at the time. I really didn't give much consideration to the practicality or quality of it.

As a "Juggler" SX 7, my Sexual instinct inclines me towards challenge and excitement, and living in the moment. I have an eye for aesthetically pleasing things. It is always a battle not to indulge what I am attracted to. I spend frequently because the buzz from a new purchase wears off quickly.

As a "Juggler" SX 7 with a Self-Preservation blindspot, I have little concern for security. I am much less apt to bargain. If I am drawn to something, I'll get it whether there is money or not. Some things I won't buy because they are too expensive, but then I will buy something absolutely ridiculous like $300 cowboy boots. I love restaurants and traveling and clothing. It is agony not to eat out a lot. I love the energy and aliveness of being out and about – the people, the waiters, the action, the buzz. If there is money in the bank, it gets spent. I don't care about savings. I hope things will sort themselves out. Sometimes, I'll get down to the wire and become anxious about money, but then the problem resolves and it's all okay. Living on the edge doesn't scare me. It makes me feel alive. If Self-Preservation is my middle instinct, I have a mild concern for security. I am more apt to bargain for good values and be less generous about money. I may stockpile resources so that I have the option and flexibility to do what I want.

Domain 3 – Earning

The way I go about earning money reflects my *Optimizing* strategy. I enjoy jobs where I can be creative in making things better. My mind is always working and I can juggle a lot of different things at the same time. Because I am always thinking ahead, I am very fast moving and busy. I am great at generating new ideas, and getting things going, but not as strong at tying things up. I change jobs a lot because I am always trying to make the situation better for myself in some way – better pay, better hours, better career opportunities, etc. I'm always trying to come up with a better combination of factors than what I had before. I want to be free to do something better if it comes along. The blessing and the curse is that I tend to know a little about a lot of things, so choosing one career path can be difficult. There are costs to jumping around though. I may not make as much as someone with greater seniority, and I don't cultivate the deep roots, familiarity and knowledge that would come from staying in one place. I have a tendency to be a jack of all trades, master of none, and can lack confidence in my personal value.

> For me, choosing a job is not always about income and money, it is also about meeting my requirements in terms of hours and excitement, the experience and the comraderie and what I can offer.

As an "Optionee" SP 7, I can be a very hard, ambitious worker when I want money. I am willing to take a job that is convenient and expedient. It doesn't have to be something I have a deep passion for. It just has to have the right mix of factors that suit me. If it doesn't work out, I'll find something else to do. I always try to keep my options open. I don't want to be a slave to a 9-5 schedule. Job flexibility is as important to me as the money I make working. I like to do things in clever ways to avoid drudgery. I want to be able to make a lot of money for the least amount of work.

As a "Playboy" SO 7, I want to contribute to the world. I am versatile and can make money in different ways. When Self-Preservation is the middle instinct, I am willing to work hard in spurts, but I also want to have a decent lifestyle. I prefer not to do grueling work. I'd rather charge more per hour so that I can work less. But there is a sadness about money that comes from a sense that I cannot honor my fire. I don't trust that I can do what I dream of and I am scared of trying. My dreams feel out of my reach. When Self-Preservation is my blindspot, I am troubled about charging for my value. I feel like I'm worth people's love, but not their money. It can be difficult to ask for my value because I doubt that I am wise or valuable. I don't take myself seriously. Sometimes I even get surprised when I am paid. I have a perception that money just comes when I need it, but not by anything that I do for it.

As a "Juggler" SX 7 with a Self-Preservation instinct in the middle, I have a thirst for challenge and stimulation. I like living a fast life and I'm a risk-taker. My natural optimism keeps me focused on the possibilities and potential upside rather than the downside. To me, there is no limit to how much money I might make. The sky is the limit. My Sexual instinct leads me to work intensively for weeks or months, and then get so burned out that I have to take a few weeks or months off to recharge. Then I go back to that cycle again. I enjoy the rush of being able to make a lot of money fast and I love to test my abilities. I like putting deals together quickly, working the system, being creative. I don't have the attention span for methodical, stable work. I gravitate towards the juice that comes from the challenge of making things better. I like complexity and thrive on it. I have the ability to see things that others don't see. I have so many ideas bounding out of me. People often tell me I'm nuts, but I don't care. I can look at something, immediately see what's not working, and then come up with all kinds of ideas for how to improve it. I am not a maintenance or routine person because that type of detail work feels suffocating. But taking the time to slow down and do some regular maintenance, such as sales calls, organizing, and relationship building, can be very good for me. It allows me to connect back to my heart, relax, and create rapport with others. My tendency to set big goals and orient to the big gap between where I am and where I want to go keeps me running fast, but in scarcity mode. I want to fly to my goals, but I never seem to be able to go fast enough. This makes me inclined to cut corners and do things expediently.   When Self-Preservation is my blindspot, I don't associate my passion with money. I just pursue things that fascinate me. I don't want to have to think about money and doing things that would require me to sacrifice my freedom, my expression, my schedule. I want to work on my own terms when I need to. For me, the upside of new experiences trumps any potential downside. If I hit a roadblock, I simply adjust course and keep moving.

Domain 4 – Beliefs

I perceive money as both an expression of my freedom and the ticket to my freedom. As an expression of freedom, I believe I should be free to use money as I want to and make money as I want to. I believe I should resist committing myself physically, financially, or psychologically to anything that might constrain my freedom or reduce my options. I refuse to be a slave to money or anything else for that matter.

As a ticket to my freedom, I believe money helps me to push away the unpleasant aspects of life and avoid deprivation. Having resources helps to dampen the severity of crises. If I have savings, then I can weather periods of disability, illness, or unemployment. If my car breaks down, the heater fails, or the plumbing bursts, I can use my money to solve problems. I need money to respond to life as it happens, in order to keep my life happy, joyful, and free. Money is therefore the ticket to my freedom, not only because it allows me to get away from trouble, but also because it allows me to have what I want.

But neither beliefs about money are in fact true. In fact, these two beliefs contradict one another. If I "express" my freedom by spontaneously spending my money, then I will not have savings to respond to emergencies and crises. And if money is my "ticket" to freedom, then I must accept constraints on my current spending and job options. What I don't see is that money is neither an expression of my freedom nor a ticket to my freedom.

I have a tendency to view money as an object that frustrates me – I believe that more money always give me more freedom. In this context, I always have a relationship to money that is characterized by scarcity. My *Optimizing* strategy of more, more, more, and better, better, better, means that I will never be satisfied with what I have. The paradox is that when I equate freedom with the lack of constraints, then I cannot perceive how freedom can be experienced within constraints. The truth is that living in the world of five senses is a constraint. The material world is a constraint. Life itself is a constraint. We live in human bodies that are constrained by physical properties, aging, and limitations. Constraints are a natural aspect of life and do not prevent me from being gratified, satisfied or fulfilled. I must learn to move past my fixation on constraints and freedom, and my growth edge is to figure out what real freedom is.

Domain 5 – Understanding

I am a fast and clever learner who is able to recognize concepts and understand quickly how to apply them. My desire to learn and understand money stems from my beliefs about money. If I believe that money is simply an expression of my freedom, I may not have a great deal of curiosity about how money works. I will most likely feel that a passing, superficial understanding is sufficient for me. On the other hand, if I believe that money is my ticket to freedom, I can get very motivated to learn about it. I will want to understand how to make more money and use the markets to become wealthier. I'm not so interested in learning for learning's sake, but learning for the sake of some end. The focus is always on what is practical and useful, with little patience for the abstract or seemingly irrelevant.

I do have a tendency to avoid thinking about things that might scare me. I don't want to look, just in case there is a nasty surprise. I don't like to think that I am wasting money, but when I can't explain where the money went, I can feel anxious about money and my ability to control my spending. I am conflicted because I don't want to look at the money stuff, but I do want to know how things are. What keeps me from looking is that the truth can be rather unpleasant. But avoiding and postponing can cause problems, including credit card debt and bankruptcy.

Domain 6 – Risk Management

I don't tend to think about worst-case scenarios, but if I have a dominant Self-Preservation instinct, I tend to be more concerned about risk management than not. As an "Optionee" SP 7, I want to make sure I have basic insurance. Whether I consider it my backup of last resort depends on what other resources I have. Two SP 7s explain their differing philosophies about insurance, which both boil down to maximizing options:

> I like to have lots of insurance to feel secure. I don't trust cheap insurance. I like to get maximal insurance coverage. That way, I don't have to budget carefully, because I know that I have insurance to rely on.

> I prefer to self-insure and count on money in my own bank account to feel secure rather than rely on costly insurance policies. I'd rather get the cheapest insurance required with the highest deductibles to minimize my insurance costs and maximize my savings.

As a "Playboy" SO 7 or "Juggler" SX 7, I will be less concerned about managing risk than a SP 7. I'll be more inclined to trust my social network as a SO 7, and to trust my own resilience as a SX 7.

> A worst-case scenario might happen, but I think it is crazy to worry about it in advance.

> Considering the trouble I might get into or how I might be rendered insolvent with one bad turn of the economy is just not natural for me.

Domain 7 – Planning

Because of my optimism, quick mind, and desire for satisfaction, I can quickly see the gap between how things are and what is possible. When I am healthy, I am able to balance planning ahead with savoring the moment. When I am less healthy, though, I can't balance now with later and almost all my attention goes towards the future.

As an "Optionee" SP 7, I pride myself on being a good planner. I like to set goals and plan how to reach those goals. My goals may center around work, money, or other Self-Preservation topics. But my plans have more to do with keeping me excited and anticipatory than they do with necessarily achieving particular goals. They have more to do with future possibilities than they do with being locked on a certain path. I stick to a plan if it serves my purposes, but I might also throw out my plans if something better comes along, or I get bored and lose interest.

As a "Playboy" SO 7, I am less goal-oriented around money. I tend to take the short cut and the path of least resistance. I get distracted and my intentionality gets diffused. I am basically optimistic that things will turn out okay. I don't like to worry in advance about things, and I don't want to be 100% committed to a particular path.   Long-term planning feels like it will limit me. I don't want to be a micro-planner; I am more motivated by learning, being of service, empowering others. I have visions and broad ideas, not specific, precise plans. The actual path forward can stay blurry, because I know instinctively that I am going to make it up as I go along anyways. I like to keep the future exciting and unknown. Retirement, for example, seems so far away and vague.

> I am afraid of being stuck somehow when I do long-term planning. Long-term planning seems boring to me. The straight line projections for 5 or 10 years feels very limiting.

As a "Juggler" SX 7, I am oriented towards challenging goals, but I am not planful. I have a vision of how I want things to go, but I don't map things out.   For example, I want to make a lot of money and I aim high, setting challenges for myself. But I will not be very linear in my path towards my goal. I aspire to do financial planning, but find the structure of planning too restrictive. I would rather save a chunk of money when the money is available, rather than deprive myself when money is tight. It feels easier to increase my earnings than reduce my spending. If I want something, I buy it, and catch up later. It is not fun to plan methodically for spending. I put money into retirement savings, but I don't look at that account so I won't be tempted to take money out.

Domain 8 – Wealth Building

I enjoy being spontaneous. I tend to diffuse my power by letting my energy dissipate in many different directions rather than harnessing it around one focus. Focusing in one direction rather than taking the easiest, most expedient path is a growth edge for me. This requires settling down, making choices, and following through. Can I harness my power and my money by being intentional and not squandering my potential? I must learn to invest in a path of action and stay on track, without worrying that the grass is greener somewhere else. I am generally not interested in empire building. I treasure my freedom and I don't relish the burden of being responsible for others. I treasure my ability to do what I want with my time. However, my creativity, energy, and vision often lead to economic success, and I may find myself leading a burgeoning business empire. But if I am not careful, I could squander my wealth-generating potential with high spending. What mainly motivates me is the desire to do something to make life better, to create a better experience for people. As I mature, I also see the value in serving not just myself, but others as well, and being a stable and dynamic participant in a bigger community.

As an "Optionee" SP 7, wealth building is interesting insofar as it enables me to avoid deprivation and have freedom and options. I may find myself focused on making more and more money, but never feeling satisfied. If I get caught up in an unfulfilling rat race, then it's time to ask where real satisfaction comes from. A lot of personal growth can occur by asking and answering this question sincerely. To the extent that wealth building feels like a constraint on my freedom, I want to ignore this Domain, preferring instead to travel, have experiences, and have fun. If I find myself continually trying to avoid being "tied down," then it's time to ask myself where real freedom comes from.

As a "Playboy" SO 7, I am basically optimistic and not so concerned about wealth building. I tend to make investment decisions superficially, and find myself making and losing money quickly. With extra money, it is fun to gamble and take risks. If Self-Preservation is my blindspot, I won't think of money so much in terms of financial freedom and options, but more in terms of how I can be stimulated and challenged. I do wonder why I don't have more financial assets though.

As a "Juggler" SX 7, I am not necessarily drawn to the responsibility and burden that power brings. I want the freedom to pursue challenges that excite me. I tend to be a solo flyer. I like investing in things like art and property that are visual, pleasurable, concrete, and tangible. Retirement and the stock market are not so appealing. For the stimulation and freshness of the challenge, investing to build something big can energize me in a way that market investing does not. I want to be a part of the action. But having and running an empire is not my main motivation. It's the challenge and stimulation that appeals, more than the wealth and power itself. If I've enjoyed many opportunities to create large amounts of wealth but squandered the wealth quickly, this is my wake-up call to ask myself how I have failed to cultivate wealth as a resource for myself. With a Self-

Preservation blindspot, I have very little interest in planning ahead or saving, either for a rainy day or for options and resources. I simply want to enjoy life now. What are my beliefs about money that make me believe that I should not or could not build wealth for myself?

Domain 9 – Balance

A large part of my appetite for money and for life is fueled by my sense of how wonderful and free life can be. My zest for life fuels my visions and big dreams. I can be a very creative about finding a job. If I need to save money, I can be very creative about how to cut back my spending. If I need to get a loan, I can be very resourceful. I am great at brainstorming out-of-the-box possibilities. I may make mistakes, but then I move on. My appetite for getting what I want gives me the energy to be creative, efficient, focused, determined and activated. On the other hand, my energy to get what I want can also drive me to make messes and be selfish. My selfishness comes from fear. I fear that my creativity might dry up, that I might run out of money, or not deserve money. I fear that I won't be able to make my dreams come true, and that I will become trapped by my life.

> I usually feel I have plenty. My deeper feeling is that I have what I need. I feel I am on the right track. I could have less and I could live simpler. I don't need a big house with all this stuff. I might even prefer a smaller house. But my ego voice worries about what is going to happen and doesn't trust what might happen.

I feel it is my birthright to be satisfied. Anything that stands in the way of my satisfaction is an obstacle to be overcome. I look outside of myself for gratification and satisfaction, but I assume that I am the only one I can rely on to get my needs met. My scarcity mentality comes from my feeling that I cannot be deprived. I worry that things will run out. I often find myself in a feast-or-famine cycle. When the money is coming in, I just want to enjoy it, not save it. When the money is tight, then I have to pull in the belt. This pattern is generated by a scarcity perspective and an unwillingness to be constrained. In searching for meaning outside of myself through experiences and material things, I can feel hollow inside. There is a lot of activity and movement. I do not take time to savor life and I have difficulty committing to one path.

In reality, I am abundant and grateful, but my perception of abundance is not there. I may never feel content. It's more about the challenge for me. I like to stay in the buzz, intensity. I am not comfortable with stability. With abundance, there would be no challenge, and then what would I do with myself? Until the money is actually there, I feel directed and focused. If there were abundance, I might lack direction and focus. What would I do? Abundance reminds me of being directionless.

5. THE PARADOX

The fundamental paradox is that *Optimizing* never leads to fulfillment. It can only lead to hunger and dissatisfaction. Not only is the actual outcome the opposite of my original intent, but it can never be otherwise. What is freedom? Is freedom the absence of constraints and boundaries? Is freedom about having more options and choices? Is freedom something that I have to create? Or is freedom something that is always available to me? *Optimizing* is supposed to help me get satisfaction and joy. But when I overdo this strategy, I actually feel less satisfied and joyful. My denial of my intrinsic self-sufficiency keeps me continually hungry.

The paradox is that *Optimizing* causes me to disconnect from the thing I care most about, which is finding satisfaction and joy. There is a part of me that knows that I am already free and not deprived. But honoring this part of myself would create conflict with my ego structure, and that tension would be too much for me to bear. So instead, I continue looking for more satisfaction. I sense that I am being blackmailed into *Optimizing* and that this entire structure is built on fear, but I do not know how to move past the fear. The more I fear being hungry, the more gluttonous and ravenous I become.

The paradox is that in always paying attention to my lack of satisfaction, I forget to savor and appreciate what is already in front of me. In always trying to have options, I cannot settle on the one option that might be completely satisfying. In always trying to be free and spontaneous, I cut myself off from the natural balance between freedom and constraints. In always wanting more, I cannot avoid being frustrated. My resistance to deprivation causes me to feel more deprived, which is the very thing I am trying to avoid. In learning to live within boundaries, I can focus on what is right in front of me. In learning to minimize my needs, I become not more deprived, but more satisfied. This satisfaction brings more appreciation and serenity to my life.

6. BREAKING THE VICIOUS CYCLE

In order to break the vicious cycle of my personality, and move from Fear to Love, I must embrace and resolve the fundamental paradox of *Optimizing*. I have spend my whole life trying to get satisfaction. Yet, all this energetic acquisitiveness has not fulfilled me. What incredible possibilities could exist if I didn't have to resist deprivation? In rejecting deprivation, I have also kept away the love. As I throw off the shackles of my personality and orient to my true nature, I begin to own the whole me. When I do this, I move past my story of being constrained and deprived.

My journey with money is a journey to real freedom. I learn to stop constantly seeking more, and savor life. I learn to pay attention, to settle down. To allow everything to become what I have been looking for. I feel every moment as precious and lovely. I let go of my own plans and participate mindfully in the continuity of life as part of the dynamic nature of the universe. I am no longer dissipated and frenetic. I am confident that I will be nourished as I participate in the unfolding. I experience my vaster identity and participation, and feel the grandeur and beauty of life. In embracing these truths, I can move past my old beliefs and patterns and welcome abundance, prosperity, and love into my life. I can begin to feel joyful and serene. But this is not comfortable or easy. I feel the pain as my ego resists losing its job. I feel remorseful about how I have lived my life and hurt myself and others. I am scared that I won't be able to survive on my own deeper knowing alone.

When I live abundantly, I don't need work at being satisfied and free because I already am. I don't need to plan, anticipate, or control. I simply participate in the brilliant, intelligent unfolding of reality, and savor the preciousness of each moment. I don't need to create freedom for myself. I sense endless options, and know that I am not confined by anything. I know that my consciousness is limitless, unbounded, and endlessly creative. I participate in the unfolding of life and know that my needs are always met. I am able to make commitments, take a stand, and be here with it all, exactly the way it is.   No running away. No denying. No fearing. I don't avoid or deny any of the unpleasantness because I am part of it all. By being here fully, I am vital, grounded, and awed by it all.

	Brief Description
"Optionee" SP 7	If I don't have options or can't exercise my options, I feel boxed in. Sometimes I exercise my freedom by spending frivolously, and sometimes I exercise my option to be free by saving money. I can be very ambitious and hard working when I want something. I'm always looking to improve my material situation.
"Playboy" SO 7	My life is a whirlwind of social activities, and being organized is a challenge. When money is plentiful, I tend to relax and enjoy it, but when money is tight, my anxiety kicks in and I try to be more careful. I want to be of value and contribute to the group. I am not so goal-oriented around money. Long-term planning feels limiting.
"Juggler" SX 7	I want the freedom to pursue what excites me. I tend to fly solo. Often I juggle multiple projects simultaneously. My life moves fast. I do not have the patience for details. I have an eye for aesthetically pleasing things. I love to shop. I spend frequently because the buzz from a new purchase wears off quickly.

Type 7	Summary
Gift	Enthusiasm and openness to new ideas.
Unconscious Belief	I am constrained and boxed in.
Strategy	*Optimizing* – making things better than they already are, so as not to be boxed in or deprived.
Vicious Cycle	Because I cannot be deprived, I must exercise my freedom and keep my options open. I cannot commit to one path or savor what is in front of me. This causes me to be hungry and unsatisfied, so I feel deprived.
Defended Against	Having minimal resources.
Operationally	• I must break free. • It's up to me to get what I want to be satisfied. • I focus only on areas where I anticipate satisfaction and fulfillment.
Paradox	*Optimizing* does not generate satisfaction.
Breaking the Vicious Cycle	I must recognize that I can be free within constraints, including my life in this body. My job is simply to be a part of the unfolding.
Direction of Growth	Being contained and disciplined allows me to be grounded and manifest my dreams.

CHAPTER 14

EXERTING

Type 8

1. GIFT

My gift is my strength and self-reliance. I know what I want and I know how to get it. I am bold, decisive, direct, and I don't rely on others. I move swiftly to get things started, to build, fortify, and protect. I don't dither, worry, or fear. I make things happen. I live my life boldly. I believe in creating my own destiny and have confidence in my power to determine my own course. My confidence gives others confidence. At my best, my presence reassures others and empowers them to take action and persevere. The world needs me to lead it, guide it, and give it confidence. The world needs me to be here, both at the front of the line leading, and at the back of the line bolstering. The world needs my courage to fight the enemy, take on challenges, and make the world a safer, juster place.

2. STRATEGY

My life and money strategy grow out of my sense of the critical importance of strength. The world needs my strength. I believe it is up to me to generate vitality. *Exerting* is about living big, being assertive, pushing my will into the world, and creating vitality. It is about being bold and decisive, not thoughtful and deliberate. While I am gifted at being powerful and strong, I can forget to be merciful on myself and others. My fear of being lifeless and without vitality stimulates my strategy of *Exerting*. Pulling back energetically is difficult. *Exerting* is a defense against my own sweetness, and is a distinctly forceful and direct way of going after what I want, contrasting to the indirect strategy of *Giving*. When I go after what I want, I operate as if others are objects to be manipulated as I please. I harden my heart, to others and to myself, and deny that others have feelings. But without being able to open my heart, I can not be fully here, vital, and alive.

This *Exerting* strategy creates a vicious cycle of misusing my strength to get my needs met, but leaves me unsatisfied. Thrusting my energy and will onto the world keeps me locked to a reality of scarcity. True strength is infused with love, kindness, and the ability to accept what is. It is only when I can be here with it all, with an open and merciful heart, that I can be truly strong. True power is derived from love, not vengefulness or mercilessness. It comes from those who know how to wield power wisely. It is only when I know my own mortality and fragility, that I can be here – brave, alive, vigorous, and strong.

3. THE VICIOUS CYCLE

If I were to look at my life objectively, I would notice that I have essentially been trapped in a vicious cycle of fear and scarcity. Because of this, my relationship to love and prosperity is constrained. *Exerting* is fundamentally about trying to be strong because I do not feel powerful. This orientation makes me feel angry and heavy. But my ego enthusiastically keeps this vicious cycle going so that it can keep its job. I get addicted to *Exerting*. Even though I think I am moving along, I am merely moving in place.

When we are caught in a vicious cycle where our actions validate our beliefs, it can be very difficult to extricate ourselves. When we are stuck at a certain point along the scarcity-to-abundance spectrum, it is impossible to improve our position until we get out of the vicious cycle. If we are suddenly showered with new wealth, we will most likely dissipate it so that we can get back to our old set point. So in order to create new wealth, we must first become aware of the vicious cycle we are caught in. Once we become aware, we will be in a better position to consciously unblock what blocks us, and welcome new wealth into our lives.

My underlying assumption is that world is a battlefield where the strong prevail and the weak perish. The best defense is a good offense. Do unto others before they do unto you. I focus and emphasize the areas of my life where I am competent, strong, and in control, and ignore those where I feel weak and ignorant. I can't afford to rest on my laurels, and I can't afford to be indecisive. I must control my own destiny. I can't let my emotions get to me. If I want to win, I need to stay focused, and can't be scared, sad, or sensitive. The only emotion I can afford to feel is anger, because anger gives me juice to carry forth. In hardening my heart and making myself invulnerable, I cut myself off from being affected by life. Not only do I not feel others' pain, I don't feel my own pain. But I can't afford to have mercy on myself or others if I am going to be tough and strong and make things happen.

I want power. I want to make an impact on the world. I focus on challenges that I can overcome. By putting single-minded focus and energy on my goal, I can make a bigger impact. The bigger my dreams, the more imbalance is justified today. When I know what to do, I don't want to lose any time taking action. I'm only willing to sit around considering different options and consequences for so long. It is obvious to me that the best course of action is a course that leads to victory and domination. It is difficult to yield until I have won. But I can get into trouble moving too fast. And there may be a lot of collateral damage and unnecessary losses: damaged relationships and hurt feelings from people I have trampled on my march to victory.

My driving motivation is to be powerful and invulnerable. Power gives me the ability to create my own destiny, and not be subject to the whim of others. The more power I have over people and things, the less vulnerable I am. I can be strong by being autonomous, self-reliant, and in control of my own life. I can be strong by having enough resources that I don't need anything from anyone. I can also be strong by being a protector of people in my inner circle, my immediate family, my friends, my community. I can be strong by meeting whatever comes up with fortitude and boldness and not being intimidated by danger or risk.

I am like a soldier who is more comfortable fighting than enjoying peace time. You could almost say I live to fight. I need to be pushing against something. If I am not fighting others, I am fighting life itself. I can live a Spartan existence if I have to. I don't want to get too comfortable in my life. I don't want to be vulnerable to needing people or things. It's not so relevant to me whether I enjoy things or not. I almost treat myself like a machine. It is not about whether the machine is happy. It is about whether the machine is doing what it is supposed to be doing. I see the world through steely eyes.

Yes, I can be a bully. I have no problem manipulating others and ordering them around like chess pieces as I mastermind reality. I am repulsed by slowness, wishy-washiness, and softness. I want others to be decisive and get to the point. Sometimes I can be too direct, express myself unskillfully, and hurt others' feelings. I push myself to the limit, and push others to their limits to test the boundaries of reality. These strong impulses enable me to be productive and compel me to work long hours, ignore my own physical vulnerabilities, and shut down my sensitivities to others and myself. Stillness feels like weakness, vulnerability, death. But being so much in action creates fatigue and exhaustion, which is the opposite of vitality and life. Nevertheless, it feels shameful to withdraw my energy to take care of myself. I believe I can only know my strength when I am out there using it and proving it.

Ironically, when I am on top, I am not comfortable because I don't know what to do with myself when I am not in fighting mode. My energy gets dispersed, and I don't feel sharp. I may pick a fight just to get some push back. I fear that if I get too comfortable, I might get lazy and fat, and then I would lose my edge.   The problem is that by staying in fight mode. I can never rest and relax. The constant pushing against life, work, self, and others can lead me right up to the door of death. I feel exhausted, under-appreciated, and heavy. I don't feel vital and alive, even though that's what I crave. In trying to control life, I cannot pull back my energy to receive life. Things have to go very badly for me to give up on pushing against life. The dynamic of the ego structure keeps my ego employed and keeps me perpetually fixated on strong and weak. I can never find strength for then I would have no excuse for *Exerting*. We are each caught in a vicious cycle of our personality and instincts until we decide to break free. This takes deliberate energy and momentum because the cycle is a compelling vortex. In order to create new wealth, we must see clearly the vicious cycle that blocks us from abundance. Then we must fight our way out of the vortex.

4. OPERATIONALLY

If my instincts are balanced, I will be able to attend to money in each of the Nine Money Domains in a healthy manner. My big desire motivates me to go after what I want, but also to protect and take care of others. If, however, my instincts are not in balance, then I get stuck in my type fixation and I cannot be optimally effective. My motivation to be powerful and strong manifests in different ways depending on my dominant instinct. Instead of focusing on areas that could benefit me, I focus on the areas that I can control and dominate. As a SP 8, my *Exerting* energy is focused on being strong in the Self-Preservation realm. As a SO 8, my *Exerting* energy is focused on being powerful and impactful in the social realm. As a SX 8, my *Fxerting* energy is focused on intensity and energetic charge. How my instincts are imbalanced will therefore impact how I relate to the Nine Money Domains – where I put my attention and energy and where I don't.

"HEAVYWEIGHT" SP 8	"BIG BOSS" SO 8	"HIGH ROLLER" SX 8

Domain 1 – Budgeting

As an instinctual type, I tend to follow my gut instincts. I prefer to pay attention to the important stuff, the big stuff, rather than the small details. I don't naturally orient to being on a budget. I would rather make more money than reign in my spending. My willingness to submit to a budget depends on my level of health and dominant instinct.

As a "Heavyweight" SP 8, I want to control my resources, but I don't naturally do budgeting. Budgeting requires detail orientation and attention to minutiae. Generally speaking, organized record keeping is not very interesting. I stack everything in a corner until something comes up that I have to deal with. Day to day, it's oh well, I'll get to it some day. I might be prompt about paying bills on time, or I might not be. If I am frustrated, I might express this by not being super careful about paying bills on time, especially when the penalties are not severe. It's a way to express my autonomy. I'm not big on budgeting or tracking spending. I may have no idea how much we save or spend, and may not balance my checkbook. I have an arrogant attitude. I make the money, so don't make me manage it too. I'd be willing to adhere to a budget if I believed it could help me be stronger, better protected, and more secure. I could even become the enforcer of the budget.

But if I feel that the budget has been imposed on me from outside, and I do not respect it, then I will not cooperate. Doing a budget review often is a wake-up call to me that I need to slow down. My spending tends to be high relative to my income, no matter how high my income is! When cash flow is tight, I know I have to pull back, but it goes against my grain and can be a challenge. A budget on paper feels confining and it's hard for me to keep to. Budgeting and cutting back triggers lust for me. The more dismissive I am about the small stuff, the more I am "daring" the system because I don't want to be vulnerable to anything, including money. Being dismissive of budgeting and tracking is my way of not allowing money to have power over me.

As a "Big Boss" SO 8, my focus is on controlling social resources, rather than material resources. I am not a nickel and dimer. I am a big picture person who focuses on the important things. I am only bound by my budget to the extent that it enables me to do what is socially appropriate. For example, I do care that the rent gets paid, and that I can visit my friends and participate in social events. But otherwise, I just want to be able to do what I want to do, budget be damned. I don't track or balance my checkbook because I have bigger things to pay attention to. Plus, I don't want to concern myself with what my spouse spends or have to restrict what I spend. I either throw away paid bills immediately, or put them in a box, then another box, and pretty soon there are three to four boxes, and I throw it all away. Life feels so chaotic that I spend a lot on conveniences like taxis, eating out, and unexpected things that make it difficult to plan. I'm not so interested in record keeping. If it says IRS on it, then it is important, otherwise it is not. I have lots of things taken out of my checking account automatically so that I don't have to think about them. Yes, it can be dangerous to not look, but I just don't want to worry about details. I wouldn't pay attention to the cable company raising my rates $10. That's minor to me. I ask myself, is it worth my time to make a phone call to complain? If something gets out of control, I would focus on it, but otherwise not.

As a "High Roller" SX 8, my focus is on my passion, be it a person or a subject, more than it is on resources or social power. I don't think about money a lot. I hate accounting and find it boring. Budgeting makes me cringe. I detest it and don't see the point. It can be one of my biggest breakdowns, because it has no charge for me and I don't like to pay attention to details. I have a chronic desire to find something easy that works. I want to know how our account is doing. I like to stay in control so that I can have what I want. And I am obsessive about paying things on time and in full. But otherwise, who cares? My record keeping and bookkeeping are clumsy. I know where the critical things are, but it's not a clever or fancy system. I don't put my energy on that kind of stuff because it's a waste of time, even though it's a necessity. Sometimes I lose a document and then I have to go looking for it. I rely on others to give me information about stuff I don't care about. I want to go deep. I have a neurotic focus on intensity. I don't care about the shallow stuff. I don't want to do things perfunctorily. It might take me four weeks to galvanize myself to do something that I have to do around money and bookkeeping, because it's not interesting enough. I don't have an "ask for help" instinct. Until my suffering gets high enough, I just let things go. If money is limited, I can be very creative and responsible, and make the money go farther. But when I know the money is there, my attention goes elsewhere.

Domain 2 – Spending

My expansive energy affects my spending. If I want it, I should be able to have it. My spending is instinctual, not analytical. I don't think about how I'm going to pay for something, or whether I should get A or B. I just buy what I want. I have no inclination to pull back. I assume I can get all my needs met by exerting myself. I often find myself spending a lot on my children and family as well. I'm really not careful about spending. If I had been more careful about spending, I'd have saved up at lot more at this point! My habit is to simply spend, and then figure out a way to make it up on the back end. I don't have a habit of limiting my spending. Having to go without feels unnatural.

I'd prefer not to have debt if I can help it. I don't want to owe others or rely on others. I want to be self-reliant and depend only on myself. But if I am faced with the proposition of putting something on my credit card and going into debt versus asking for money from my family, I would be inclined to go it alone. When times are tight, I work harder, push more, and am more aggressive to make ends meet. I do what I need to do. I generally won't reduce my spending or ask for help since both would feel like defeat.

I don't have any guilt or shame about wanting what I want. The only thing that stops my lust is my sense of the absurdity of my own patterns. I am bounded by logic and reason more than by shame or guilt. I can be frugal if I think it makes sense, but if there is something I want, I'm inclined to go for it.

I have no problem buying big ticket items. I don't experience any residual fear, but my desire is calibrated. I don't want to be vulnerable to wanting. Although I have strong desire, I also have the ability to cut off my desire if I sense I could be hurt by that desire. Not being able to have what I want feels like weakness and vulnerability. So with money and material objects, if I can't have it, then I will adopt the attitude that it's not what I care about anyway. I could live on very little if I had to.

As a "Heavyweight" SP 8, my *Exerting* strategy in Self-Preservation causes me to be carry a heavy load with spending. My spending is not lavish, but I do not want to be constrained. I don't need a lot, but I want what I want. I think I use my money wisely. I spend to invest in my business. I spend to take care of people in my inner circle. I take a lot of responsibility on my shoulders, and can feel that certain relationships cost me financially. I feel the burden of providing house, cars, TVs, phones, clothing, education, for my family. I also have a tendency to display some *Giving* behavior with my family. For example, I might spend a lot more on my kids than on myself, but then feel unappreciated and resentful. I want to be able to save, relax, and be okay, but because the weight of responsibility is so heavy on me, I end up working a lot, pushing myself a lot, and not relaxing. The more tired I get, the more I want to compensate by overindulging. Rather than having clear intention about what I want to accomplish with my spending, I tend to more action-oriented than deliberative. When I'm exhausted, I just go out to eat, drink, spend. I don't take time to nurture myself. Life weighs me down with all kinds of responsibilities and I can feel like I am literally working myself to death. There is not a lot of fun or lightness in my life. I'm pushing against life and *Exerting* to be strong in Self-Preservation.

As a "Big Boss" SO 8, my focus is on social power. I want to have a great reputation. I want to protect others and nurture my posse. My spending, like my eating, working, and exercising, tends to excess. My philosophy is to enjoy life now. I never think about how I'm going to pay for things. I might have 100 shoes and still, it never feels like too much. I try to limit my spending, but after a while, I want another hit. I can always have more. I love restaurants, conveniences, experiences. I like to set a tone of generosity. I like to host parties, take care of others, make sure there is plenty of food and drinks. I want to do it in A+ style. I don't want my family and tribe to feel lack. I give generously to charities, and buy lots of toys for my kids. I am not anxious about giving money to others. I am magnanimous.

As a "High Roller" SX 8, my spending is instinctive and impulsive. I want the freedom to follow my impulse. I spend on food, art, experiences, knowledge, clothing. If it's going to be mine, I want it to be nice. I am a very visual person. Liability insurance has no buzz for me; art does. I also love to travel and experience new things. I prefer learning trips to laying on the beach. At less healthy levels, I don't have a lot of control over my spending, and can get into trouble with debt.

Domain 3 – Earning

My basic assumption is that I must exert myself to get money and love. If I want it, I should be able to have it and I will earn enough to pay for it. I have no reflex to pull back from life. I am driven to be independent and self-reliant. I want to be my own boss. I don't like to take direction from others. I am confident in my ability to make things happen. I understand the generative nature of things, how one thing begets other things. I have an intuitive belief that what I do will increase my chance for large success. I have no problem generating opportunities for myself, opening doors, and going for what I want. I am not deterred by potential risk. What I see is the risk in not trying, not being bold. I set the bar high and push boundaries. I am also resilient and can bounce back. I can be unrelenting in the face of exhaustion. I just do what I do, and keep going. The problem is that I sometimes work like crazy without a lot of clear thinking about why I am doing it or what I really want.

As a "Heavyweight" SP 8, I feel responsible for making money and providing security for my family. But often work can feel like a grind and I have difficulty having fun. Fun feels like a luxury I could have when the responsibilities were off my shoulders, but I can't relax now. Even if I get beat up at work, I keep at it. Working hard is easier than working smart. I don't think to take short cuts or make things easier for myself.   I don't have a natural intuition to pace myself. I see myself working until I drop dead. I feel like a hamster in a wheel that will never be able to stop. I am not afraid of hard work, but I may push myself to breakdown. When I stop, it is to recuperate, only to get back up and go again. I work lustfully, rest lustfully, indulge lustfully. I work really hard, but I often feel like I live paycheck to paycheck. I have a difficult time balancing the fine line between challenging myself (in a good way) and pushing myself to physical breakdown. I know how to work. I don't know how to relax.

As a "Big Boss" SO 8, I am very ambitious. I can earn a good living because I can read groups well, am a great networker, and can lead others. The possibility of failure doesn't deter me. I go out and create opportunities for myself. I want to do what I want to do when I want to do it, and goof off when I want to. I make things happen, close deals, get things into the pipeline. I always assume I can go out and make more money if I have to. I believe that if I do good and important work and keep swinging, sooner or later I will hit a home run. I believe that if I get too detail-oriented and caught in the details, I'll have to take my off the ball. I want to be paying attention to the right things. I realize that swinging for the fences is risky, but I like challenges and can't imagine doing it any other way.

As a "High Roller" SX 8, I don't want to do work that does not charge me up. I can't do things I don't believe in. I have strong feelings. I don't want to punch the clock and follow rules. I can feel like I am battling the world, and beating my head against the wall. I want to make a big impact. Being an employee often doesn't work well for me. I believe in having a big vision and going all out to try to make it big. My *Exerting* energy reinforces my Sexual instinct and makes me bolder and more confident. I get a charge out of investing my money to build and grow things. I believe in leveraging up to turn small capital into large capital. I am not deterred by the possibility of failure. I love the thrill of the hunt, the charge of the challenge. If there is a set back, I just keep going. Building things is a way to channel my energy to push against things, take action, and create. I am more comfortable building than I am in being successful. Once I hit a goal, I wonder what the next goal is. It is in the building process itself that I feel most in my element.

Domain 4 – Beliefs

I am a realist, and the reality of life is that we need money to live. Everything I want and need requires money. Without money, I am not only weak, but unworthy. There'll never be enough money or enough success. I have a love-hate relationship with money. It seems that the more you make, the more responsibilities you take on, and the more pressure builds. The more successful I am, the more I need to be successful and the farther I have to fall, so the less I can afford to fail. These beliefs trap me in a vicious cycle of work, success, more work, that prevents me from ever relaxing.

As a "Heavyweight" SP 8, I believe in the value of constantly pushing myself and others. I never stop to consider the value of pulling back my energy to relax and reflect. I want to know: Can I do this? Can I conquer this? Can I hit this goal? Can I do it better than the next person? I always gravitate to the next step, what else needs to be done. I believe in constant action, pushing, and exerting. My *Exerting* personality likes to be aggressive, and is afraid of being lazy and fat. This belief that it is not okay to relax locks me into a scarcity mindset that blocks me from experiencing abundance.

As a "Big Boss" SO 8, I care more about power than money. I want to have enough money to be able to do what I want to do. I want money when I want it, but then I don't pay attention to it. My interest in money is more around how I fit into the group and not being embarrassed. I want to make sure my bases are covered so I don't have to think about it. Money doesn't intrinsically interest me. I only pay attention to it when I need more or because I want something. It is true that more money is better than less money, especially because I can have a bigger impact with more money. In terms of happiness and who you are, money doesn't mean much.

As a "High Roller" SX 8, I think money is important in allowing me to do things I want to do and live intensely, but my most important resources are my good health and energy. Being forced to slow down is a bigger crisis for me than losing money, because then I cannot control my destiny as well.

Domain 5 – Understanding

Understanding money requires downtime. Understanding is about digesting, observing, interpreting. It is not about doing. I am so busy doing that I don't have a lot of time for reflecting. I don't like to pay attention to things that aren't directly related to action, or to areas where I don't feel competent or in control. Unfortunately the areas where I don't feel competent and in control are where I need to pay attention!

> I don't have a very systematic way of understanding my money situation. I prefer to be in action mode rather than reflection mode.

> I really don't want to think about money. I want someone else to do it for me.

Especially when I am having failures rather than successes, I hate to admit that I am getting in my own way. I have a lot of difficulty asking for help. When I get stressed out, I deliberately avoid thinking about money. It's active avoidance, because nothing I do is passive. I don't make it easy on myself to step back and just see what's really going on, because I get so wrapped up in being defensive and angry. All I can see is what is in my line of vision, which is to work harder, and make more money. I also don't make it easy for financial advisors to work with me.

> All I want to know is where can I invest my money to make it grow more. The last guy was a piece of sh@% and you're probably not going to be any better. But here's the deal. I'm not happy with how things have grown. I don't understand my statements. I don't want to deal with managing the money. I want someone else to do it for me because I don't know about this world of investments, and I don't have the time to learn or manage it myself. I want to have a financial cushion so that I can slow down and stop being so busy. I don't care about all that touchy feely personal growth jibber jabber. Just make me money. And don't screw up like the last guy did.

When I get like this, please know that I don't know any other way to express myself. And I don't even know what I don't know. What can be very helpful for me is to be proactive at taking care of myself. How can I get beyond challenging others and start to challenge myself to pull back and grow?

In the areas that I care to dominate, I am motivated to learn and understand so that I can demonstrate mastery and control. In the areas that I willfully ignore, however, I have zero motivation to learn or understand. Why waste my time and attention on something that doesn't matter to me? I'm going to focus my energy where there will be a payoff in terms of control, mastery, and domination. That's how I feel about money. If I think that learning about money will help me to be stronger and more protected, then I might be interested in learning about it. Otherwise, who cares? The tragedy with this neglect is that it locks me into this vicious cycle of lustful work and exhaustion. By not taking care of money matters, I may not be able to slow down or retire when I am older and don't have the same energy I had when I was young. I dismiss the value of pulling back energetically and pacing myself. I think I can fight off death.

Domain 6 – Risk Management

I'm a realist. S*%t happens. That's obvious. But I don't worry too much about it. Depending on my instinct, I'll take the necessary precautions. But I mostly live in the now. I don't worry about things going wrong. You have to be tough and just plow through things. I'm a survivor. What I forget to consider is that there might be more support for me in the world than I can even imagine. I try to do it all alone. I have almost no instinct to ask for or receive help and support. Perhaps it's because I don't actually believe that others would help me.

As a "Heavyweight" SP 8, risk for me is everything I can't control. I don't want to be vulnerable to random external forces, so I work hard to build a fortress around me and my family that will insulate us from as much external risk as possible. Money is good for this. The more money I have, the more protection I have. Thus, risk management is about building wealth. I rely on myself almost 100%. When my wealth falls and I lose my fortress of protection, this can be devastating and terrifying. I must learn to trust that I am supported and not forsaken.

As a "Big Boss" SO 8, I perceive risk that seems even more devastating than a loss of financial wealth. My reputation and social network are what I live for. I am generous to others, and believe that they will be generous to me if I need something in tough times. As a "High Roller" SX 8, even more devastating to me than loss of money or reputation would be a loss of vitality, energy, and my health.

With a Self-Preservation blindspot, financial matters don't faze me. I hardly think about saving for a rainy day. I figure when the rain happens, I'll deal with it. I've never been one to take my umbrella with me. I have no instinct to play things safe and worry about things ahead of time. I'm tough. I can handle it. Bring it on. I dare the world. I'm not willing to pull back my lustful spending just to have some rainy-day emergency savings. That's for wimps and I'm not a wimp. But just because I don't worry about myself, doesn't mean I don't worry about others. I buy life insurance so that in case anything happens to me, my family will be protected. My mortality scares me for their sake because, if I die, I can't be around to protect them. Alone, I wouldn't feel this vulnerability. Does that fear make me take better care of my own health though? Not necessarily. My personality is strongly wired to believe that self-care is for wimps and that I'm a survivor. I don't have the skills or personality to live a low-risk life. The way I deal with risk is to work harder, not take fewer risks.

Domain 7 – Planning

I'm more of a doer than a planner. I don't like to set goals because goals can be limiting. My goal is "as much as possible." Goals could cause me to swing too low. I always want to achieve more. As I climb higher and higher, I want more and more.

As a "Heavyweight" SP 8, I would like to be able to retire, but planning for retirement feels like planning for my eventual demise, decline, and death. The reality is that my life force energy will decline over time, and I need to make some accommodations for this fact. But my personality assumes that I can keep going, keep working, keep *Exerting* forever. What I resist from a planning perspective is doing what I might have a passion for. I don't feel I can get out from under the weight of responsibility on my shoulders. How can I plan for fun and games when I have such a load to carry?

> I get depressed from the planning process. I have resistance to doing things that are at my heart's core. I like my life. I like the work I do, except that I'd like a different experience of my life. The way I move through my life feels heavy.

As a "Big Boss" SO 8, my inclination is to deal with things as I go, not plan carefully, especially not around money. I'm not good at setting financial goals. It never crosses my mind to think about the dollar goal at some particular point in time. I know I should save, but when I step out of the room, I completely forget about it. I worry more about my status, reputation, and power, than I do my financial status. I'm not a bean counter. Planning also feels a bit futile because things always come up to deter best-laid plans. I prefer to be in the moment, responsive to what comes up socially. If I have to choose between hosting an unforgettable party and saving for dental care, it's a no-brainer. I care about my reputation and don't want to look poor. I'm not going to say no to something just because it is not in the "plan." When I have what I need for the short term, then I turn my attention to other things.

As a "High Roller" SX 8, I am more spontaneous than planful. I live for today. Retirement and death seem a long way off, and I assume things will all work out. I don't want to manage my energy, manage my money, or be boxed in. I want to live my life fully now, and respond to what comes up in the moment. Because I feel confident in my own survival abilities – to meet whatever comes up – I don't feel the need to plan. I don't doubt myself, to a fault. Retirement planning feels very nebulous to me. It's as hard to imagine retirement as it is to imagine my own death. I am focused on being alive, not dying. I put money in a retirement plan each month, but there is not a lot of interest for me. The present has much more juice.

Domain 8 – Wealth Building

I naturally understand the idea of turning small into large, and leveraging one's current resources to generate greater wealth. I understand that the right investments can lead to big payoffs in the future. I intuitively understand the risk-reward dichotomy. I am intuitively willing to take bigger risks for bigger returns, because I enjoy big charges and big outcomes.

> I want to make $1,000,000 in 12 months. I can do it. It's not the having that is exciting. It's the feeling of conquest that I crave. Ok, now, can I make $5,000,000 in 2 years? I might lose money, but I will gain it back and lose it and gain it back. And hopefully each time there will be some net gains. If it's a loss, I'll just keep going. I'll take every dollar I have and I bet on black. I accept both failure or success as mine. It is the process of conquering a challenge that I like.

My lusty spending, however, can deter wealth building. When my energy is oriented to spending money, even if a lot of money comes in, a lot also flows out, and there may not be much left over. My lack of understanding about how to pace myself energetically and financially leads to over spending and over risk-taking. If I could learn to pull my energy back, and restrain myself a bit, I wouldn't have to live paycheck to paycheck.

> If I were more careful about spending, I'd have saved more at this point.

> When we lost 20% in this market downturn, it pissed me off, but I didn't panic. I just have to keep making more money. I don't see myself resting for ten years. I want to scale back, but I don't know if I'll be able to.

I naturally understand that creating and building something new requires risk, commitment, and an investment of resources and oneself. Wealth creation is an expression of our inner confidence to generate something from nothing. But to be maximally powerful and generative, we need to balance exertion and withdrawal. We need to know when to push, and when to pull back, so that our bright flame doesn't burn out. But my lusty appetite can cause me to take too much risk without fully considering the consequences.

> When the markets were hot in Nevada, we did really well. We acted opportunistically and bought two homes with almost no money down. But then the markets tanked and we got burned bad. I didn't see it coming. Money wise, it ended up being a poor decision. But I am super optimistic. I feel wealth can be built up over a long time, but it can also be built up in a short amount of time. I am focusing on rebuilding right now. This is a fun stage for me. I always have a lot of ideas for things I would like to do.

My distorted, personality-driven thinking is that I must keep myself in scarcity in order to be vital and alive. If I don't have anything to push against, I will become fat and lazy. I will not be the lean, hungry, fighting machine that I must be in order to be vital and alive.

> My philosophy is that if you create a vacuum, you need to fill that vacuum, so if I spend a lot of money, then I will have to fill the empty pot with more work, and that keeps me on my toes, and I like that. If I was complacent, then I wouldn't have the motivation to make money. I would sit around and read books. Our high spending rate keeps me on top of my game. I need a battle to fight. Without a battle, the air goes out of me. Though I can't think of the last time there wasn't a battle to fight.

The truth is that it is not our *Exerting* that makes us alive. It is our experience of vitality that makes us feel alive. We cannot artificially reproduce vitality. Unconsciously, my aversion to financial success comes from my fear of pulling back energetically. A large part of my journey with money is to learn how to relax and let my armor drop. If I do not spend so lustfully, and allow savings to build up, I will actually discover that I can cultivate wealth and feel more alive when I am *Exerting* less! And I can begin to connect to this sensation of being at peace and at one with things, rather than separate and apart.

Domain 9 – Balance

I do not experience much balance. What I am mostly familiar with is separation, opposition, and difference. My whole life has been about pushing up against other people and things, engaging in challenge, being strong by staying in battle mode. I worry about getting lazy if I relax. I try to stay on my toes, stay sharp, motivated, and focused. Balance requires being able to rest, relax, blend in, harmonize, and not push against everything. This Domain is a big growth edge for me.

As a "Heavyweight" SP 8, I have a strong sense that money is a scarce and finite resource in this world. If I had triple what I have right now (financially), I'm still not sure I would have enough. The sense that I must continue *Exerting* to get my needs met keeps me in scarcity mode and prevents me from being able to experience prosperity. When I focus on getting what I want, I forget that I might already have what I need.

> I used to feel there was never enough and worried about providing even though I was making a good income. It drove me to work very hard. It was constantly

exhausting. It felt like a grind, a chore. I'd wake up, get my head beat up, and then do it all over again the next day.

The problem is that if I attach my value to money or something outside of me that I cannot control, then I set myself up for disappointment and anger. It is only when I can begin to unhook from my need to control the world that I can begin to take in what is around me with appreciation and wonder.

As a "Big Boss" SO 8, I am less focused on money, and therefore more able to feel abundance. I am generous with my time and money, and appreciate what I have. I trust in generosity and energy flow. I don't need much material stuff for myself. My lust is for social power more than for material things (though I do like my shoes and books). I like to use money for the greater good. I don't want to be hedonistic. Money comes in and money goes out of my life. I don't worry much about money. If I don't have what I want, I will figure out a way to get it.

As a "High Roller" SX 8, my Sexual instinct is to chase the possibilities and not worry about what might go wrong. If it does, something else will come up and give me new options. I believe that if I pay attention, income will happen. If I don't pay attention, it still might happen. Possibility trumps problems for me. I believe things will bounce back and recover. The less attached I am to things, the stronger I can be. By focusing more on my business strategy and customer service, rather than on money and the bottom line, I believe that I will be able to generate more abundance. I am really resilient and optimistic. I can make what I need to happen happen. I feel I can spend, even if I have nothing. I don't know why that is. It never occurs to me that there is not enough.

5. THE PARADOX

The fundamental paradox is that *Exerting* never leads to real strength. It can only lead to pushing and exhaustion. Not only is the actual outcome the opposite of my original intent, but it can never be otherwise. What is strength? Is strength something I have when I push hard? Is strength something I have when I control things? Is strength something that I must prove? Or is strength something that we all have? *Exerting* is supposed to make me feel stronger. But when I overdo this strategy, I actually feel less vital and alive. The defenses I've employed bring about the very deadness and dullness that I fear.

The paradox is that *Exerting* causes me to disconnect from the thing I care most about, which is finding my strength and true power. I fail to see how I have forsaken my own sweet nature. I forget that my being strong does not come from *Exerting* at all. There is a part of me that knows that I am not mean-spirited or an intimidating bully. But honoring this part of myself would create conflict with my ego structure, and that tension would be too much for me to bear. So instead, I continue pushing and *Exerting*. I sense that I am being blackmailed into *Exerting* and that this entire structure is built on fear, but I do not know how to move past the fear. The more I fear being lifeless and without power, the more I push, exert and dare.

The paradox is that in always pushing against life, I do not leave room to enjoy life. In always battling to win, I actually lose. In always paying attention to how I can be tough, I fail to recognize that my so-called enemies make my life real and worth living. My pushing so hard causes me to become more lifeless and dead, which is the very thing that I am trying to avoid. In learning to pull back my energy, I bring more life and vitality into my soul. In learning to be more withdrawn and curious, I become more connected. In relinquishing power and control, I feel more alive.

6. BREAKING THE VICIOUS CYCLE

In order to break the vicious cycle of my personality, and move from Fear to Love, I must embrace and resolve the fundamental paradox of *Exerting*. I have spend my whole life hiding my sweetness. I have been made inhumane by my need to be tough. How can I admit my own delicacy and vulnerability? What incredible possibilities could exist if I could honor my sweet and loving side? In keeping my sweetness and empathy at bay, I have also held away the love. As I throw off the shackles of my personality and orient to my true nature, I begin to own the whole me. When I do this, I move past my story of being sinful, rejected, and unloved.

My journey with money is a journey to mercy and innocence. My journey to mercifully embracing my vulnerability and sweetness requires me to connect my body to my head and heart. By doing this, I begin to have a more spacious sense of my life. I can step back and know that we are all mortal and delicate. Instead of being lustful in getting my needs met, I can relax, knowing that what I need is here for me. I don't need to work at being strong and in control. When I witness pain, sadness, and mortality, I can be with it all, which takes strength and love.

I am part of the strength of the universe. I don't need to work hard to be strong and appreciated. Strength is not about doing but being. Our nature is strong. In surrendering to my core nature, I stop resisting the truth. I become embodied Love, with compassion in my heart, wisdom in my head, and well-being in my body. I now occupy a much vaster reality. I experience my vaster identity and participation, and feel the vitality of being here right now. By having empathy for others, I begin to feel my own heart more. This enables me to be fully present without trying to cover over the pain. I can accept my own mortality. In embracing these truths, I can move past my old beliefs and patterns and welcome abundance, prosperity, and love into my life. I can begin to feel more sensitive and wise. But this is not comfortable or easy. I feel the pain as my ego resists losing its job. I feel remorseful about how I have lived my life and hurt myself and others. I am scared that I won't be able to survive on my own deeper knowing alone.

When I live abundantly, I know that I am part of a merciful universe. I can be sweet and gentle, without being gruff and angry. I can connect to my vulnerability and mortality, and own the whole of me. When I can be fully me, I can connect with others. I no longer need to push against the world, separated from others. By accepting my own mortality and innocence, I can be at one with the world, in harmony with it all.

	Brief Description
"Heavyweight" SP8	I want to be in control of my resources. My spending is not lavish, but I do not want to be constrained. I take care of people in my inner circle, and feel laden with responsibility. I feel that certain relationships cost me financially. I tend to push myself and others hard and work till I am exhausted.
"Big Boss" SO 8	I am a big picture person who focuses on controlling social resources rather than material resources. I don't care at all about details. I am not a nickel and dimer. I want to set a tone of generosity and magnanimity. I protect my posse.
"High Roller" SX 8	I play big. I do what charges me up, and take big gambles. My Sexual instinct reinforces my type energy, making me extra bold, confident, and impulsive. I like to invest my money and myself to build and grow things. I love the thrill of the chase. If there is a setback, I just pick myself up and keep going.

Type 8	Summary
Gift	Making things happen with my confidence, boldness, strength.
Unconscious Belief	The world is a battlefield where the strong prevail.
Strategy	*Exerting* – pushing against the world to make things happen and feel alive.
Vicious Cycle	Because I want to feel alive, I exert myself and push against the world. I cannot relax or rest. This causes me to be exhausted and depleted, so I feel lifeless rather than alive.
Defended Against	Being sweet and vulnerable.
Operationally	• I must control my destiny. • I cannot afford to rest or relax. • I focus only on areas where I am strong and in control.
Paradox	*Exerting* does not generate vitality and strength.
Breaking the Vicious Cycle	I must recognize that real strength is loving. I can be more vital and alive when I open my heart and stop pushing against the world so much.
Direction of Growth	Pulling back my energy allows me to be connected rather than separate so that I can be at peace with the world.

CHAPTER 15

SETTLING

Type 9

1. GIFT

I have an innate sense of the importance of being grounded, relaxed, and at peace. I don't need to live a big, flashy life. I don't need to strive for validation, and I don't want to get caught up in worrying. I can rest, relax, and take time to just be here. I am able to appreciate the blessings in my life. I am okay as I am and can be quite happy with lots of different situations.

I am able to experience what is good in this world. I don't feel obliged to rush or strive or be somewhere else because where I am is a very good place to be. In this world where everyone seems to want more now, I am a healthy antidote. I can be here without needing things to be different. I can go with the flow and just enjoy how things are.

In being at peace with myself and the universe, I give the world peace. I can hold space for others and their differences. I can see the good side of different points of view. I can integrate contradictions and see what is shared in common. I bring peace to the world.

2. STRATEGY

My life and money strategy grow out of my sense of the critical importance of being at peace. At the unconscious level, I register the world as fragmented and conflicted, though I deny this feeling at the conscious level. At the conscious level, my belief is that I can generate peace. *Settling* is about accepting life as it is, without fighting what is. Others might think I am a bit stubborn in my unwillingness to be disturbed. What they miss is my desire to live from a place of harmony and wholeness, where I can be in the flow of life.

An aspect of *Settling* is my ability to see the silver lining in everything. It's about recognizing that things do generally work out for the best. This is why I can be comfortable with things just as they are. I believe we should let life unfold as it will. Sometimes the best outcomes occur without any goals or striving. Sometimes things don't go as planned, but then something better comes of it. My approach to life is more organic than structured.

Settling is a defense against trying to be seen and is the opposite of *Striving*. In *Settling*, I reject my desire to be validated. Feeling that there is no hope to be seen and validated, there is no point in being proactive. I am happy to let myself and other things be as they are. Fixing, changing, improving all require a sense of what is wrong. But I don't see anything seriously wrong with the way things are. I don't see the point of fixing things that aren't broken.

I assume that both my internal and external worlds are in conflict and disharmony and need to be held at bay. I take it upon myself to create peace and harmony in this conflicted world by *Settling*. I deeply fear a life that is disturbed and not harmonious. But being at peace is not really about being undisturbed. Being at peace is about embracing life fully, not about letting our fear of being disturbed keep us from engaging. It is about being in the flow with what life brings us. If we are really at peace, then we do not perceive everything as potential disturbances, and we do not hide from disturbances by staying attached to our local sanctuary, either internally or externally. If we have to hide to get peace, we are not in fact at peace. We are only at peace when we can be with the pleasant and the unpleasant, the comfortable and the disturbing, with equal poise.

The difficulty with being engaged in this way is that I must leave the comfort that I am familiar with. An orientation to being in the flow requires being willing to be bothered, troubled, disturbed, conflicted. I prefer the peaceful to the conflicted, so I prefer to stay in my comfort zone.

For me, having peace is about staying with what I am familiar with. I don't associate it with being curious, open, and energized. For me, peace is more like being asleep than awake. Staying awake is difficult because I would have to trust that it's worth the trouble. If it's not worth the trouble to be awake, then it's difficult to show up and engage.

3. THE VICIOUS CYCLE

If I were to look at my life objectively, I would notice that I have essentially been trapped in a vicious cycle of fear and scarcity. Because of this, my relationship to love and prosperity is constrained. *Settling* is fundamentally about holding myself back from life. But in being this way, I continually reinforce my assumption that disturbances must be avoided. This orientation supports my inertia. But my ego enthusiastically keeps this vicious cycle going. I get addicted to *Settling*. Even though I think I am okay, I am not as okay as I think.

When we are caught in a vicious cycle where our actions validate our beliefs, it can be very difficult to extricate ourselves. When we are stuck at a certain point along the scarcity-to-abundance spectrum, it is impossible to improve our position until we get out of the vicious cycle. If we are suddenly showered with new wealth, we will most likely dissipate it so that we can get back to our old set point. So in order to create new wealth, we must first become aware of the vicious cycle we are caught in. Once we become aware, we will be in a better position to consciously unblock what blocks us, and welcome new wealth into our lives.

My underlying assumption is that I am not valued, loved, or seen. I just want to sleep and be undisturbed. Staying asleep allows me to avoid feeling the pain and hurt of not being loved. Shutting out the world and creating a comfortable place makes life tolerable. I do not overtly rebel, but I do not embrace life either. I just try to make myself as comfortable as possible. I take the path that is the least challenging and strenuous. I don't want trouble or conflicts. To have my peace, I just want to get along.

I can be quite stubborn in my complacency. No one is going to dislodge me from my state of peace. Let them try. *Settling* is my way of trying to be okay, no matter what the cost. Complacency is rooted in the belly center. My belly center supports my being how I am, attached to things the way they are, ignoring disturbing thoughts and feelings. My inclination is to be laid back, calm, not grasping or trying too hard. What I do not perceive is how hard I work at being okay. I skate on the surface of life, doing what is necessary, but not completely buying into it, not fully embracing it, always maintaining skepticism. The more I fear being disturbed, the more conflict-averse, resistant, inertial I become. This constricts me and dampens my life energy.

I believe that I can't afford to say no, but I can't say yes either. I cannot embrace anything earnestly because nothing seems certain. Fuzzy boundaries, fuzzy thoughts, fuzzy numbers all seem safer because they do not require sharp divisions. It is hard to take a stand for myself because this would create divisions between me and others. My lack of clear boundaries, however, creates a problem for me because I don't know how to protect myself, except to hide inside myself. Similarly, I resist striving and setting big goals that could generate disappointment.

No matter whether I am dealing with people, ideas, or things, I try to avoid conflict. I avoid conflict within myself by ignoring ambivalent or contradictory feelings and thoughts. I avoid conflict with others by avoiding difficult people, avoiding difficult conversations, and avoiding using the word "no." I don't often say "yes," but I try to avoid conflict by not saying "no." I avoid sticking my neck out in situations that might bring disappointment, frustration, or humiliation. I avoid noticing things that might disturb me or cause conflict. If I don't see anything wrong, then then there is nothing to fix. I also resist imagining new possibilities that might entail difficulty or trouble.

I also resist difficult emotions because they feel dangerous and risk cutting me off from my sense of inner peace. I resist being vigilant because I might notice something that causes me to be anxious. I secretly resent pessimistic people. They bring me down and I don't like being down. I resist being angry because this would disturb my peace. I resist strong desires because I might be disappointed. I resist shame and embarrassment because I would feel bad about myself. I resist seeing my own culpability in things. By not connecting to my true feelings, I have difficulty moving past my inertia.

My driving motivation is to be okay. I don't want to exert myself. I don't want to strive for validation and I don't want to set my sights too high. I don't want to try to control things to be a certain way or want something so badly that I risk disappointment. The kind of planning for the future that makes sense to me is open, big-pictured, but somewhat fuzzy. General intentions are better than specific numerical goals. I prefer to create my own path through an open horizon and be optimistic.

I don't try to be heroic or put myself on the line. By avoiding conflict, I hope to maintain my inner peace and continue along smoothly. I can easily perceive how things are going well and how things do generally work out for the best especially because I can be quite happy with lots of different situations. When someone asks me where I want to go for dinner, or what I want to do this weekend, I usually respond "Whatever you want." Since I could be happy with a lot of options, there is no point fighting about it.

I don't get hung up on being a winner or loser. I do not feel compelled to conform to external standards of success. For me, everyone can be a winner in their own way. The idea that there is only way to be "successful" seems silly. I do not need to project an image of success and I do not feel the need to impress others. I know what I want to do and I know when I've done a good job. My best motivation comes from within me, not from the outside. Narrowly defined goals lead to conflict, tension, and disappointment. Because I naturally orient towards maintaining harmony for myself and others, it seems obvious to me that success should be broadly defined. Then it is easier to reach a win-win situation for everyone.

> I don't invest in one position or outcome, so more outcomes can be defined as successful. I don't have to have everything all at once. I can have things over my lifetime.

Being able to define success broadly also enables me to justify being inertial. Since things are okay right now, I do not need to do anything differently. There is a sleepy stubbornness in the way I refuse to embrace change. Once I am doing what I am doing, I float along in that mode because I don't want to upset my routine, habit, and idea of how things should be. I don't like to be disturbed. I have a large zone of satisfaction. Some people find me exasperatingly unambitious because even though I am very talented, I do not reach for the stars. I know that achieving would disrupt my comfortable life and could end in disappointment. Why would I do this when I am happy with things the way they are?

My persevering and patient nature has a downside. The more I fear being disturbed, the more resistant and inertial I become. Even if things aren't working well, I settle for things the way they are. I don't deliberately resist change. I just find ways to procrastinate or be preoccupied with other matters. Things have to go very badly for me to be motivated to disrupt my life and try something new. The dynamic of the ego structure keeps my ego employed and keeps me perpetually fixated on peace and conflict. I can never find peace for then I would have no excuse for *Settling*. We are each caught in a vicious cycle of our personality and instincts until we decide to break free. This takes deliberate energy and momentum because the cycle is a compelling vortex. In order to create new wealth, we must see clearly the vicious cycle that blocks us from abundance. Then we must fight our way out of the vortex.

4. OPERATIONALLY

If my instincts are balanced, I will be able to attend to money in each of the Nine Money Domains in a healthy manner. If, however, my instincts are not in balance, then I will get stuck in my type fixation and I cannot be optimally effective. My motivation to be undisturbed and at peace manifests in different ways depending on my dominant instinct. Instead of addressing areas that need to be addressed, I tend to focus on my routines and habits. As a SP 9, I am motivated to be comfortable. The more convenience, pleasantness, and ease, the better. As a SO 9, I want to be in harmony with the groups that I am a part of. Money for myself is not a large part of my focus. As a SX 9, I like to draw intensity and energy towards me. How my instincts are imbalanced will therefore impact how I relate to the Nine Money Domains – where I put my attention and energy and where I don't.

"STEADY" SP 9	"UNSUNG HERO" SO 9	"GROOVING" SX 9

Domain 1 – Budgeting

I don't stress too much about money and I don't live by a strict budget because that would be a burden. As a "Steady" SP 9, I have an intuitive sense of whether I am within my budget or not. I want things to be easy so I don't want to put myself on a tight budget where I would be stressed out. I try to make sure there is enough money to pay the bills. I keep track of receipts, invoices, expenses for tax purposes, and have a basic idea where the money is coming from and where it is going. I am fairly organized; for example, I have files so I can find what I am looking for. I seldom bounce checks. As long as the bills are paid on time and I am taking care of matters, I don't need an explicit budget. What's the point of knowing how much we spent on groceries last month? Spending money should serve my basic needs without stressing me out. Savings goals and budgeting both feel counter-intuitive and a bit counter-productive. If the point of having savings is so that you can worry less about money, then worrying about money so that you can have savings seems backwards. I would rather not "live on the edge" financially because that would add a lot of stress and difficulty that I don't want in my life. I would rather be self-sufficient than go into debt to buy something unnecessary. I can be happy with what I have. So it is not a problem to be frugal.

> Why would I want to live beyond my means? That would only add stress and difficulty to my life. I try not to get into bad habits that will be difficult for me to break. For example, I always pay off my credit cards. Because once you can't pay, your interest rates goes up and it becomes a difficult habit to break, so I just don't go there.

> When I have less money, I simply lower my expectations and adjust my lifestyle to match my means.

> I am not very proactive about things, more just checking on things. I am pretty low intensity about my emotional reaction to things. Sometimes my emotions might trigger me to a more action orientation, but it is spiky, and takes a while to build up. Decision making mode – there will be a maturing process for the decision. I don't make decisions right away.

As an "Unsung Hero" SO 9, I tend to be more disorganized and unstructured about finances. My Social instinct is more interested in connecting to and supporting groups and family than it is in taking care of my personal well-being. I can be rather neglectful of money, and get disorganized about paperwork, paying bills, and other financial matters. I may run up credit card balances, not pay my bills on time, get overdraft notices on my bank account, pay finance fees, and forget about money that I owe others. I only have a loose structure for receipts, invoices, expenses for taxes. I have difficulty with boundaries, including financial boundaries. Things tend to be a bit fuzzy for me. My easy-going spending can get away from me. My spending may be greater than my income, but I may not do anything about it. I can get caught up in the habits of my life, going through the motions. The more stressed out I get, the fuzzier things become, and the more difficult it is to pay attention to the details of money. Without routines and structures, I can get very disorganized and find myself procrastinating on tasks I know I should get to. I'll hang on to checks that should get deposited. I don't pay attention to how much is in the bank. I forget to pay bills. I always intend on doing these things, but somehow I have trouble activating. I find it difficult to muster energy for myself.

> I am fuzzy, fatally optimistic, and trust that there will be enough. I make estimates about money. I might know the ballpark only, but would be content with that. Record keeping seemed less important. But in the long run, fuzzy doesn't work. I've gotten into big trouble being fuzzy with numbers.

As a "Grooving" SX 9, my Sexual instinct is more focused on relationships and passionate interests than on money. I have trouble getting worked up about money. It's just not that interesting to me. I get preoccupied with more interesting things. It's better when bill paying and savings are automated so I don't have to do anything. I want to conserve my energy and just not worry. It is such an effort to sit myself down and pay bills. I don't know why. It's not like I'm not good with numbers, but there's something about paying attention to money that feels particularly challenging. I can get organized for a while, but when I get stressed, my organization falls apart. I don't like to owe money, and feel it is wrong to spend more than I make, but things often get the best of me and I have to pay the consequences with late fees and penalties. I don't keep records. I try to pay bills right away to get rid of the burden. It makes me happy to pay it and I feel grateful I have electricity. There is a rebellion in me against budgeting. When I have money, I want to spend it. I find myself getting into debt because I am not paying attention and then I have to dig myself out of the hole again and again.

For me, it takes such a conscious intention to sit myself in a chair and do money-related things. My bills stack up and I wait till it's the day for bill paying. But I may forget it's my bill paying day. It is really difficult to make myself focus on paying the bills. I strategize out my due dates. I've tried using structures to keep me organized. I will hang on to checks and not deposit them for a while. I may have no idea how much money is in the bank.

I have had trouble getting worked up about money. I live on the edge, and I never know how many days away from not making it I am. Money is not fun for me. Paying the rent and counting money is boring to me. I am more interested in my relationships, friendships, groups I socialize with. Yes, I wish I had more money to be secure, but I don't orient towards having a secure life.

Domain 2 – Spending

I am reasonably easy going with money. As a creature of habit, my spending tends to be routinized. Money for me is about being comfortable and easy-going. But, sometimes, I splurge like a "successful" person on a fancy restaurant meal, a status car, or a McMansion. As a "Steady" SP 9, the way I am frugal is to reign in my needs and expectations. I adjust my lifestyle to match my means. I don't feel the need to impress others, but I do like to spend for comfort and convenience. If there is something that I or a family member really wants, I am willing to spend money on it. I can be frugal about certain things, and quite loose about other purchases, especially for things that buy convenience and happiness. I have spikes in my spending. Mainly I eat at reasonable places, but then I might eat somewhere really expensive. I can be frugal at home, but when I am traveling, I want to enjoy myself. As an "Unsung Hero" SO 9, I spend more for comfort than well-being. For example, I eat out and money gets away from me easily. I am generous to others. I am also aware of social trends and want to fit in. As a "Grooving" SX 9, I want to enjoy the moment, and don't hesitate to spend on experiences, art, good food, relationships. If I have the money, I will spend it. I'm not good at pacing myself.

Domain 3 – Earning

When it comes to making money, I am a persistent worker, but I do not have high ambitions. I don't like to brag or promote myself. I am more internally motivated than externally motivated. If I am in a groove, doing what I am good at, I am not inclined to disrupt my life by changing my job, routine, or location. Persistence and patience are my strengths. I believe that I will be rewarded for my good work, and I actually enjoy working, even doing things that other people might consider tedious. It is more difficult for me to set something up or begin something new. Sometimes I will even turn down a promotion, especially if it is a job where I would have to persuade others or stick my neck out. I prefer jobs where I know what I am supposed to do, and I can do it my way. I like my autonomy and independence, and I like seeing things to completion. I also enjoy positions such as teaching or ministry where I have my autonomy, but also have the support of a larger institution. I hope my effort and excellent work will be noticed and rewarded, but I am not willing to assert myself to ensure it. I don't like being pushy, because I don't want to trouble others. I hate to bother people with reminders and nagging, even if they owe me money. I would prefer someone else to do this dirty work.

As a "Steady" SP 9, I want work that I enjoy and am good at, with good hours, decent pay, and a comfortable lifestyle. I love supporting my family. I don't have to love my work, but I have to enjoy it. I don't want a job with long hours, a stressful commute, being on the line of fire. I don't need high visibility to feel good about myself. I want to be competent and successful, not a star with all the pressures that come with stardom. Even though I may be an expert, I don't brag. I expect others to notice my good work and reward me appropriately, without my having to push for it. I don't like to feel taken for granted.

> I've turned down manager jobs many times. Leadership catches trouble if we fail, not me. Going to a new job requires rebuilding relationships and selling. I like being an introvert and sitting at my desk.

> I am uncomfortable selling myself. I would prefer all my business to be word of mouth. I want to sell what I do without feeling bad. My pitch is not about "overcoming objections." It is more about being in alignment with what I value.

As an "Unsung Hero" SO 9, I want to care for and contribute to the group and be in harmony with others. I am soft in terms of holding boundaries for myself. My work energy is around social causes, meeting the needs of people who need help. I am not oriented so much to how much money I make. I trust that if I have to make more money, I'll find a way to do it. I don't worry about money a lot, even if I don't know exactly where it's going to come from or where it is going to go. It'll work out somehow. It is a challenge for me to be aggressive about making money. If I knew what to do, maybe I would do it. But even simple things like following up on a phone call or email when I'm owed money can be challenging. I don't like conflict and imagine that asking for something might cause conflict. Is my need more important than their need? I have an internal conflict about things like this. It is challenging for me to consider that I should come first. The other person's agenda always seems more important. It is difficult to stand up and say "This is important for me." I guess it doesn't feel okay to take care of me.

As a "Grooving" SX 9, doing something that I am passionate about is more important than how much I am paid. I keep doing what I love to do and hope money shows up. I never ask for a raise. I don't want to sell myself. I want my work to speak for me. It is difficult to push for my own well-being. Enough money usually shows up to allow me to keep doing what I love to do. I don't want to assert myself, show off, be in the limelight, or put myself on the line. I have difficulty connecting to my activation energy which makes it difficult to get off my butt to find work. If I am in a groove, it is easy to keep going. But looking for work and changing direction is difficult. I often wait for another person's energy to help activate me. It's not so much that I lack confidence, but I don't like to assert myself. I don't put myself out in the world clearly. I depend on others responding to me to get excited. Because my belly center tends to be cut off from my head and heart center, I have difficulty connecting my hope and feelings for money with action. So, even though I love to make money and spend money, I can't get activated to make more money or ask for more money.

Domain 4 – Beliefs

Money is supposed to make my life easier. If I have money, then I don't have to stress about it, pay attention, or think about it. The less I have to worry about, the better. On the other hand, it feels a bit greedy to want too much money. I don't want money to be a source of conflict between me and others. I want to be a good provider and I don't want to be the bad guy or set limits on others. As a "Steady" SP 9, I want money to give me stability and security. Security for me is mostly defined in terms of comfort, convenience and physical well-being. As an "Unsung Hero"

SO 9, I believe that money is for comfort, sharing, and social marking. I am aware of the symbolic nature of money and how money can convey respect, approval, and validation. I am also aware of how money can become a source of conflict, tension, and disagreement, so I tread carefully. Upholding boundaries around money does not feel as important as allowing things to unfold as they will. I tend to be very generous because I believe it is important that money gets spread around, not hoarded. Closed systems are dead systems; open systems are alive systems. As a "Grooving" SX 9, I want to be merged with my passion, be it a person or hobby or work. Money allows me to have the kind of experiences that I want to have. It's for stimulation, beauty, play, relaxation, having a good time. Money is more important and meaningful to me when I am in a good relationship. Otherwise, I am not so motivated about money. I don't stop to consider what more I might want from money. All I want is to be in my groove and not be disturbed. I don't really think about what larger possibilities might exist.

Domain 5 – Understanding

I can see things, including money, from multiple perspectives. As a "Steady" SP 9, I tend to be pretty objective, logical, clear-headed, and detached about money. I don't get too excited when the stock market falls or rises. I don't believe I can time markets. I stay the course and don't get emotional. If the market falls, I am more likely to view it as a buying opportunity than a reason for panic selling. I know all investments are risky, even bank accounts and t-bills because of inflation, but I also believe that sensible investing does pay off over time. I am happy with average returns, and pleasantly surprised by better-than-average returns. One of my strengths is my ability to see things from different angles and to recognize tradeoffs. Because I don't get too invested in any one position, many outcomes can be defined as success. I may do lots of research and consider things this way and that, but then hesitate and procrastinate, not out of worry, but out of inertia.

As an "Unsung Hero" SO 9, my understanding around money can be quite fuzzy, which prevents me from making clear decisions and taking clear stances. This lack of clarity and precision can really hurt me. It is difficult to get energized about what I need because I don't like fighting, pushing, or going after things. I feel like I have to "pump myself up." My fuzzy thinking can interfere with my understanding of how money works and how to deal with money. Being optimistic, I tend to just trust there will be enough, without worrying about details. I have a deeper-seated anxiety that money is scarce, difficult, and not easy, but because I don't want to deal with this anxiety, I cover it up with fuzzy optimism that can get me in trouble.

As a "Grooving" SX 9, my inclination to merge with the object of my passion makes it difficult to be objective and understand money clearly. Investments may be a foreign world to me. With Self-Preservation in my blindspot, I may feel like I do not understand money at all. For example, I might have no idea that if I am one day late with my credit card payment, I will be charged a $35 penalty and a 22% interest rate! Since it was my fault and I don't like conflict, I wouldn't fight it. But I might be so angry at the credit card company that I pay what I owe and cancel the card. Money can be a huge source of anxiety for me, so I push that anxiety away and zone out from money and anything having to do with it. Of course, that doesn't make it easier to take effective action around money.

Domain 6 – Risk Management

My general optimism causes me to habitually see the silver lining because I don't like to worry or get worked up about things. My inclination to manage risks depends on my dominant instinct. As a "Steady" SP 9, I want to be self-reliant. I'd rather anticipate potential disruptions and take care of them than leave things to chance. I want autonomy to do what I want, and not have others tell me what to do. I buy insurance to protect me from possible disruptions in my work, health, and lifestyle. As an "Unsung Hero" SO 9, I am more concerned about fitting in and reciprocity. I feel supported by others and don't worry much about potential problems down the road. I don't like anxiety or disruptions, so I procrastinate. I suppose there are ways that I have taken risks with myself and my life, and it seems to have worked out fine, but mostly I wasn't awake enough to even know that I was taking a "risk." As a "Grooving" SX 9, most of my attention is on being in the moment, not thinking about what-ifs. So I'm pretty oblivious to potential disasters that might be looming. My support is in my relationships and in my passion for beauty and depth. These give me a resilience and ability to bounce back. I don't have much of an orientation to managing risks, since I hardly perceive the risks as risks. I depend on others to energize me. It can be very difficult to get motivated to do things on my own. What I do worry about is that others will not choose me. This is the biggest risk in my life.

Domain 7 – Planning

I am more in the moment than in the future. When I do plan, I prefer loose intentions to concrete plans. My inclination is to allow life to unfold and go with the flow. I don't need things to go a certain way, because then I would be stressed out if things didn't go my way. As a "Steady" SP 9, I try to build up a stash of savings so that I can be flexible as the need arises. I don't necessarily have any specific goals, though I might plan for retirement in a general way. My weakness in this Domain is that I do not have grand visions about the future, and I do not get easily excited about what's possible. My strength, though, is that when I do have a sense of the direction to move in, I am consistent, persistent, and patient. I am like the slow turtle that wins the race. I set goals, but not too rigid goals, because goals that are too specific can work against you. I believe that if I just persevere, eventually things will work out.

As an "Unsung Hero" SO 9, planning feels more like dreaming than anything concrete. For example, I might feel that "I'd love to go to Spain," but not feel that "I must go to Spain." So I would have to pull these energies off two different shelves and put them together before I would ever actually go to Spain. Sometimes they don't get put together. My planning is more like wishful thinking than definite goals. I often see the big picture, but I am not so good at setting specific agendas, goals, deadlines or doing logistics and scheduling. Even if I have goals, I don't necessarily have the proactive energy or discipline to get there. Defining what I want is difficult because there are so many different results that could be good. Overall, I feel that life works out okay, and even if there is a setback, what happens can more than make up for that setback. I might not know what to do, but over time, the way to do it shows up.

As a "Grooving" SX 9, I am not very future-oriented or planning-oriented. Planning requires connecting my thoughts about the future to actions in the present. I am not very good at changing course. I just don't think about things, like food or money, until I have to. I don't calculate precisely. I don't have concrete goals. I might realize I need to make more money, but I won't have a specific goal like make an extra $800 a month. The problem is that it is difficult to muster up the energy to achieve goals. Connecting to bigger, more attractive goals would help pull me out of the fogginess. Unfortunately, I don't tend to get connected to bigger goals on my own. I need others to bring energy to a situation for me to get activated. Worrying about the future is not enough to motivate me to save. For example, even though it only takes one phone call to set up a retirement account, it might take me three years to make the call. It's amazing how difficult thinking about the future is for me.

Domain 8 – Wealth Building

As a "Steady" SP 9, I cherish my autonomy and want to build up my wealth as a resource for autonomy, comfort and ease. My philosophy is slow and steady wins the race. I am a patient, long-term investor. I have no desire to rush out of the starting gate or get somewhere fast. I am "built for comfort, not for speed." For me, savings by definition is what is left over. I refuse to be tight for the sake of saving. After all, the point of money is to provide ease and comfort. I put money away when I can and don't get too anxious about how much I am saving or how my investments are doing.

> I don't diversify as much as I probably should, and I might think harder about investment options, but I tend to ride stuff down vs getting out. There is a huge inertia piece. I put 7% into my 401K per year and then ignore it.

> Savings is a residual. I believe in investing and then ignoring it and assuming that the money will be there when you need it. It is not something I plan for or have goals about.

I am a patient investor and take the long-run perspective. I invest and forget. I am not the type of person who tracks my performance carefully or jumps in and out of the market. I am willing to invest in stocks and accept their volatility, but I don't get ecstatic when prices go up and I don't panic when prices go down. I don't like to change things just for the sake of change. In fact, my *Settling* resists change. I believe that buy and hold makes the most sense. I don't want to be bothered and I am not proactive about investment decisions. If the basics are covered, then I'll be fine and everything will work out. My investing strengths are that I am persistent, patient, and consistent. I am optimistic in that I have a sense that everything will be okay, whether things are going well right now or not. I don't monitor or even calculate my total wealth. I just enjoy what I am doing and am confident that I have enough money to be comfortable. I don't see the point of artificial targets and stressful challenges. There is no point worrying about details and trivial expenditures. Does it really matter if I buy an appetizer at dinner? I am reluctant to strive for more. I feel like, who am I to complain or deserve more? My life is blessed as it is. I am okay just as I am.

As an "Unsung Hero" SO 9, wealth building for my own sake feels a bit selfish. Wealth should be shared. What's mine is yours and what's yours is mine, and we are all one big family. As a "Grooving" SX 9, I am inclined to use the money I have and not do a lot of planning and saving for tomorrow.

Domain 9 – Balance

My optimism orients me towards abundance. I have a sense that things are okay, things will work out, and there is nothing to get stressed about. I like to look on the bright side. I don't like being around negativity. When I need something, the abundance in my life always seems to provide. When I look at the big picture, I know that support has come from all directions. When I am not resolutely blocking out disturbances, but allowing myself to be in the flow of life, I am especially able to experience prosperity and feel supported. I feel gratitude and trust. I feel directed, empowered, and connected to all of it – my family, my community, my country, the planet, the divine.

As a "Steady" SP 9, what keeps me in fear and scarcity is the concern about having no money. This drives me to be a bit selfish and tight and unable to allow myself to fully be in the flow. I am generous in terms of my time and energy, but not so much with my money. When my wealth drops, it makes me anxious even though I don't want to let it get to me. When things are good, I am apt to relax and get complacent. I don't get too down or too up. The world has a lot of problems, but if they don't affect me, I don't stress about them. I settle for what I have. I like playing sports, being with my kids, having a nice cup of coffee, being comfortable, enjoying earthly pleasures. I am a very grounded, earthy kind of person. Life feels real to me, not at all like a game.

As an "Unsung Hero" SO 9, I feel connected to groups. Sometimes I feel like I am nothing but a cog in the wheel, that no one is listening to me, and that I don't matter. What keeps me in scarcity mode is feeling unconnected and unseen. As a "Grooving" SX 9, I feel the beauty of nature, food, friendships, travel. I don't equate abundance with money alone. Living on the edge gives me juice and excitement, even if it adds some stress and hardship to my life. I don't know why things can get so difficult. I don't have a sense that I am struggling, but I don't have a sense that I am doing that well either.

5. THE PARADOX

The fundamental paradox is that *Settling* never leads to the peace and harmony I am looking for. It can only lead to feeling disturbed and out of touch. Not only is the actual outcome the opposite of my original intent, but it can never be otherwise. What is peace? Is peace what I get when I've blocked out all disturbances? Is peace something that I can create? Is peace something that has to be generated? Is peace a scarce commodity that can be preserved? Or is peace something that exists here for all of us always? *Settling* is supposed to help me get peace. But when I overdo this strategy, I actually feel less at peace and less whole. In defending against my intrinsic gloriousness, I want to stay asleep. I do not trust that I am seen and supported.

The paradox is that *Settling* causes me to disconnect from the thing I care most about, which is being in the flow, balanced, and whole. There is a part of me that knows that I am whole and part of the oneness. But honoring this part of myself would create conflict with my ego structure, and that tension would be too much for me to bear. I sense that I am being blackmailed into *Settling* and that this entire structure is built on fear, but I do not know how to move past the fear. The more I fear being disturbed, the more I stubbornly dig my heels in and resist what is going on around me. In continuing to search for peace, I can never actually experience it.

The paradox is that in always paying attention to how I can be undisturbed, I forget that I am already at peace. In always trying to resist the flow of life, I do not participate in life as it unfolds. In being unengaged and stubbornly inertial, I actually cut myself off from life. My resistance and unwillingness to say yes to life causes me to become more disturbed and conflicted, which is the very thing that I am trying to avoid. In learning to set boundaries, I become not more separated, but more connected. When I go with the flow, engaged and alive, I am more balanced and whole.

6. BREAKING THE VICIOUS CYCLE

In order to break the vicious cycle of my personality, and move from Fear to Love, I must embrace and resolve the fundamental paradox of *Settling*. I have spent my whole life stubbornly trying to be undisturbed. What incredible possibilities could exist if I didn't have to resist disturbances? If I could awaken, I could be fully present. In keeping the fear of disturbance at bay, I have also kept away the love. As I throw off the shackles of my personality and orient to my true nature, I begin to own the whole me. When I do this, I move past my story of being disturbed and disconnected.

My journey with money is a journey to real peace. My journey to experiencing wholeness requires me to connect my body to my heart and head so that I can be centered and balanced. When I am simply here, I am awake to everything. I am no longer numbing out and falling asleep, because I am confident that I am loved, seen, valued. I trust that I can simply be, without resisting anything. In surrendering to my core nature, I stop resisting the truth. I become embodied Love, with compassion in my heart, wisdom in my head, and well-being in my body. I now occupy a much vaster reality and feel real peace. In embracing these truths, I can move past my old beliefs and patterns and welcome abundance, prosperity, and love into my life. I can actively engage in life. But this is not comfortable or easy. I feel the pain as my ego resists losing its job. I feel remorseful about how I have lived my life and hurt myself and others. I am scared that I won't be able to survive on my own deeper knowing alone.

When I live abundantly, I know that I am part of the beingness of the universe. By stepping into my full potential, I can fully accept my glory and light and recognize that I am the hope of the universe. This enables me to be fully awake and present under all conditions. By engaging with life, my real oneness develops. From here, I am able to connect to all that is good and right, and be a part of the natural intelligence of the universe.

	Brief Description
"Steady" SP 9	I try to be fairly organized about money so that I do not have to live on the edge and get stressed out. I want to be self-sufficient. I am fairly frugal, though I will splurge on occasion. I adjust my lifestyle to match my means. I don't need to impress others. My motivation is to be comfortable and easy-going, and enjoy my life.
"Unsung Hero" SO 9	I am quite generous to others. I find it difficult to put a lot of attention on my own well-being. I feel that everyone should share and act as a family. I am pretty easy-going with my spending, and financial matters can get a bit fuzzy for me. I go with the flow and trust things will work out money-wise, even if I don't have a lot.
"Grooving" SX 9	I love money, but I have difficulty getting worked up about it. I can find it difficult to put energy on money matters, because I get preoccupied with other things. I am passionate about my work, and hope that money will show up for the work I do. I have difficulty pushing for my own well-being. If I am in a groove, it is easy to keep going. But it is difficult to change directions. I don't like to sell myself. I want my work to speak for me.

Type 9	Summary
Gift	Being relaxed and at peace.
Unconscious Belief	I am unseen.
Strategy	*Settling* – being okay with what is and not going for more.
Vicious Cycle	Because I must avoid being disturbed at all cost, I must stay away from conflicts, strong boundaries, and stay in the gray. Everything is fine as it is and it is difficult to initiate things and get activated. By avoiding disturbances, I can keep the peace, but this keeps me out of the flow of life.
Defended Against	Being outstanding and shining.
Operationally	• It's up to me to create the peace. • I must not get riled up and let disturbances get to me. • I take the path of least resistance and go with the flow.
Paradox	*Settling* does not generate peace.
Breaking the Vicious Cycle	I must recognize that the universe is intelligently ordered. It is not up to me to fix what is wrong. My job is to be a part of the intelligent order.
Direction of Growth	Waking up allows me to align with what is right and good.

Frequently Asked
Questions

1. Why are the Nine Domains important to our understanding of money?

The Nine Money Domains, derived from the general Enneagram model, give us a clear and precise map for how to have a healthy relationship to money. In sets of three, we are guided to move from surviving to purposing to thriving. Survival is about making and spending money. Purposing is about clarifying our money beliefs, understanding, and commitments. Thriving is about manifesting our dreams and living in the flow. I don't know of any other map that is as holistic or accurate as this Nine Money Domains model.

2. Why are the three instincts important for our understanding of money?

Our instincts drive us unconsciously to be well, to be social, and to procreate, amongst other things. Without acknowledging our instincts, we would be leaving out a big piece of the story about humans and money.

3. What's more important for money: instinct or type?

That's a tough call. What I can say is this. A story of the nine personality types *without* the instincts would be insufficient to explain our essential differences around money. Our personality types are basically a response to and a rationalization of our imbalanced instinctual attention. In a nutshell, here's what I think happens. Because we get so freaked out about surviving in this scary world as babies, we conserve our energy by putting our attention on one instinct alone. But because we do this, we are not as effective as we could be. As a result, we feel a loss of connection to our true nature, and we turn to our ego strategy to help us meet our needs – by being correct, giving, striving, special, strong, etc. Our money strategy describes how we relate to money to address our dominant instinctual concern.

4. What's the difference between the Nine Domains and the Nine Types?

Although they are both derived from the general Enneagram model, they are conceptually quite distinct. The Nine Domains describe the nine aspects of money that are each equally important for having a healthy and prosperous relationship to money. The Nine Types describe the nine different money strategies we tend to display as humans.

5. What's the relationship between the Nine Domains and the Nine Types?

Good question. Even though these are conceptually distinct, there is indeed a relationship between the two. What I have found is that each of the Types has a special "home" that corresponds to the Domain of their number. So a Type 4 will tend to be very comfortable in Domain 4, a Type 8 will be comfortable in Domain 8, etc. But just like the homes we grew up in, just because we are comfortable, doesn't necessarily mean we have a healthy relationship to our home. We can have all kinds of bad habits and unhealthy patterns that make being home "comfortable," but less than optimal. We might learn to live with criticism, co-dependency, even abuse, and be "comfortable" with it. But that doesn't mean it's the best thing for us. In the same way, Type 4s may be comfortable searching for personal meaning, but it doesn't mean that their money beliefs in Domain 4 are authentically connected to what is personally meaningful for them. Developing a healthy relationship to our "home" Domain is our first order of business, but it is aided by doing our work in the other Domains, especially in the Domains of our "arrow" numbers.

6. How did the structure for the book emerge?

Another good question! It was definitely a struggle. Don Riso told me that the key to a good Enneagram book was to have a strong framework. I knew that the instincts were important. I knew I wanted to write about the personality types and their respective relationships to money. But I didn't have a way to tie it all together with the important money concepts from financial planning and economics, like spending, saving, planning, budgeting, investing, etc. It felt clunky to write about the types and money without having a compelling structure. I had essentially written a full manuscript in Spring 2010, but wasn't thrilled about the chapters. Then I went to the July 2010 IEA conference and Don Riso happened to be speaking publicly for the first time about the Nine Domains of the Enneagram. He said that the Nine Domains represented nine distinct archetypal energies that describe any healthy system, be it a corporation, a team, or an orchestra. He also said that the critical work ahead for the Enneagram community was in the *application* of the Nine Domains to real world matters. That's when things clicked for me and I realized how important it was to think discretely about the Nine Domains of Money and how important it would be to carefully explain how Domain 1 described the energy of budgeting, Domain 2 described the energy of spending, etc. So I set myself to this task for the next two months. As I wrote about the Domains, I began to notice the themes of surviving, purposing, and thriving emerge organically from the sequential nature of the Domains. After that, things just fell into place naturally. I knew that the next task would be to write about the nine types. I knew that for each of the nine types, I would have to write about the different instincts, dominant and blindspot, in each of the Nine Domains, making sure to give the instincts fair and even treatment, and not over-emphasize Self-Preservation alone, which is a more money-focused instinct. Amazingly, the correlations and relationships started falling into place naturally, as if these things were just waiting to be organized neatly. But I have to remember that nothing was obvious to me when I first began. I had no idea at all how any of it would turn out!

7. What methodology did you use for your research?

Initially, I thought I would run a quantitative study, and have hundreds of people answer an online survey and see what statistical relationships I would find between personality type and financial behavior. But in order to do this type of study, I'd have to know people's personality types and what questions to ask. I had some inkling that different types related to money differently, but beyond that, I did not have well-defined hypotheses to test. I didn't have any well-established theory or hypothesis, for example, of how a 5 would relate to spending or savings differently than a 2. So a quantitative study at this initial stage was out. I didn't feel I would be able to learn what I needed to learn that way.

So I decided to interview people. I interviewed, by phone or in person, about 160 people over a two-year period from Fall 2008 to Fall 2010. I interviewed people who knew their Enneagram type. I also asked them what their dominant instinct was. If they didn't know their dominant instinct, I explained what the instincts were and how we tend to behave if we have a particular dominant instinct. I asked them to rank which one seemed to be most dominant in their lives and which they tended to ignore. I asked them questions about their relationship to money. I promised each interviewee complete confidentiality. From my experience as a financial planner, I had some idea of the types of questions to ask. In 45 minutes to 90 minutes, I asked them how they kept financial records, stayed organized, tracked finances. I asked them about their relationship to budgeting, spending, earning, saving, investing, risk management, insurance, planning, retirement, wealth building. I asked them about their beliefs about money and their understanding of money. I asked them where they fell on a scale of 1 to 10 from scarcity (1) to abundance (10) and why. Luckily, I had generally organized my interview questions by Domains, though I hadn't really thought of them as "Domains" until the Fall of 2010.

After I interviewed each person, I transcribed each interview and labeled the document by type and instinctual stack, and recorded the interviewee name, date, type, and stack in a spreadsheet. After interviewing and transcribing all the interviews, I still had no idea what I was going to find. I put all the Type 1 interviews in one document, all the Type 2 interviews in a second document, all the Type 3 interviews in a third document, etc. Then I began to "process" the interviews. It took several passes of reading and interpreting the interviews to make any sense of them with respect to type and money. Still, things seemed pretty jumbled, not that coherent. Then as I was preparing to give my talk for the July 2010 IEA conference, and began making slides about instincts and type, I had a big "aha" moment. As I was sorting through the interviews by dominant instinct, I saw for the first time some very clear money patterns emerge for Self-Preservation dominant and Self-Preservation blindspot types. Those who were dominant Self-Preservation were much more likely to think about saving, planning ahead, and budgeting, and be self-reliant about money than those who had a Self-Preservation blindspot. This was very exciting. After months of doing this research, a clear pattern had emerged! Once I could see these Self-Preservation patterns clearly, I realized that there were similar patterns for those with dominant Sexual instincts and those with dominant Social instincts. What I noticed for dominant Sexual types was a tremendous boldness and resilience, and for dominant Social types, a marked generosity and sense of reciprocity. Now things were really starting to click.

Once I could see the instinct patterns with money, I could then begin to filter out how these dominant instincts were causing "wrinkles" in the patterns for the Types. I started to methodically study the withdrawn types, 4, 5, and 9s, because they were so intriguing and different to me. They seemed to be much more relaxed and sometimes unmotivated around money in a way that piqued my curiosity. As I spent more time processing the interviews for the 4, 5, and 9s, I began to see some commonalities in their level of assertiveness, planfulness, and desire for money. Then I did the same for the dutiful types, the 1, 2, and 6s. The 3, 7, 8s, were more straightforward in some sense because they were the "opposite" of the withdrawn and dutiful types. I essentially used a qualitative sociological methodology to understand this topic.

8. How has the process of writing this book affected you?

I'd have to say that the biggest change was having to get inside the world of the withdrawn types. Having to do that fundamentally altered my sense of reality. I couldn't hold on to my old views about about planning, control, and the future after going through that process. I've also learned to ask for help and be supported by others in terms of asking for interviews from friends and strangers, and to feel a part of a larger world. And I've learned to focus and sustain my attention on something I really care about.

9. Why did you write about the types in the first person?

I used a first-person voice because I wanted to give the reader a chance to really understand from the inside out why people are so different with their motivations and behaviors around money. I thought this would be the most effective way to understand the different types and really get inside their head. I also thought that by seeing things from the first person perspective, we could really understand each type's pain, but also see through their pain to what more is possible.

10. What do you hope people will take away from reading this book?

I hope people get the idea that we are each and every one one of us on a journey from Fear to Love. We were born into these separate physical bodies, and that makes us afraid for our lives, trying to survive. We get all these great tools to survive with, but if we focus too much on surviving, then we block ourselves from the bigger Love that is possible. I want people to take away the idea that by seriously addressing and improving their relationship to money, they can begin to move from Scarcity to Abundance, Surviving to Thriving, and Fear to Love. It's hard work, but it's worth it. We should live and thrive as we were meant to.

11. What do you hope this work will accomplish?

My hope is that this work will stimulate a continuing conversation about types, instincts, and money that will allow us to uncover some real truths about individual and social financial behavior, that will not only help us as individuals, but inform financial planners, economists, and academics. If anything you read in this book resonates or doesn't resonate for you, helps you or doesn't help you, please share that with me and the community at www.MargaretSmith9.com/EnneaMoney. The more dialogue we have about this, the more we will be able to learn. There are so many more questions that we could begin to address if we knew more about personality, financial choices, and financial well-being, like: Why is there poverty? What can we do to stimulate socioeconomic mobility? Why do countries get mired in economic stagnancy? What does our personality or a country's personality have to do with any of this? The only way we are going to answer these big questions is if we come together as one collective mind.

Resources

At www.MargaretSmith9.com/EnneaMoney, you can take a test to find out what your money type and instinctual stack are. You can also learn about workshops and coaching services offered. And you can order this book in larger quantities at a discount. You can follow on Twitter @EnneaMoney, and participate in further dialogue at www.Facebook.com/MargaretSmith9.

Suggested Enneagram books

- Almaas, A.H. *Facets of Unity – The Enneagram of Holy Ideas*. Boston: Shambhala, 2002.
- Goldberg, Michael J. *The 9 Ways of Working*. New York: Marlowe & Company, 1999.
- Lapid-Bogda, Ginger. *Bringing out the Best in Yourself at Work*. New York: McGraw Hill, 2004.
- Riso, Don Richard, and Russ Hudson. *Personality Types: Using the Enneagram for Self-Discovery*. Mariner Books, 1996.
- Riso, Don Richard, and Russ Hudson. *The Wisdom of the Enneagram*. New York: Bantam Books, 1999.
- Riso, Don Richard, and Russ Hudson. *Understanding the Enneagram: The Practical Guide to Personality Types*. Mariner Books, 2000.

Suggested Personal Finance books

- Gawain, Shakti. *Creative Visualization*. Novato: Nataraj Publishing, 2002.
- Gurney, Kathleen. *Your Money Personality*. New York: Doubleday, 1988.
- Kahler, Rick and Kathleen Fox. *Conscious Finance*. Rapid City: FoxCraft, Inc, 2005.
- Kessel, Brent. *It's Not about the Money*. New York: Harper One, 2008.
- Kinder, George. *Seven Stages of Money Maturity*. New York: Dell Publishing, 1999.
- Needleman, Jacob. *Money, Money, Money*. Carlsbad: Hay House Inc, 1998.
- Needleman, Jacob. *Money and the Meaning of Life*. Crown Business, 2004.
- Nemeth, Maria. *The Energy of Money*. New York: Ballantine Wellspring, 2000.
- Price, Deborah. *Money Magic*. California: New World Library, 2003.
- Twist, Lynne. *The Soul of Money*. New York: Norton & Co., 2003.

About the Author

Dr. Margaret Smith is an intuitive money coach, teacher, and inspirational speaker who works at the nexus of money, personal growth, and spirituality. She leads workshops on transformational journeys with money. She is principal of EnneaCoaching, a coaching and consulting firm which provides Enneagram training seminars, workshops, and coaching for companies and individuals seeking to understand their personality style at work, in leadership, and with money. She is a Certified Riso-Hudson Enneagram Trainer™, a Certified Financial Planner™, and a former Economics professor. She was financial planner and coach for Smith Financial Place from 2005 to 2010. She is a Certified Integral Coach™ through New Ventures West, one of the country's

premier coach training institutions. Dr. Smith received her PhD in Business Economics from Harvard University, and her BA, *summa cum laude*, from Yale University. She has spoken at International Enneagram Association conferences and has published various articles on real estate and finance in academic journals. She is married and mother to four children, ages 4, 7, 10, and 12. She lives in Claremont, CA and enjoys tennis, white water rafting, digital photography, and traveling. To learn more about Dr. Margaret Smith, please visit www.MargaretSmith9.com.

a	b	a
LHI	IIII LH	II sX
swore	SP	Blind

Made in the USA
Charleston, SC
22 February 2011